Evil Eye in Christian Orthodox Society

Evil Eye in Christian Orthodox Society

A Journey from Envy to Personhood

Nikolaos Souvlakis

berghahn
NEW YORK · OXFORD
www.berghahnbooks.com

First published in 2021 by
Berghahn Books
www.berghahnbooks.com

© 2021 Nikolaos Souvlakis

All rights reserved. Except for the quotation of short passages for the purposes of criticism and review, no part of this book may be reproduced in any form or by any means, electronic or mechanical, including photocopying, recording, or any information storage and retrieval system now known or to be invented, without written permission of the publisher.

Library of Congress Cataloging-in-Publication Data
A C.I.P. cataloging record is available from the Library of Congress
Library of Congress Cataloging in Publication Control Number: 2021015492

British Library Cataloguing in Publication Data
A catalogue record for this book is available from the British Library

ISBN 978-1-80073-118-9 hardback
ISBN 978-1-80073-119-6 ebook

To Rev. Dr Nikodemos and Kirsty

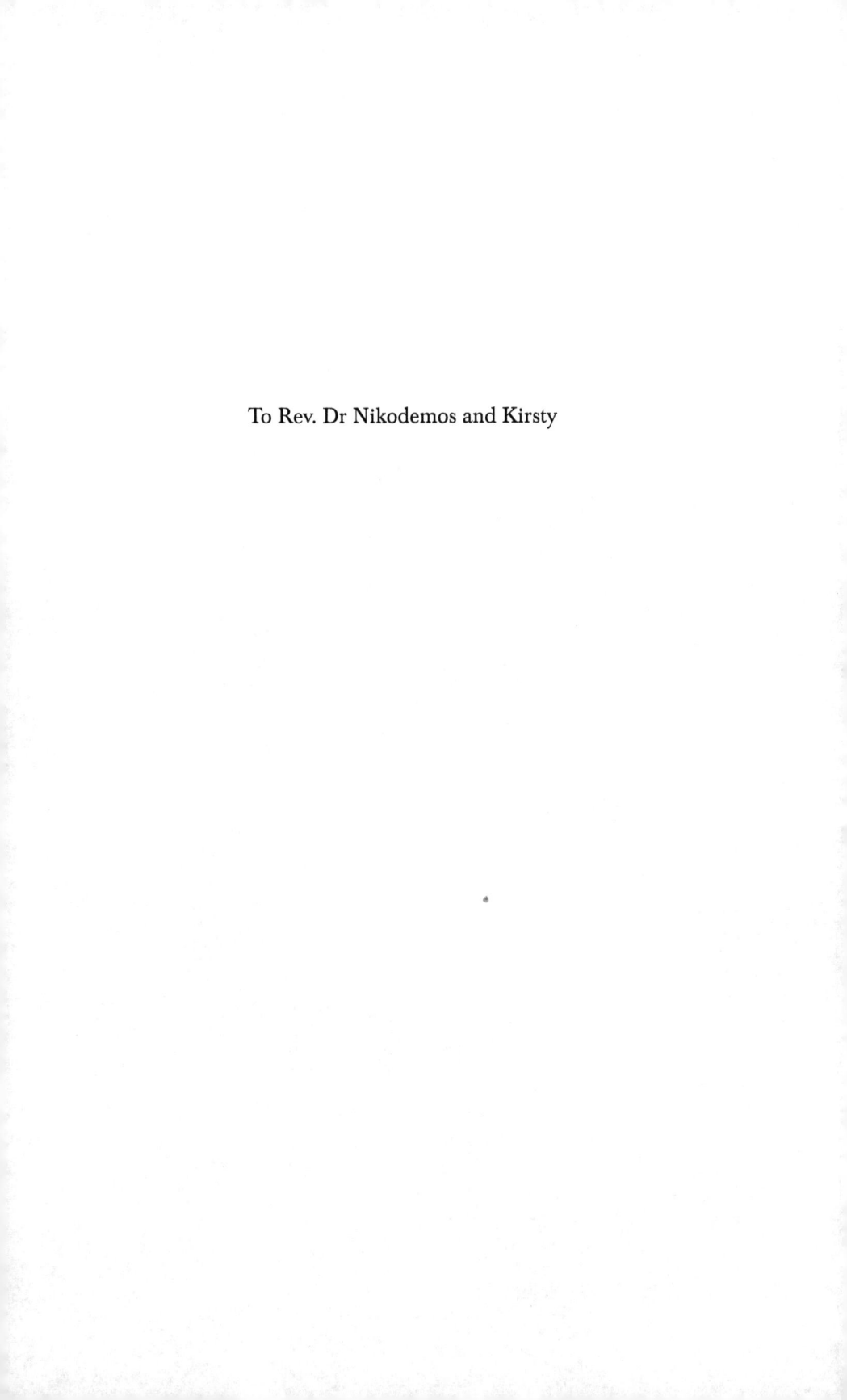

Contents

List of Figures	viii
Foreword *Kirsty Annable*	ix
Preface	xi
Introduction	1
1. The Selected Region, Informants' Demographics and Methodology	42
2. Informants' Different Attitudes and Understandings Regarding the Evil Eye	80
3. Fieldwork Observations: Symptomatology of the Evil Eye and Sociocultural Views	129
4. Personhood and the Evil Eye	169
Conclusion	208
References	219
Index	241

Figures

1.1.	Informants' education	49
1.2.	Age and employability	50
1.3.	Age and gender	50
1.4.	Occupational and population distribution	51

Foreword

Kirsty Annable

In this book, Dr Souvlakis, drawing from his expertise as a psychoanalyst, forensic psychologist and anthropologist, takes the reader on a journey to Corfu, Greece, where he explores the link between the evil eye within Eastern Christian Orthodox traditions and the development of personhood.

Addressing a gap within existing studies and literature, his book challenges the common perception that the evil eye is globally experienced and understood in certain ways. The book engages with different social groups, such as clergymen, folk healers, mental health professionals and laypeople – groups which experience the phenomenon in a variety of ways, not because of their different socio-economic backgrounds but because of the transhistorical and trans-generational heritage of the individual.

Dr Souvlakis' writing captivates the reader on a quest that goes beyond historical views to show that the evil eye is not purely triggered by envy, admiration or jealousy, but in fact is a phenomenon related to the individual's shame and existential anxiety of 'being' seen by the others' 'I'. Following an ethnographic methodology influenced by psychological and social anthropology, Dr Souvlakis argues that the phenomenon of the evil eye offers insight into human existence and its tripartite elements: soul, mind and body.

The book is essential for anyone interested in anthropological research, including social, religious and psychiatric anthropology, and for individuals interested in the evil eye. Corfu is a region that historically has not been under Ottoman rule or any Islamic influence, making it a particularly interesting location for this study of the evil eye. Bringing together the evil eye and an Orthodox perspective gives Dr Souvlakis scholarly authority and uniqueness.

Evil Eye in Christian Orthodox Society: A Journey from Envy to Personhood is a pioneering work of research, bringing to the forefront a different meaning behind the evil eye that is not just about envy and calamities, but a journey inwards in the attempt to explore one's self and better understand one's personhood. The reader will discover how Dr Souvlakis develops an interdisciplinary dialogue and brings a fresh view of the phenomenon of the evil eye as a facilitator of well-being processes, rather than a generator of calamities.

Ms Kirsty Annable is a psychiatric anthropologist and psychotherapist and clinical practitioner at National Health System.

Preface

This book engages with the phenomenon of the evil eye, which can be traced back to 5000 BCE and is still a current anthropological phenomenon. It is a global phenomenon that is closely linked to the malevolent glare. Many traditions believe that being cast under the evil eye results in calamities or bad luck. It is also commonly believed to be a supernatural phenomenon that inflicts harm on others when cast. This book, however, investigates the evil eye in a Christian Orthodox environment, and the findings reveal something different than simply the bad luck and calamity that are associated with the phenomenon.

The book, which is divided into an introduction, four chapters and a conclusion, examines the effect of the evil eye on individuals' mental health and personhood. It poses the problem of how the evil eye fits into the ethnographic arena as a key question that forges a fundamental link between the disciplines of mental health, theology and psychology. It is the argument of the book that the evil eye is an essential and fundamental human phenomenon; therefore, any scholarly field touched on in this book must consider the insight it provides into the development of personhood. For the purpose of the ethnographic research, which has also been anthropologically informed, the phenomenon of the evil eye is approached from multiple disciplinary perspectives. Psychological ethnography – the main ethnographic subfield in which my research is situated – engages with the evil eye as a central and fundamental phenomenon in relation to understandings of personhood, even though understandings of the phenomenon itself might differ at times. However, in order to comprehend the phenomenon of the evil eye from a psychological-ethnographic point of view, dialogue across various disciplines is required. The phenomenon is explored within the existing literature, showing how it is understood from different points of view (e.g. theologically, existentially, socially) and by different scholars. In particular, my research investigates the phenomenon of the evil eye within the Eastern Christian society of Corfu and considers its effect as a mirror of the individual psyche. It is a pioneering study which seeks a better understanding of the evil eye, not as a negative effect on an individual's mental state, but rather as a process of understanding personhood. Hence, through ethnographic fieldwork, I examined the symptomatology that develops when someone suffers from evil eye possession, and also focused on building a better understanding of the causation of the symptoms rather than understanding the symptoms per se. The main aim of the fieldwork was to examine how the informants engaged with and discussed the phenomenon in their everyday lives. In other words, an investigation of these expansive questions is confined to building a better understanding of the evil eye as it continues to be an influential phenomenon in people's everyday lives. The book discusses the specific geographical area of Corfu, Greece, where the phenomenon is very prevalent, as indeed are religious practices in general. Corfu also exhibits an increased interest in mental health, while at the same time folk traditions and healing processes appear to maintain their influence. However, just as the ethnographic field endeavours to deepen our understanding of subjectivity and personhood, so too is this fieldwork directly and indirectly concerned with the phenomenon of the evil eye as it pertains to the concept of being and the experience of being human. It is argued that the concept of the evil eye enables an insightful connection to be made between personhood, anxiety and 'I' (eye). There are cross-disciplinary commonalities and differences in the process of exploring and understanding the phenomenon.

The existing literature reveals that there are different approaches and interpretations of the phenomenon of the evil eye, due to the fact that its functionality may have been misunderstood; rather than causing calamities to befall individuals, it instead facilitates meaning-making in the human quest for personhood. The question of the evil eye can be explored through the ages and across different schools of thought. It has attracted interest and intrigue, and it has challenged and formed the foundation of theological and philosophical inquiry into personhood and mental health. Even though the evil eye defies conclusive investigation and analysis, it has become embedded in concepts of what constitutes a person, and therefore it cannot be ignored. It is central to the disciplines involved in this book and the underpinning fieldwork, but it also facilitates a better understanding and expression of personhood.

The phenomenon of the evil eye is conventionally associated with calamities, fear of denigration, object-worship and the supernatural. Humanness, the pursuit of personhood and the striving for meaning are all, at least to some extent, influenced by the evil eye: the need to be seen but also the fear of being seen may be discerned, at times obviously, but often indirectly and disguised in symptomatology and in various manifestations. Thus, ethnographic questions relating to the phenomenon have exercised scholars across disciplines; however, in attempting to understand the phenomenon, attention has not been given to its internal meaning, but only to its external manifestations and societal influences. The book seeks to understand the phenomenon in relation to psychical manifestations and responses to the evil eye, in the light not only of theology but also of ethnography, mental health and psychology, all of which attempt a realistic and mystical representation of human personhood. Attention will also be given to transcultural and transhistorical influences that have made the phenomenon possible.

What is the evil eye? It may be argued that this is too broad and perhaps too vague a question; therefore, an attempt to explore and answer it in any comprehensive way might not be realistic. To understand this phenomenon more deeply requires an interrogation of the meaning of the evil eye that is sufficiently comprehensive as to reflect and represent all of its aspects and natures. The current literature focuses on some aspects of the evil eye, but fails to capture the true nature and purpose of the phenomenon. This book acknowledges the evil eye's complexities but also accepts limitations and inconclusiveness with regard to a theoretical and definitional inquiry into the question. It therefore adopts a narrower and more focused approach to investigation of the phenomenon. The research is thus placed within a geographical, theological and historical framework, and seeks to discover how the phenomenon is viewed, experienced, explored and analysed by the informants within this framework. The book proposes that the central element of the phenomenon is not simply the understanding of it and of how it affects individuals and societies in forming a better understanding of mental health, the way people interact with each other and the society in which they live; it further suggests that the significance of the phenomenon lies in the incontrovertible confirmation of its centrality in human experience.

The book starts with an introduction to the evil eye, which gives a thorough account of the existing literature concerning the phenomenon, not only in Greece but globally. This chapter presents facts and beliefs with regards to this subject both within the micro-context of Greek society and culture and in the global context. Even though the evil eye has sparked interest in the field of orthodox ethnography, little attention has been paid to its indigenous conceptual schemata. The concept of the evil eye appears to convey some grand emic terms but fails to convey the broader ramifications of these terms (Crick 1976; Spooner 1976; Maloney 1976). The chapter starts with a general introduction, which leads to a global approach to the evil eye and its effect on mental health. I then zoom in on the phenomenon, and the literature takes a close-up view prior to it being examined within Greek culture. The phenomenon is examined from antiquity (classical Greece) to modern times. The chapter also gives an account of the position of the church and religion in relation to the phenomenon, in which it is linked to healing rituals and spiritual protection. Finally, the chapter concludes with a description of the history of mental health in Greece and the contemporary situation, leading to a discussion about current understandings of the evil eye in Greece and its influence on individuals' well-being and mental health.

Chapter 1 focuses on the methodology of the research, explaining the research question and the way in which the collected data was analysed. I give an explanation of the chosen research design and outline the importance of the research. The purpose and scope of the fieldwork are stated, alongside a thorough description of the procedures that were followed prior to the fieldwork. A description of the inclusion and exclusion criteria is also given in this chapter, and I also introduce myself as a researcher, explaining my position as a psychological- and social-ethnographic researcher. Finally, an account of the history of, and influences within, the field is given, including its demographics as they have manifested in recent years. In this section, the results from the fieldwork are presented systematically; all the observations and journal notes are presented and articulated. The data is revealed and emerging theories are put forward. The chapter engages with attitudes towards the evil eye, and analyses the phenomenon as observed and examined in the fieldwork. In addition, interviews with four major social categories are also analysed in order to better understand the phenomenon of the evil eye. The experiences and reflections of these four categories of people – namely, laypeople, clergymen, folk healers and mental health professionals – are thoroughly analysed in order to bring to the forefront their attitudes on the subject.

Chapter 2 begins the analysis of the data, which takes the form of the attitudes that individuals and groups have on the evil eye. To this end, the chapter negotiates the positions that clergy, laypeople, mental health professionals and folk healers take in regards to the phenomenon. The chapter is interested in the similar attitudes that each group has on the evil eye, rather than the differences between each informant, which is the focus of the following chapters.

Chapter 3 examines the general understanding of the evil eye, engaging in a dialogue with the phenomenon, its motives and its triggers, as it is experienced and observed in the field. Thus, this chapter highlights the phenomenon's inconstant dialogue with contemporary Greek Orthodox views as derived from field observations. Particular interest is paid to the general attitudinal similarities among all the social classes of the participants in regard to the evil eye and how this will inform our understanding of the phenomenon.

In Chapter 4, I engage in an ethnographic and philosophical dialogue on personhood in relation to the evil eye, highlighting the relationship between the evil eye and personhood in the contemporary area of Corfu as observed according to Eastern Orthodox perceptions and beliefs. Finally, the Conclusion discusses the results in detail. The analysis presented here appears to go against the traditional view of the evil eye as a source of calamities and misfortune. The fieldwork revealed that in fact, the evil eye facilitates an inner journey for individuals to reach a deeper level of understanding of self and personhood.

Introduction

This chapter engages with the dialogue that has developed among scholars and throughout history on the phenomenon of the evil eye, giving an account of the evil eye as it has been observed globally in order to provide context for the investigation undertaken in this study. In addition, it aims to give an account of preventative measures designed to protect individuals from the evil eye and ways of casting the evil eye away from an individual. I therefore analyse the Greek Orthodox Church's views in this regard, since Eastern Orthodoxy is my main focus in relation to the phenomenon of the evil eye. Finally, the chapter explores current views of the evil eye in contemporary Greek society. However, before embarking on the analysis of the evil eye it is vital to establish the language that I use to express the phenomenon. Therefore, what follows is a general explanation of the phenomenon as it has been observed in the Greek tradition.

The evil eye (*Vaskania*, Βασκανία) is an enduring phenomenon which survives even into the twenty-first century, as science gains more and more credence among non-Westernised societies, and more specifically within Greek culture. In the century of rationality and at a time when there is a deep-seated desire to explain and explore everything, the phenomenon of the evil eye remains alive in Greek society; it is a phenomenon that fails to find an explanation and still remains as part of the folk religion in most individuals' consciousnesses. Campbell (1964) and Du Boulay (1974) both assert that the presence of the evil eye in societies is generally attributed to Satan. Such a definition reflects the Greek tradition and the way that the majority of Greeks operate. However, it would be rather naïve to take this position at face value without any further analysis and exploration. The definitions given by Campbell and Du Boulay lack gravitas and fail to capture the spirit of contemporary Greek society. One of the major characteristics of the evil eye is that the individual on whom it has been cast is demoralised and lacks social and personal worth. Even though Du

Boulay focuses on a link between societal belief in the evil eye and Satan, a more recent study conducted by Wazana (2007) separates the phenomenon from satanic manifestations, arguing that the evil eye is a human vice and sin. In other words, Du Boulay and Wazana humanise the phenomenon, stating that the evil eye is the manifestation of Satan within human beings and that it is nurtured by their destructive impulses (Thanatos). Even though destructive impulses seek integration with life impulses (Eros), Blum and Blum (1970) point out that the evil eye cannot be seen separately from its epiphenomenological folk tradition. They insist that the evil eye is strongly related to psychological and physical illnesses; it would therefore not be ethical to examine the epiphenomenology of the evil eye without investigating the true meaning of the phenomenon as it exists within the deeper level of individuals' consciousnesses. Consciousness is not just transgenerationally and transhistorically configured; it is also a reflection of the society that fosters it. I therefore see the phenomenon within the cultural context of Greek Orthodox tradition.

Even within the current scientific era, Greek society has maintained a strong superstitious and religious culture, the antecedents of which predate Jesus. The Greek Orthodox Church's teachings have been strongly criticised by postmodern Western scientific and religious societies as primitive. However, the answer to these critics is that the teaching by both Eastern and Western churches on the subject of the evil eye has been socially learned, and this is a process which has been transferred from generation to generation (Dionisopoulos-Mass 1976; Elliot 1991, 1992). Greek Orthodox scholars argue that criticism of a particular culture requires a thorough understanding and investigation of its values, goals and purpose of existence; otherwise it is a critique without validity (Ware 1996; Cunningham 2002). It is only through a deep understanding of the ethnographic and anthropological elements of a culture that scholars can achieve cultural validity (Summer 1906). In addition, Rohrbaugh (2006) points out that even though it is commonly accepted that there are cultural differences between East and West, Western societies tend to underestimate these differences when they encounter the phenomenon of the evil eye. Such a limited view does not allow biblical scholars, for instance, to identify and understand evidence from the Bible which is not included in its Westernised interpretations. This attitude leads to a misunderstanding of the tradition of Eastern Christianity. On this point, it is important to mention that Eastern Orthodoxy portrays Satan and evil powers as real beings, who can cause severe problems and significant mental health issues to individuals. On the other hand, Western societies approach Satan and his powers metaphorically. Satan is portrayed in a symbolic form as an internal vice, which can be triggered by specific events in one's life and lead to behaviours harmful to oneself or others; part of this vice is the evil eye (Russell 1986). This major difference in the interpretation of Satan has created a misunderstanding between West and East, and to an extent hinders the progression of our understanding of the evil eye. Western societies believe that Eastern societies are underdeveloped in response to the treatment and understanding of evil and satanic presence, while Eastern societies believe that Western beliefs and traditions are impersonal and that satanic powers are real; in order to be spiritually healed, people need to be treated appropriately, whether by mental health professionals or purely by clergy (Page 1995; Pilch 2000).

Keeping in mind a general understanding of the evil eye and how it is broadly viewed by Western and Eastern societies, and before the particular analysis of the evil eye within the context of the Greek Orthodox community of Corfu – the geographic area where my ethnographic study took place, and the significance of which is explained in the next chapter – it is important to explore the commonly accepted link between the evil eye and superstition.

SUPERSTITION AND SUPERSTITIOUS BELIEFS

Superstition appears to have been present in societies since the earliest years of humanity. Superstitious beliefs have been passed from generation to generation, and it is asserted that they have reached their latest form in connection with religious beliefs about the evil eye. Rituals related to superstition have both positive and negative influences on a person's well-being and religiosity, or their practice of religion (Matute 1995). One of the scholars who has investigated the links between superstition and behaviour is Neil (1980), who maintains that superstitious beliefs affect an individual's behaviour and determine their psychological and social status. Neil, as well as Matute (1995), despite investigating superstition and its basic functionality, fail to approach the phenomenon from its existential elements, which can affect the individual's worldview. These scholars reveal that in societies where there is fear, superstitious beliefs have a positive effect as they appear to decrease the high levels of individual anxiety stemming from the fear of the supernatural. They go further and state that the supernatural is closely related to the severe anxiety which stems from the individual's fear of uncertainty, and therefore that superstition gives them an illusory sense of control over the situation. However, they do not pay attention to individuals' narratives about the evil eye, but rather focus on a generalised view of superstition. To remedy this omission, the present study pays direct attention to individuals' reactions in order to investigate whether the evil eye is in fact a superstitious belief in individuals' consciousnesses.

In the Greek Orthodox tradition, the fear of the unknown within the field of superstition is most directly related to demonology, which is arguably the bridge between superstition and witchcraft. Demonology is the interest that individuals exhibit in understanding the rituals by which they can summon and control demons – in our case, the evil eye. Jahoda (1969) suggests that fear of the unknown and witchcraft exist simultaneously and that they are often considered to be the same phenomenon; this has been observed since the beginning of human history. Jahoda adds that superstition can be observed in three major fields: religious, personal (esoteric) and cultural. However, he is interested in the objective understanding of the phenomenon of superstition, and does not demonstrate any interest in its subjective manifestation, upon which the current study focuses. On the other hand, superstitious beliefs such as the evil eye cannot be taken separately from the society in which they are manifested, and most importantly, without paying attention to specific cultural elements. Consequently, superstition is defined in this book as a cultural belief formed in pre-scientific civilisations to minimise fear of the unknown, and mostly to control the future.

Sharmer (1998) adds that superstition is not only about controlling the future, but rather is about dealing with misfortune while at the same time building hope into the individual's life. Sharmer's addition to the understanding of superstition helps to build a picture of superstition that is related not only to the fear of the unknown but also to misfortune. Consequently, Sharmer argues that the evil eye appears in individuals' consciousnesses when their existence is threatened through unknown future events. I broadly agree with Sharmer, but I take a more anthropological approach when examining the effects of the unknown in the individual's consciousness and understanding of their existence.

In this more thorough examination of superstition, Sharmer (1998) asserts that superstitious beliefs are injected into society to ward off misfortune and the evil eye and eventually bring good luck, hope and happiness. However, Vyse (2000) and Zusne and Jones (1989) suggest that superstitious beliefs are influenced by society, demographics and emotional instability and are not simply concerned with bringing about happiness. It appears that Sharmer's understanding of superstition fails to reflect societal and existential exigencies. What follows therefore aims to investigate the nature of the evil eye's existence in contemporary Greek society, examining its societal and cultural elements in order to challenge Sharmer's assumption that it is simply concerned with bringing hope to individuals.

I therefore suggest that the evil eye is the projection of individuals' emotions onto superstitious beliefs: emotions such as fear, happiness and rage are externalised in order to avoid looking inwards at one's own consciousness and understanding of self. Saenko (2005), in his study on superstition, makes a pioneering connection between superstition and individuals' internal fear of being in touch with their difficult feelings, triggered by the unknown. However, Saenko does not pay attention to subjective difficult feelings and truth as triggered by the evil eye, nor the manner in which the phenomenon interacts with a society at large, something that the current study aims to investigate. In fact, Saenko is interested in the cognitive understanding of the phenomenon of superstition and the development of coping strategies based on such understanding. The behavioural aspects, which are significant for the purpose of this chapter, comprise the rituals performed by individuals to defend against misfortune and the evil eye. On the other hand, Žeželj et al. (2017), investigating Saenko's views on superstitious aspects of behaviour, argue that individuals develop certain linguistic and symbolic data associated with objects or behaviours which are believed to bring misfortune. Concurrently, this book is interested in the investigation of the Christian Orthodox linguistic and symbolic data that interact with the belief of the evil eye, since no precedent exists in the literature for an examination of religious language in regard to the phenomenon (Ajzen and Fishbein 2005; Skinner 1938, 1948, 1953; Bandura 1963, 1977).

It is also important to mention at this point that positive psychologists argue that behaviourism is a historical discipline in psychology and therefore that illusion of control through learned behavioural mechanisms should not be considered a valid or, in fact, reliable approach to superstition and the evil eye (Cervone et al. 2006; Murphy 2009; Carver and Scheier 2001; Rogoff 2011). They also point out that human beings have inherited an intrinsic motivation that awakens a psychological need for control in situations of ambiguity and doubt, something that is strongly connected to the current research on the evil eye. Whitson and Galinsky (2008) show that an individual's psychological need for control is strongly correlated with superstitious beliefs. In their experiment to prove such a hypothesis, their participants performed superstitious rituals when they had no control of a situation. In addition, they started to see images and believe in events or phenomena that were not real. Whitson and Galinsky's participants also developed anxieties and phobias if the superstitious rituals were not performed. Most of them developed a strong religious belief as a way of achieving certainty in their everyday life through the church's rituals and beliefs (Case et al. 2004). However, the literature reveals that despite societal progress, advanced superstitious beliefs are nevertheless resilient phenomena that manifest in different societies and cultures around the world (Newport and Strausberg 2001). Gallup and Newport (1991) link religiosity and superstition, and define religiosity as religious practices and attendances. Thus, in their study, they reveal the positive correlation between superstition and religiosity, whereby individuals with high religiosity or spirituality also have strong superstitious beliefs. Ross and Joshi (1992) extend Gallup and Newport's findings, revealing that individuals who have undergone some sort of trauma find comfort in religious beliefs in their attempt to comprehend their reality and control their future; therefore, the maintenance of superstitious beliefs does not originate by chance, but is rather a last-ditch attempt to control the future and deal with their current pain. Influenced by these studies, this chapter pays particular attention to the Greek Orthodox tradition in its investigation of the evil eye. Indeed, this book as a whole presents a pioneering study in which for the first time the evil eye is considered under the umbrella of Greek Orthodox tradition.

Up to the present point, this chapter has examined superstitious beliefs as they have been observed by various scholars. According to these accounts, it is obvious that there has been a strong correlation between the development of superstitious beliefs and times of ambiguity and fear regarding the future. Such fear triggers an innate human characteristic: to control or eliminate anything that threatens the existing status quo. Superstition and the evil eye have therefore been strongly related to cognitive elements that attempt to give illusory control to individuals and to develop hope, which would enable them to counteract their anxieties regarding the unknown. As mentioned in this section, superstitious beliefs can be related to religious beliefs and rituals; further analysis of the relationship between folk-religious and religious beliefs follows in the next section.

RELIGION AND FOLK RELIGION

In the attempt to further examine the phenomenon of the evil eye, it is important at this stage to investigate folk-religious beliefs and their relationship with religious beliefs and rituals. This section illustrates the relationship between the evil eye as a folk-religious belief within a social context and the religious rituals relating to the evil eye. The first pertinent reference comes from Herbermann, who in 1912 introduced to his field the different forms that folk beliefs can take. He states that there are various folk beliefs which refer to inappropriate worship of the transcendent God: namely divination, idolatry and the occult. He explains that inappropriate worship of God commences when external factors are incorporated into the worship; then, idolatry commences, especially when it is suggested that certain objects are considered divine. When believers seek to acquire knowledge about upcoming events in their lives through religious rituals, this is considered divination. Rituals that appear to be supernatural are those which, through the use of black or white magic, cause good or evil outcomes in an individual's life. Within this school of thought, the evil eye is a form of divination upon which rituals are followed in order to interfere with one's reality and to manipulate it.

Folk religions have therefore existed within religious realms from the very earliest ages of humanity. This is witnessed in the Bible, where people attribute power to phenomena such as curses and blessings. Many individuals in the Scriptures clearly recognise that great power follows curses, and they experience fear regarding these curses. In the New Testament, assurance was given that there would be no other curses for the New Jerusalem (Rev. 22:3). In the history of Christianity, there has been no clear differentiation between religion and witchcraft: Christian doctrine has not been clear on what is religion and what is folk-religious belief, miracle or magic (Darmanin 1999). Therefore, one can conclude that superstition can be manifested in religious practices and rituals. However, it is still not clear whether folk-religious beliefs are positively correlated with religion(s) and religiosity. Further exploration is needed in order to better understand the difference between the two.

In the centuries following the writings of the New Testament, and especially during the Middle Ages, believers attributed unexplained phenomena either to God or to evil powers; their comprehension of the world was thus an amalgamation of Christian and folk-religious beliefs. During this period, the major teachings of Christianity became influential, and simultaneously reinforced belief in folk religions and rituals. During these dark times, negative philosophy portrayed God as a persecutor, cruel but also benevolent. The polarised medieval image of God gave rise to folk-religious beliefs about the wrath of God, which were maintained by some dedicated Christians for many years, up until contemporary times. Many of these beliefs upheld the idea that the suffering in the world is caused by satanic powers (Bornstein and Miller 2009). The era that followed the Middle Ages was characterised conversely by individuals' greater focus on science and an immense interest in explaining the secrets of the universe. Nevertheless, the view that folk-religious and religious beliefs could not be seen as separate persisted in the Enlightenment period. Parish and Naphy (2003) suggest that during the Enlightenment period, Christians believed that any other religion outside the Christian doctrines was nothing but folk religion and was therefore heretical. Individuals therefore developed certain fears attached to difference and the other.

In the twenty-first century, with its focus on religious freedom, it has become obvious that what is religion for one person is folk religion for another.

However, it seems at this time that many religions have adopted some form of folk-religious belief. Darmanin (1999) argues that Protestants consider the devotion paid by some Christians to saints and icons to be folk religion, or even sometimes heretical practices; some religious people consider the Aborigines' religious rituals to be folk beliefs. In order to understand the multifaceted nature of folk beliefs, an exploration of their origin is necessary. Folk beliefs take so many forms because they are strongly influenced by their social construction and the cultures in which they manifest. However, such a complex phenomenon as folk beliefs cannot be analysed and witnessed simply by focusing on social-construction theories and culture. Buhrmann and Zaugg (1981), after many observations and studies in social-construction theories, argue that it is not only social construction which feeds folk beliefs, but also the individual's internal fear of the unknown. Their proposal is an invitation to see the phenomenon from a more esoteric view than a mere social-constructivist approach affords. Unfortunately, Buhrmann and Zaugg maintain the premise that religious beliefs prolong and feed the fear of the unknown, which draws attention to folk religions and the supernatural. Even though there is a link between religion and folk beliefs, there are also fundamental differences. Religion is strongly related to morality, while folk-religious beliefs are not. In addition, folk beliefs appear in times of fear and doubt, whereas religion is a continuous practice and can be observed in different expressions of life and emotions (Malinowski 1954). Therefore, religion reinforces belief and trust in God, which in fact is not overpowered by events stemming from bad lack. Hood, Hill and Spilka (2009) suggest that religion is a social construct arising from society and culture; this is in contrast to folk-religious beliefs, as it is often not known why a person develops such beliefs.

Up until now, there has been no clear distinction between folk religion and religion(s) (Hood, Hill and Spika 2009). Some religious leaders and adherents would argue that there are indeed fundamental differences; however, others can argue that there are in fact fundamental similarities as well. If neither necessarily links with the other, it is easy to state that there is no link between the two. However, this might be a naïve conclusion, as religion(s) and folk religions can have fundamental similarities. Folk religions have been related to individuals' attempts at controlling their fear of the unknown. Folk beliefs are a phenomenon, observable in many aspects of life, whereby an individual attempts to exert control over things that upset their psychical equilibrium. Folk beliefs give the individual a sense of power or control, but what is that control? Lefcourt (1982) argues that an individual's awareness in regard to the level of control they have over a situation is called the locus of control. The internal belief through which they develop a sense that they can manipulate external events to produce positive or negative results is called the internal locus of control. On the other hand, the belief that a person's fate is shaped by forces beyond the human realm is the external locus of control. Neuropsychologists argue that there is a correlation between the locus of control and folk beliefs: in situations where control has been lost, human beings tend to create an illusion of control through folk-religious beliefs (Tobacyk, Nagot and Miller 1987).

Humans' fear of the unknown and their need for control originate in an internal desire to be in charge of every aspect of life. For this reason, people usually practise different rituals in order to gain an illusory sense of control over events. One can therefore conclude that evil eye rituals are in fact related to an illusory sense of control over the unknown effect of the phenomenon in someone's psyche. Such a conclusion has not attracted much scholarly attention, and the current study views its further investigation as vital, as it could provide significant insight into human functioning regarding the evil eye. However, psychological ethnographers argue that individuals become omnipotent and even exhibit narcissistic traits in order to control the unknown and manipulate external events that cause them distress due to the individual's primary anxiety (Segal 1982; Rachman 1997). Psychologists believe that the infant lives in a stage of megalomania and formulates the fiction of omnipotence – in other words, the illusion of control. The function of omnipotence is crucial for the child to survive the anxiety and threat of the unknown. The child therefore develops this megalomania, thinking that when they cry, they control the external environment with the result that their needs are gratified; the carer reacts to the infant and attempts to satisfy their needs. If the child does not develop sufficient strength of ego to sustain the frustration of the unknown, and does not develop a mediator between reality and fantasy, then the illusion of control takes a more sophisticated form in adulthood through folk beliefs and a boundary-less and bodiless self (Ferenczi 1963; Rachman 1997). Therefore, it is believed that adults develop neurotic omnipotence as a relic of their old illusion of control, which might now take the form of evil eye. Through this later illusion of control, it has been argued, the individual seeks reparation for the early trauma of losing their function of omnipotence in combination with the not 'good enough' mother (Ferenczi and Rank 1986; Winnicott 1965, 1971; Phillips 2008). This book – influenced by the above psychological theory – investigates adults' views of the evil eye with the aim of better understanding how these relate to the effects of childhood megalomania and boundary-less self. So far, psychological ethnographers have not investigated the phenomenon of the evil eye in terms of the effects that it might have on adults' bodiless selves and childhood megalomania under the umbrella of a particular religious system of beliefs.

Folk beliefs can therefore be observed across different aspects of someone's life. Most of the time, these beliefs can be linked with religious beliefs; however, this is not necessarily the case. The primary trigger for folk beliefs is the fear of the 'other' and the unknown, and they therefore give individuals hope and a false sense of control. At times in an individual's consciousness, the evil eye is a form of folk-religious belief. Although the evil eye is the primary focus of this study, it has not yet been explored; thus, the following section is an attempt to summarise global manifestations of the evil eye, before the focus of the chapters settles upon the geographical area of Corfu.

GLOBAL MANIFESTATION OF THE EVIL EYE

The ways in which the evil eye manifests globally are another important aspect of the current argumentation, as they provide the context for the research that underpins the following chapters. They underscore the importance of revisiting the phenomenon and exploring it with regard to the individual's existential anxiety and personhood. The various global manifestations highlight the deep roots that the phenomenon has in humanity's consciousness and the ways in which it can affect individuals' well-being. Finally, exploring the global manifestations of the evil eye in advance of a microscopic investigation of the phenomenon in the selected geographic area allows the reader to comprehend the phenomenon in different cultures, while at the same time inviting further investigation and evaluation of the differences and similarities of the phenomenon as a cultural construct.

Herzfeld (1981) argues that the phenomenon of the evil eye should be examined on the basic assumption that it is a cultural phenomenon, and therefore that it is imperative to investigate its cultural elements. This suggestion shapes the methodology underpinning my research, which examines the phenomenon holistically and with a multidisciplinary approach within the specific cultural context of the Greek Orthodox tradition. However, an opposite view to Herzfeld's argues that a complex phenomenon such as the evil eye cannot be examined simply according to ethnographic facts; that would be naïve and would cause scientific confusion (Beidelman 1970; Ardener 1970). Such a close-minded approach has meant that the phenomenon of the evil eye has sometimes simply been linked with witchcraft in some cultures. The specific symptom of misfortune, which is closely linked to the evil eye, is attached to a specific social dysfunction, with the result that the phenomenon cannot be examined in isolation from its society or its hermeneutics (Crick 1976). Therefore, numerous cultures believe in the evil eye, especially pagan and tribal communities.

Tribal communities bring to the forefront another element of the evil eye: envy. The tribal communities of the Baharvand and the Basseri believe that *nazar-e*, which is related to the evil eye, is closely linked to envy. Many studies in Africa have observed and examined the evil eye, and suggest that belief in this phenomenon has significant similarities worldwide. Thus, Amanolahi (2007) suggests that in almost all African societies, the evil eye is mostly associated with jealousy and envy, and that it can be cast either consciously or unconsciously. Due to the social dynamic within social micro- and macrocosms, some people are more predisposed to casting the evil eye on others (Westermarck 1926, Evans-Pritchard 1937; Ullmann 1978; Edwards 1971; Foster 1972; Spooner 1976; Dundes 1981). However, it is commonly agreed that globally, the core element of the evil eye is envy.

In Latin America today, and more specifically in the Mayan tradition, there is an argument that the evil eye is closely related to witchcraft or black magic. The Mayans' understanding of the evil eye is closely related to the fear of calamity connected with envy. However, Mayan folk tradition adds that it is the community's belief system that can bring harm (mental or physical) to individuals, and introduces the idea of '*k'oqob'al, a K'iche*': 'someone is making you sick'. Nonetheless, the notion that 'someone is making you sick' does not explain the phenomenon well enough, as many unexplored aspects of that statement require further investigation. It does show, however, that Mayans associate sickness – such as *k'oqob'al*, which comes from the '*mal de ojo*' (evil eye) – with magic. It also suggests that the *mal de ojo* can be caused by a person's 'overlook' (Maloney 1976).

Similarities to the Mayan view on the evil eye can be seen in Eastern traditions, and more specifically in Muslim Turks. Turks believe in *nazar*, which can be interpreted as 'gaze'. *Nazar* is strongly related to the evil eye. The Ottomans believed that the evil eye was fuelled by individuals' fear of dying – a fear which implies that an individual can die from a gaze, but also can suffer from severe illness as a result before dying. However, Turks believe that the cause of harm through another's gaze (positive or negative) is unconscious; the idea is that *nazar* strikes when no one is waiting for it, and the phenomenon is therefore associated with the fear of the unknown (Berger 1977, 2011; Dundes 1981). In addition to Muslim traditions, Wazana (2007) investigates the phenomenon within the Jewish tradition, arguing that the evil eye appears many times in rabbinic literature. The Jewish tradition adopts the same view as that of the Muslim Turkish and Mayan traditions: that the evil eye is a strong societal belief, which can severely affect a person's health or even an inanimate object. Jewish ideas differ, however, from those of the Greeks in regard to the evil eye's manifestations; Jews are not cognitively concerned about the effects of the evil eye on themselves but rather with the development of defences with which to protect themselves from the evil eye. The evil eye appears in Jewish texts, as for example: 'the census is controlled by the evil eye; and it happened in the days of David' (2 Sam. 24:1–10) (Rashi on Exod. 30:12; Rashi on Num. 24:2; Num. 22:41, 23:28, 24:2).

Similarly, in the Ethiopian Orthodox tradition, the evil eye is associated with *buda* (Finneran 2003). According to the Ethiopian tradition, *buda* is related to madness and causes people to be cast out, and this stems from a powerful evil eye. Roberts (1976) explores the Ethiopian tradition further by examining the galvanising energy of *buda*. He states that *buda* is fuelled by envy and therefore that it is through *buda* that individuals can cast the evil eye; *buda* is caused by and can cause serious damage or mental illness only when individuals are madly envious of material things or qualities that they do not possess. Vecchiato (1994) focuses on times and moments when individuals are more vulnerable to the evil eye, such as during mealtimes, emotional periods and the period of crop raising.

While Ethiopians link the evil eye with *buda*, Arabs associate it with '*ayn*'. According to Arabic tradition, the evil eye is known as *ayn* and consists of two different elements, which can be taken as different types of the evil eye. These elements find similarities in the Greek Orthodox typology of the evil eye *(matiasma, vaskania)* (Abu-Rabia 2005; Vecchiato 1994; Dionisopoulos-Mass 1976). The two types identified in Arabic tradition are the '*insiya*' and the '*jinniyah*'. The first refers to the human kind, and the second to jinns in an apparent similarity to the Greek *vaskania*. On the other hand, Bedouins oppose the typology offered by the Arabs, and are more interested in classifying the evil eye according to its power. They classify it according to three different categories based on the power that it emits or the power possessed by the envious person who casts it. The three categories are unconscious, hereditary or conscious . In the first category, an individual who admires an object or another human being can cast the evil eye without actually wanting to. In the second category, the individual is aware of their power to cast the evil eye, as they have inherited that power. Therefore, their presence in a group of people signifies a bad omen. The last category, which is seen in the Bedouin tradition as the most dangerous, is when someone suddenly appears in a person's path and casts the evil eye. This third category is also linked with magic (Briggs 2002; Edwards 1971). There are also some similar beliefs to the Jewish and Turkish traditions which come from the Gaelic islands; here, the phenomenon is approached more religiously, and the evil eye is not seen as anything other than a look cast over Jesus' property (Black 2007). Such an approach suggests that human beings are Jesus' property and are controlled by him; it is therefore Jesus who allows the phenomenon to affect his people, perhaps to punish or teach them.

Similar beliefs about the misfortune that accompanies the evil eye come from the East. As we observe in the Bedouins' belief system, folk beliefs strongly associate misfortune with the evil eye. Bedouins believe that the evil eye is a fatal force that can ruin individuals' lives and even cause death. During his fieldwork, Abu-Rabia (2005) came to an understanding that the evil eye is like a sharp beam of light, which can be seen, felt and activated by individuals' fear of possession and by their strong religious beliefs. On the other hand, Finneran (2003) focuses not on individuals' experiences of the evil eye but on its manifestation within ecology. He argues therefore that the evil eye can be blamed for social and environmental disaster. Finneran agrees with Abu-Rabia that in the Bedouin tradition the evil eye is strongly correlated with jealousy and envy, which can be conveyed through a 'strange gaze'.

Another, slightly more philosophical view of the evil eye comes from the Balkans. Albanians base their belief about the evil eye on their philosophical understanding of limited good, or in more general terms, in limited earthly resources (Peterson-Bidoshi 2006; Foster 1972). They believe that there is a finite amount of good resources available to them, and that therefore those who gain more of these resources do so at the expense of others losing them. Albanians believe that the evil eye is part of the equation of liquid (life) and dryness (death), which stems from the Sephardic Jewish tradition (Levy and Levy 2002). Hence, Albanian people believe that the evil eye can dry life out through the power of the envious glance. The evil eye dries up an individual's body fluids, causing them to feel either physically or psychologically drained. Draining can also be observed in the animal kingdom; animals such as cows, llamas and camels try to protect their young by spitting on them; and there are also animals which spit at humans when they look at them. Romanian tradition adds that envy is not the primary fuel of the evil eye; looking at, praising or admiring someone is enough to put an individual in danger of having the evil eye cast upon them (Onians 1988; Garrison and Arensberg 1976; Dundes 1992b). Romanians take a more physiognomical approach to the evil eye and its power, which complements the Albanian view. They believe that those with green eyes are prone to cast the evil eye, while those with brown eyes might not have such power. It seems that green eyes are fairly rare in Romania; this is thus a preconception and superstition about something that is out of the ordinary. In addition, there exist folk beliefs according to which those with joined eyebrows are able to cause fatalities through the evil eye. It is also believed that the evil eye is not intentional, and that it can be caused even by those with good intentions (Arensberg 1965; Onians 1988; Peterson-Bidoshi 2006).

Parallels to the dualistic take on the evil eye in Albania can be found in the Islamic tradition. Al-Ashqar (2003), in an attempt to investigate the phenomenon of the evil eye in Muslim tradition, focuses on the Koran. Therefore, a close investigation of this text forms part of Al-Ashqar's research. His particular attention to Al-Hijr (chapter 15), verses 26–27 resulted in the statement that Muslims believe in a parallel universe where evil spirits and angels coexist in opposition. They believe that jinns are forms of spiritual entities that function as human beings and exist in the human world; they cannot be seen, even though they can see the human world and interact with it. In the Islamic tradition, it is argued that the evil eye absorbs energy not from the eye of the person but from the spirit (*nafs*), which works through the individual's eye, and that jinns are responsible for this (Abu-Lughod 1988; Abu-Rabia 2005; Abu-Saad 2002).

It appears that the evil eye has received global attention throughout history. The phenomenon declares its presence in many cultures, exhibiting similarities in beliefs and rituals, but also fundamental differences. The fact that the evil eye appears to be very present in the modern era signifies its importance, but also how deeply it is embedded in individuals' consciousnesses. However, to be able to comprehend the development of the evil eye through the years, it is paramount to understand its history. Therefore, the section that follows investigates the phenomenon in antiquity.

THE EVIL EYE IN ANCIENT GREECE

It is important to consider at the outset the origins of the evil eye, as this will assist comprehension of the phenomenon's development in later years and its manifestation in individuals' lives. The evil eye is not just a phenomenon that has been developed in contemporary urban societies; rather, its presence can be observed across history, with the first reference to the evil eye occurring in antiquity. At the same time, the long history of the phenomenon not only signifies its importance, but also how deeply it is rooted in individuals' consciousnesses and the collective unconscious.

One of the first references to the evil eye has been noted by Dickie (1991) in his studies of classical Greeks such as Herodotus and Socrates, who undoubtedly believed in the power of eyesight or overlook as a source of harm. In their writings, there was an immense negative power attached to the phenomenon, which was reputedly able to destroy people and cities. Dickie also suggests that the classical Greeks had certain beliefs with regard to the powers of the eyes, and that these beliefs originated in Egypt, and more precisely in Ptah the Opener. Ptah was recognised as the father of all gods and human beings, and he gave birth to all gods through his eye. This meant that emanations coming from the eye were the most potent (Massey 2012). One should be afraid of the Opener's wrath, as he is able to see and destroy. However, Epictetus (2012) does not agree with the physical attributes of the evil eye, suggesting instead that eyesight is the source that gives flow to the *pneuma*. Epictetus maintains that *pneuma* is transmitted from an object or a living creature to the brain and back again through the eyes. There is a certain flow of energy between objects and *pneuma* which interconnects all people. Epictetus develops this theory about *pneuma* further, contending that it cannot be considered in isolation from the evil eye, as at times the evil eye is its vehicle for communication from inanimate objects to animate ones and vice versa. However, he debates the reasons for the existence of the evil eye in the arena of *pneuma* and thereby links *pneuma* with the power of the evil eye, which can affect a person's mental health. Democritus follows Epictetus' understanding of the evil eye, but he is mostly preoccupied with (and in fact, is one of the first to introduce) the notion that the evil eye must have different levels of effect on individuals; he adds that the evil eye has different levels of transferring energy among creatures (Cartledge 2011). Plutarch, however, takes a different approach to the above scholars, suggesting that eyes produce the most effluxes, which can be projected in the form of a fiery beam (ibid.). Here, Plutarch introduces the notion that would later be known as noetic science, the power of mind; and in this book, eyes have been approached as a phenomenon which emits energy and activates a chain of events that might affect another individual or an object.

Following the classical Greeks and their attempts to explain the evil eye brings only confusion, because they approached the phenomenon differently to those in the present scientific world, focusing their attention on individual subjectivity instead of trying to understand it from a universal standpoint. They understood the phenomenon as part of a person's being and existence, and this led to different explanations and manifestations being assigned to the evil eye to those that we witness today. Such different schools of thought signify the complexity of the phenomenon of the evil eye, but also show that it has different functions. Nevertheless, it is undeniable that common manifestations are observed which can be described universally as envy and pride (Crick 1976; Berger 2011; Murguia et al. 2003). The evil eye was linked to religion, which then allowed it to be applied only to mortals in classical Greek antiquity. Gods and goddesses were governed by different rules to those of mortals, and therefore even though they could be affected by the evil eye, they also controlled it. There is a significant reference in Homer's *Iliad* (2003), where he describes Athena's eyes: 'terribly her eyes shone' (1.172). Here, Athena has been assigned the power of a gaze that can cause death, and in fact is seen to be wielding it. This passage is one of the first references in which the evil eye is attributed godly characteristics and assigned to the goddess of wisdom and diplomacy. According to Aeschylus, deities applied the evil eye to cause pain to humans, to punish or teach them. Aeschylus writes in *Agamemnon*: 'struck from afar from any God's jealous eye' (1994: 947). Even though these two references from the Greek Classics describe gods using their eyes to punish or cause misfortune to humans, it could be presumptuous to assign this to the evil eye; however, we cannot ignore the fact that for the first time, we are confronted with the power of the eye to strike from afar. It also introduces us to the fundamental anxiety that if the gods were jealous, they could inflict misfortune and torture on humans through the power of the eye; the punishment, therefore, can strike at any time and from afar, leaving human beings in the absolute darkness of the unknown.

Reviewing the literature, it is revealed that in Greek mythology the evil eye is strongly linked to the story of Narcissus, whose name has been used by scientists to describe a mental health disorder – the narcissistic personality disorder, as outlined in the *Diagnostic Statistical Manual* (APA 2013; Calimach 2001; Conrad 2012). According to Greek mythology, Narcissus was a young man who was so handsome that in the end he became fascinated by himself, falling in love with his own reflection and pining away to death, leaving behind only a flower (Conrad 2012). This is one of the earliest stories that surfaces when investigating the evil eye in ancient Greece. Following the case of Narcissus, the classical Greeks believed that overlook or fascination could cause a person to undergo misfortune or petrification. In other words, overlook or fascination could steal an individual's cognitive capacity to think and therefore exist. The classical Greeks believed that the evil eye could be cast not only by one individual onto another, but also by an individual onto their own self. However, the condition in which the evil eye is activated is one in which anger or envy exists in a person's psyche. These feelings have historically been attributed to fear and danger and have therefore been thought to cause misfortune to people. Narcissus' story, however, highlights for the first time another element of evil eye by suggesting that fascination is activated when there is a hunger for possessing; those who are highly praised by others or by themselves are more likely to experience the evil eye. Similarly, Eutelidas caused a fatal illness to himself by admiring his golden hair and face in his reflection in a stream; the case of Eutelidas is considered one of the first references to the evil eye (fascination) and its association with fatal illness and disease caused to oneself. Theoclitus also gives an account of fascination through the story of Damaetas, who fell in love with his own beauty and reflection. The interesting aspect of this story is that he was aware of the fascination, and in order to prevent any disease or misfortune he would spit on his chest three times; by doing so, he believed he was preventing fascination. The reason that he spat three times on his chest is still unknown, but what is clear from his reaction, other than the specific interest that ancient Greeks had in the power of numbers, is that even in ancient Greece there were certain rituals deployed in order to prevent fascination. There is also another interpretation of the evil eye in Greek mythology in addition to the one introduced by Narcissus. While Narcissus represents the evil eye through admiration, one of the most famous gorgons in Greek mythology explains the phenomenon through a broken heart, which was turned into stone and in its turn produced anger and envy. The term gorgon (Γοργώ) can be used to explain how anxiety provokes the power of the evil eye that gorgons could cast; the word derives from the Greek word Γοργώ, which means dreadful (Wilk 2000) and the reference is to the gorgon Medusa, who could turn people into stone through her gaze alone.

The evil eye emerged not only in Greek mythology but also in the works of great classicists such as Aristotle, Agamemnon, Plutarch and others. Plutarch, in his *Morals and Symposia*, makes reference to the evil eye in his interaction with his friend Soclarus during a supper in the Mertius Fiorus. He asserts that those who are under the influence of fascination are talking as if they are not themselves. Further analysis of such a statement brings to the forefront the dissociative attitudes that a sufferer of the evil eye might exhibit. Plutarch indicates here that those who have been cast with the evil eye have lost touch with reality; this is another reference signifying that the evil eye can affect someone's mental health. The description of these situations declares the presence of the evil eye and the way it affects an individual's well-being. As Plutarch states, those affected by the evil eye have no control over their actions and speech (Plutarch, 2012, 2013). Another account of the phenomenon is given by Heliodorus (1997) when Calasaris' daughter suddenly becomes severely ill. When she is asked what the matter is, she replies that she has been exposed and therefore seen by people, suggesting that the evil eye has been drawn upon her because she has been seen by others. Calasaris' case introduces the hypothesis that the evil eye can cause illness or bring 'madness' to someone. Calasaris' daughter also gives a rich description of the evil eye, asserting that malign influences affect the air that someone breathes. This poisonous air penetrates the eyes and therefore takes the royal path to the individual's psyche. After such an intrusion, the individual carries the noxious elements of envy within themselves. Heliodorus, however, for the first time links the evil eye with love, as in the case of Narcissus, and not with envy or admiration. He continues this thought by stating that such love is affected by envy and attracts malevolent love, even though the initial aim was to define the person in the physical world by providing love and portals such as 'mirrors' in order to be seen via their eye's reflection.

In his research on mental illness, Cartledge (2003) proposes that illness in Greek regions can be caused in individuals who have been praised or admired, supporting the theories about the evil eye and illness caused by admiration. The cause of this illness is the benevolent admiration of others, which is linked to the evil eye. From this, it has been concluded that the evil eye should be seen as having other links to mental illness than envy or menace, and I give credence to this idea. The belief system which links the evil eye to different causes of mental illness is explored throughout this book. Cartledge maintains that envy and pride constitute the fundamental elements of the evil eye and proposes that in ancient Greece, people lived with the fear of the evil eye, a condition that led them to rule their lives based on the concept of hubris. Hubris was strongly linked with arrogance and pride; it was a disrespectful act towards the gods, who would then unleash their wrath upon individuals to teach them a lesson. Hubris was therefore the cause of a person being overlooked by the gods, something which then caused them to enter the world of ghosts or the hallucinatory world (Cartledge 2003). The ancient Greeks feared the evil eye because of the illness that it could cause in others or themselves. Through hubris, one can see that there is a strong link between mental illness and reality. The Greeks were afraid of hubris because of their fear of not being in touch with their reality and themselves. However, it is not clear from the ancient Greek texts what caused the dissociation and delusional state that individuals experienced when possessed with the evil eye.

Reference has been made to the evil eye in antiquity and the effect that it had on the everyday life of Greeks. It is important to understand the phenomenon and its influence on the lives of individuals; thus, the next section gives an account of the evil eye and what might fuel it, according to current literature.

The classical Greeks through their writings clearly identified the importance of the eye and the ability to see the other. They also argued that the evil eye was not just concerned with envy and jealousy, but also with love and the innate need that humans have to be seen. The evil eye therefore becomes something more than envy; it becomes love, and at times broken love. The classical Greeks also attributed the power of the evil eye to gods and goddesses, associating it with divine powers. The paradox therefore arises of how all good gods and goddesses can have malicious attitudes towards humans as expressed through the evil eye. When engaging with the phenomenon of the evil eye and the Classics, one can observe that the evil eye fosters good and bad at the same time. This is the fundamental belief of dualism; thus, particular attention should be paid to the relationship between the evil eye and dualistic beliefs. Such an approach informs my research, which attempts to investigate the phenomenon of the evil eye by analysing the ways that its characteristics are manifested and coexist in one body, as in what follows.

DUALISM AND THE EVIL EYE

Paramount in Greek folklore and tradition is the belief that both good and bad influences can be part of an individual's psychical reality. Based on social-constructionist theory and alchemical beliefs, human beings try to find order in a capricious, chaotic and limited world. The mysterious forces of nature can only be faced, and in fact controlled (or at least that is what is believed), by mystical societal structures. Social morality itself is thus now subject to good and evil; the battle between good and evil cannot be perceived in Corfiot tradition in any other way than as the battle between survival and extinction, which is one of the core beliefs of Greek folklore (Russell 1998; Plato 2003). Soon after Plato introduced the theory of dualism of mind, Greek thought began to take the form of pairs of polarised concepts, often in conflict; the forces of cold and heat, God and evil, wet and dry, and so on (Plutarch 2002). This section aims to negotiate the relationship between dualism and the evil eye.

The theory of dualism of mind introduces humanity to the idea that the earth is limited in its resources. Thus, if human beings lose control of their impulses and inhibitions, they are confronted with the danger of exhausting the earth's goods. Plato (2003) proposed the notion that envious impulses could be fuelled by greed, which could lead to death. The idea of limited resources later creates tension among societies; this tension appears to cease with the development of the psychical defence reaction formation. This is because people develop gratitude as a means of surviving the evil eye and the death instinct that drives the actions that will exhaust the earth's resources. Thus, envy has become associated with gratitude. However, gratitude related to fear of the evil eye can cause mental illness, because the individual lives in constant fear that the increase of one's happiness comes at the expense of someone else's misery; therefore, calamities are caused to them both (Dundes 1992a; Walcot 1978). Greek Orthodoxy was influenced by platonic dualism when it proclaimed the teaching that those who have two of something should give one away. Only then does envy not take a malevolent form, and the chances of the privileged person being overlooked are reduced (Walcot 1978).

Dundes (1992a) was influenced by dualism, and the theories that subsequently followed that way of thinking were attempts to analyse the evil eye in that context. Dundes is particularly interested in the theory of 'wet and dry' and tries to apply it in his understanding of the phenomenon of the evil eye, especially during the Hellenistic period and the conceptualisation of the phenomenon. Dundes (1992a) and Onians (1988) point out that the Hellenists viewed the evil eye as a form of 'dry'; they state that the evil eye exhausts the fluids of the land, or the vital fluids necessary for the existence of human beings. Onians also indicates that headaches are a minor symptom that one can experience due to lack of vital fluids; he believes that they are caused when the brain's fluids are dried up. He expands his theory, stating that the dryness is caused by overlook (positive or negative), which activates the evil eye. Dundes, in agreement with Onians, suggests that the limited resources of the earth have an impact on the fluids of humans. The evil eye thus drains individuals' fluids, which are fundamental for life. Greek historical thinking, which might have affected Greek Orthodox teaching, held that cremation hastens the process of drying and goes against the natural process by which it occurs. It violates and prematurely liberates the soul, and this is one of the reasons why Greek Orthodoxy does not accept cremation; it is also one reason behind the particular interest in the phenomenon (Dundes 1992b).

Following an exploration of antiquity in relation to the evil eye and the platonic theory of dualism, we have been confronted with different ideas about the evil eye and what triggers it. In addition, this section demonstrated that the evil eye is a phenomenon which supports a dualistic belief that the threat of extinction looms if the battle between good and bad does not develop into a dialogue and ultimately lead to peaceful coexistence. Such thinking led this research to investigate whether the manifestation of the evil eye perpetuates an internal fear of 'death' in individuals' psyches. However, nothing has been mentioned so far as to how the evil eye is manifested in the broader geographical area of the Mediterranean, and more specifically in Greece, and how the phenomenon is related to Orthodoxy and Greek society. This is the aim of the following section. In addition, the next section examines the ways in which the evil eye is manifested in individuals' everyday lives. Such understanding facilitates a negotiation of the importance of the phenomenon in regard to its influence over humanity.

MANIFESTATIONS OF THE EVIL EYE IN THE MEDITERRANEAN AND THE GREEK ORTHODOX FAITH

This section aims to give a brief introduction to the relationship between Greek Orthodox faith and the evil eye in the wider area of the Mediterranean. In the Mediterranean context, Jones (1951) suggested that belief in the evil eye evolves in people's consciousness, giving rise to the fear that some people possess eyes from which just a glance can cause calamities or even death. However, Jones' argument was met with scepticism and received a lot of criticism. Even though some scholars agreed with Jones' proposal that belief in the evil eye is a universal phenomenon, others argued against this view, stating that belief in the evil eye is culturally constructed, and that even though it is a transcultural phenomenon, its identity is formed by the society in which it takes place (Bohigian 1997b; Roberts 1976). Marchese (2001) disagrees with Roberts' (1976) argument that the evil eye is not universal. I agree with Marchese in supporting the hypothesis that the evil eye might appear in most cultures globally, but also concur with Roberts that its functionality and purpose cannot be seen as universal, and that the specific cultural context in which the evil eye manifests needs to be examined in order to develop a comprehensive understanding of the phenomenon. In order to understand the phenomenon we might therefore need to investigate it through its origin in the Mediterranean regions, where it endures even in present times (Murdock 1962; Galt 1982).

In the Mediterranean region, people appear to believe that an evil eye sufferer can only be treated by what is known as folk medicine or by a healer (Herzfeld 1981). A healer is either a priest, or anyone who has experience and can apply different rituals based on the evil eye's severity. However, this view has been characterised as historical and without statistical reliability; therefore, Wing (1998) suggests that more research should be done in regard to the evil eye and biomedical treatment, as it appears that folk healers are engaging in medieval methods which may be risky for the sufferer. Wing's view, however, does not pay respect to the ethnographic characteristics that the evil eye might adopt; he is looking instead to categorise or quantify the phenomenon. For this reason, due to the mental health aspect, which is subordinated to the evil eye, and also given its ethnographic validity, it would be appropriate to place the healing process of the evil eye within the ethnomedicinal field. Recent research by Seremetakis (2009) supports the notion that even though biomedicine influences almost all urban societies, Greece appears to resist this influence; therefore, Greeks still seek treatment from folk healers in relation to the evil eye. On her trips in Greek villages,

Seremetakis observed evil eye exorcism via the telephone. The sufferer has quick and easy access to the healer through modern information technology. Seremetakis argues that the evil eye is not just universal, but rather is also adjusted to the cultural circumstances which have enabled the phenomenon to survive. She therefore invites us to engage with the evil eye as an archaic phenomenon which not only declares its presence in the current time, but also interacts with technological matters and affects individuals' mental health.

One of the most prominent things that keeps individuals' interest in the evil eye alive in the Mediterranean is the introduction of the phenomenon into pop culture. Divination and the evil eye appear to be a point of interest for the Mediterranean media and in Mediterranean literature. Jones (1951) gives a historical overview of the phenomenon and how it was transferred across different areas. He also talks about the effect that Mediterranean people have on other cultures and mentions that immigrants brought with them their belief in the evil eye, which has slowly impinged on their new social contexts. It is important at this point to focus on Christian Orthodox religious beliefs and how they are related to the evil eye, as this is the focus of the current study.

It has been observed that the Church has a strong relationship with the practices and beliefs associated with the evil eye (Hardie 1981). Furthermore, while Kingdon et al. (2002) proposes that churches within the Eastern tradition consider the belief to be superstitious, she also notes that there is incongruence between the doctrinal teachings of the Church and everyday practices. Therefore, on the one hand the official Church does not engage with the phenomenon, despite the fact that it might recognise it; on the other hand, there are rituals and charms that priests engage with in order to cast out the evil eye from believers. In addition, Kingdon makes the observation that monotheistic religions such as Christianity and Islam engage with the phenomenon of the evil eye in their everyday existence without any attempt to suppress it, and therefore create certain behavioural attitudes towards it, which become implanted in individuals' consciousnesses. To strengthen this argument, it has been observed that everyday rituals – as performed by religious leaders – and the charms with which they are executed not only aim to resist and suppress the phenomenon but in fact reinforce its existence (Tripp-Reimer 1983). Up until recent times, Christianity has had a substantial place in the lives of Greek Orthodox people. Hence, many protective charms can be seen in homes; these consist of crucifixes, saints, pieces of saints' clothes and similar objects. One significant observation that can be made in the Greek Christian tradition regards the role of the Virgin Mary in protecting someone from the evil eye. Tripp-Reimer (ibid.) maintains that the Virgin Mary in Christianity, and especially in the Greek Orthodox and Catholic traditions, has the ultimate power to protect someone from *matiasma* (giving the eye).

What makes the phenomenon psychologically and ethnographically important and interesting is the complexity of its diagnosis and treatment. Even though the rituals adopt prescribed and at times similar patterns, every healer, whether folk healer or priest, develops their own style and methods in order to identify and heal the evil eye (Appel 1976; Quave and Pieroni 2005). However, the commonalities come from the symbolism of the elements and materials used for the casting out of the evil eye. Appel (1976) proposes that in the Christian tradition, the number three plays a significant role as it represents the Holy Trinity, and water's purifying powers represent the first sacrament of exorcism, namely baptism. Once again, the wording used in the exorcism rituals may vary from caster to caster; however, there is a congruence between them since they all appeal to the Holy Trinity. Seremetakis (2009) highlights the incongruence between everyday life and the doctrinal Eastern Christian life, explaining that Eastern Christian priests go so far as to use and accept special prayers for protection in the case of demonic affliction that might be manifested in the form of the evil eye. Therefore, Seremetakis concludes that Greek Orthodox priests have designed and use their own rituals to exorcise the evil eye, calling sufferers victims of the evil eye. Such a major involvement of the Church in the evil eye facilitates a separation between the phenomenon and Westernised biomedical models of maladies, while at the same time it increases the manifestation of the evil eye in these societies.

In regard to the evil eye, there is some truth to the idea that the phenomenon finds supporters in the upper classes or among those who have stronger influence and a higher socio-economic status. However, such a view appears to be historical, and recent studies suggest that the evil eye may be observed across all social classes and educational backgrounds; therefore, the current study does not exclude any individual based on their sociocultural background (Appel 1976; Seremetakis 2009). Greek tradition contains many accounts across all educational backgrounds and social statuses which tell of misfortune due to the possession of the evil eye.

The evil eye is strongly connected with faith in modern Greece, and it is seeded into people's unconsciousness through faith, culture and tradition. Aquaro (2001) asserts that envy is present in every society and culture, as it is part of human nature; at the same time, it appears to be central to the fallen condition of humankind in Greek Orthodoxy. There is a belief in Greek Orthodoxy that there is no need to explain or investigate what is obvious (ibid.). However, envy is a dominant element of the evil eye, which can cause death or illness, and envy appears to be the primal sin of human beings. While in Western societies there is a belief that original sin makes people guilty of sin, the Greek Orthodox Church holds that all human beings are subject to the curse of sin. We (human beings) feel guilty in trans-generational reality because of Adam's sin and his fall from the Garden of Eden. If envy is now the main sin of Adam and Eve and the one which caused their fall, then the whole understanding of Jesus' sacrifice and redemption is open to another interesting interpretation; that is, that Jesus Christ was sacrificed to save humanity from the same feeling of envy that led him to death. If this is the case, death, envy and the evil eye can be used interchangeably (ibid.). Theophilus of Antioch was one of the first Christians to suggest envy as the motivation of Satan in sending the serpent into the Garden of Eden (Russell 1981). St Basil the Great devoted a whole treatise to discussion of the phenomenon of the evil eye, envy and death.

It was later that the Greek Orthodox Church developed the Euchologion (Ευχολόγιον), which includes prayers against the evil eye. However, Canon 61 of the fifth Ecumenical Council forbade and designated as heretical everything that had been constructed by humans or used by humans in order to protect sufferers from the evil eye. This meant that the use of magic and amulets was forbidden (Ware 1993). The use of blue amulets, which is common among Greek Christians and in Eastern societies, fell into the same category of magical amulets and is therefore not accepted by the Greek Church, according to St John Chrysostom in Homily 8 of Canon 3:5–7. During the Byzantine era, a peacock or a peacock's feather afforded strong protection against the evil eye. It was said that peacocks had the divine power to cast away the overlook (Peabody 2001). Nowadays, Greek beliefs in the evil eye are an amalgamation of folk tales told throughout the nation's history. Such amalgamation causes confusion, as each region has different beliefs and rituals for protection.

The existence of belief in the evil eye in the Mediterranean region has been briefly discussed. The evil eye has been explored in relation to the Greek Orthodox tradition and how it can affect individuals in their everyday lives. At the same time, this section explored some Christian Fathers and the prayers that they used in order to treat the evil eye and its manifestation. According to Aquaro (2001), the evil eye is strongly linked to envy and jealousy, which in effect was the origin of the evil eye, as revealed in Genesis. Other Christian references, such as the Euchologion, have been discussed. What follows digs deeper into the Greek Orthodox tradition and its relationship with the evil eye.

THE GREEK ORTHODOX TRADITION
AND THE PHENOMENON OF THE EVIL EYE

This section focuses on the Greek Orthodox Church's understanding of the phenomenon of evil eye. The Church officially recognises two types of the evil eye. The first type is *vaskania*. This refers to the jealousy and envy felt by some people for things they do not possess, such as beauty, youth and courage. The Church has many prayers for protection from *vaskania* and for offering a cure from it. The second type of the evil eye is *glossofayia* (those who constantly talk about others' happiness and possessions) or *koutsompolio* (those who have malevolent intentions when they talk about others). However, the Church prohibits believers from consulting those who practise folk rituals and witchcraft to cast out the evil eye, as this is outside the religious beliefs and rituals of the Church (Dionisopoulos-Mass 1976; Papademetriou 1974).

The Greek Orthodox Church did not initially accept the belief in the evil eye, as this goes against its main belief in the Divine. However, the silent prayers which clergy read during the Divine Liturgy clearly declare that the Church strongly believes in the power of the evil eye as a morbid corollary of envy. Dundes (1992a) maintains that in the Greek Church there is a secret rite – which is passed from generation to generation – with which adherents may perform a sort of exorcism of the evil eye. Charles (1991) adds that the rite of exorcism of the evil eye is not solely the purview of a priest, but may also by carried out by an old woman devoted to the Greek Church; this has, however, been declared heretical by the Church. Dundes (1992a) argues that Greeks have been influenced by those who believe in witchcraft and who think that old women possess the knowledge and experience required to perform such rituals, as well as the ability to interfere with a person's psychical life and cause calamities. Taking influence from Dundes' fieldwork on the evil eye and his observations of the rituals of casting it, my research is concerned with the determination of the different types of informants. The present study is therefore interested in revisiting Dundes' idea about those who can cast the evil eye and how they interact with each other.

There is a paradox, however, within the Greek Orthodox Church regarding the evil eye. On the one hand, the Church is sceptical and at times critical in regard to the phenomenon, but on the other hand, there are prayers to protect the faithful from it. At face value these may seem opposing beliefs, but further examination reveals that it is more a case of different approaches. The Church accepts the idea of the evil eye, but not the fact that a simple look can cause misfortune or even death; it accepts belief in the evil eye under the umbrella of envy and demonic possession. However, St Nikodemos of Mount Athos, in his teaching, specifically mentions the two different types of *vaskania* and envy. Influenced by St Nikodemos, the Church holds the view that envious human beings, or even demonic powers, need mediation, which both humans and demons find through the use of the evil eye. In St Basil the Great's exorcism prayer there are particular descriptions of the evil eye as a representation of demonic powers, as in the words: 'Who shall bind you that dares envy to plot against His image'. The Greek Church does not believe that the evil eye can kill a person or cause any mental health problems; such a belief is instead a pagan one. However, the Church does believe that those who envy someone or something a great deal can cast the evil eye, which causes physical and mental harm.

It is worth mentioning the connection between one of the major Orthodox saints, namely St George, and belief in the evil eye and mental health (King Solomon 2008). According to Aquaro (2004), there is a strong connection between the fear of the evil eye and St George. St George is often represented on a horse, killing a dragon or a demon, but one might wonder about the connection between the saint and this creature. The answer lies in the story of King Solomon. Ankarloo and Clark (1999) reveal that King Solomon played a leading role in Hellenised Christian magic. In the apocryphal book of Solomon's Testament, the reader is exposed to the great powers that King Solomon possessed in order to exorcise satanic forces; this is where the evil eye belongs (King Solomon 2008). King Solomon gains power over the demons after an interview with them, upon which he builds his theory of demonology; it is only through knowing the demon that someone can gain control over it. According to King Solomon, Beelzeboul is the demon who is responsible for the evil eye, envy and death. He also suggests that there is another demon, who is called Envy; he is headless and has the ability to steal human beings' mental capacity by possessing them through their eyes. This is one of the first references in the Greek Orthodox tradition to suggest that the evil eye can cause mental disorders. However, the headless predicament appears to have a long history in Greek Orthodoxy. St George and King Solomon appear to have a strong connection with the headless demon, as they are both attributed powers against the demon Envy, the headless beast. Hence, they both became the protectors of those who had lost their mind (Ankarloo and Clark 1999; Aquaro 2004).

Greek Orthodox tradition and beliefs are therefore strongly correlated with the evil eye. Schmemann (1974) maintains that Satan was sufficiently wise and divine to know God well enough to decide to go against him. Therefore, he and other angels opposed God and became the perverted version of the angelic order. Satan was not created evil but chose to be so. This belief is linked to the theory of dualism regarding good and evil. Potentially, all human beings are predetermined to be good or bad, and can therefore cast the evil eye onto others out of envy; all human beings can be envious, but the story of Satan provides another version of the evil eye, one which introduces the idea of free will. Human beings have free will, which enables them to oppose good by entering the ranks of evil. Through the evil eye, satanic powers aim to prevent human beings from working towards heavenly goals; demons do not want people to enter the place from which they have fallen. According to Papademetriou (1974) and Cunningham (2002), the evil eye can take the form of demonic possession as a method of preventing someone from being in a relationship with God. The Greek Orthodox Church thus acknowledges and accepts that the evil eye is strongly linked with demonic influences.

Ware (1996), a highly respected Orthodox theologian, asserts that Satan is not just an idea to be played with, but is a real being; he is among us and can be experienced through emotions and behaviours. Such a belief is shared by the Greek Orthodox Church, and it maintains the idea that anyone can be possessed by demons at any point. Ware extends his argument, stating that the Lord's Prayer (Matt. 6:9–13) identifies Satan as a real being: 'but deliver us from the evil one'. The end of that prayer indicates that human beings need protection from this 'evil one'. Elliot (1992) argues that even Jesus made a reference to the evil eye; he therefore maintains that belief in the evil eye was an aspect of Jesus' Hebrew culture. In the Sermon on the Mount, Jesus talked about the negative effects that possession of material goods could cause to an individual's well-being. This negative effect is caused by the overlook of others; Jesus therefore proclaimed that it is better to look for heavenly riches than earthly ones. Papanikolas (2002) attempts to interpret this particular aspect of Jesus' teachings, arguing that individuals become envious of those who have more material goods. Envy can cause people to cast the evil eye. Papanikolas develops his thinking further, stating that the evil eye weakens a person's body and soul (the person's existential core) as it acts from within both. Nicholson (1999), however, argues that the evil eye can cause people to become mentally ill, have accidents, suffer from bad luck, be possessed by demons or even die, but we need to be careful associating it with an individual's soul. On the other hand, Moss and Cappannari (1976) contradict Nicholson by suggesting that the eyes are a window to the soul, which expose the inner world and spirituality of a person to demonic influences. It is through the eye that demons find their way into a person's body and cause suffering and pain to their spirit (Papanikolas 2002; Moss and Cappannari 1976). Furthermore, the evil eye can be witnessed within Greek Orthodox tradition, which is deeply rooted in the Orthodox faith. It is still believed that people can be so jealous of others that they can cause harm to each other, allowing demonic powers to find a host within their spiritual world and cause harm through their eyes (Nicholson 1999; Papanikolas 2002).

According to Greek customs and tradition, there is a strong belief that some folk forces, commonly known as the evil eye, can rule a Christian's life. Campion and Bhugra (1997) argue that these forces are strongly linked to fear, if not terror, and are transmitted from older to younger generations. These forces are documented clearly in the prayer books used by the Greek Orthodox Church.

In our exploration of the Greek Orthodox tradition and the evil eye, and as we came to understand the actuality of the evil eye in the believer's life, it became vital that we uncover manifestations of the evil eye in the Bible – one of the most significant documents in Christianity – to further our attempt to understand the phenomenon. In this section, the evil eye has been analysed and approached in relation to its perception within the Greek Orthodox Church and tradition; this subchapter has given an introduction to the religious beliefs into which the research will dive in order to investigate the phenomenon. Little, however, has been mentioned in regards to the symptomatology of the evil eye within the Greek Orthodox tradition, or the rituals that exist to protect someone from the evil eye's symptomatology, or in fact to cast it out. For this reason, the following section discusses the symptomatology as observed in Greek Orthodox tradition and the rituals used to protect someone from this symptomatology.

THE SYMPTOMATOLOGY OF THE EVIL EYE AND PROTECTIVE RITUALS

The phenomenon of the evil eye is activated by the individual's need to possess what they do not have; such a desire can emit negative energy which can cause harm or damage to both animate and inanimate objects and subjects (Parrot and Smith 1993). Lazarus (2006), in his summary of coping strategies for dealing with stress stemming from folk beliefs, adds that an envious person – or to be more precise, an envious person's eye – can cause harm to object(s) or to other people who are in a more privileged position (such as being richer, happier or more successful) than they are. This section therefore gives a thorough account of the symptomatology that individuals experience when they are possessed or cast under the evil eye. What follows also gives an account of the rituals most frequently used to cast evil eye out from someone as observed in the literature.

Based on their fieldwork in Greece, the anthropologists Stegemann and Stegemann (1995) assert that although Greece is in a privileged geographical location, it is also cursed because its resources are scarce. Therefore, Greeks believe that social constructs such as culture, economy and technology fuel the phenomenon of the evil eye, which affects the richness of the soil. Levine and Campbell (1995) extend this argument by suggesting that social classification regarding a person's socio-economic status is a dualist construct, which supports the theory of limited resources. Hence, social classes appear to empower the phenomenon of the evil eye not only between classes but also among members of the same social class, based on belief in the cosmic balance, which originated in dualism, the theory of opposition and the alchemical basic theory of material balance. It is thus believed that when resources are imbalanced, disaster(s) can happen, and this can also take the form of mental illness or damage through the evil eye (Elliot 1992). People in Greece have been living with the anxiety and fear that the improvement of one person's social condition might be at the expense of another's. Therefore, Greeks have been causing harm to their own well-being, living with a constantly suspicious state of mind which causes friction in human relationships. Concurrently, a state of mind that fuels envy empowers the phenomenon of the evil eye (Elliot 1992).

According to the Greek Orthodox Church tradition, as seen in a study by Dionisopoulos-Mass (1976), those who suffer from the evil eye (*matiastei*, *ματιαστεί*) experience headaches, lethargy, nausea, a lack of appetite, or dizziness. It is important here to revisit Dionisopoulos-Mass's summary of evil eye manifestations, which divides the everyday manifestations of the phenomenon into two categories: the *matiasma* (*μάτιασμα*) and the *vaskania* (*Βασκανία*). *Matiasma* happens in everyday life and can be caused by anyone; the term is derived from the word 'eye' ('*mati*'), which is strongly linked to the evil eye (ibid.). *Vaskania*, on the other hand, means the tendency to kill by casting the evil eye onto someone. Of these two types of evil eye, *vaskania* is the more dangerous and can inflict spiritual suffering or even death. The symptoms associated with the evil eye have been described as psychosomatic; the most common somatic symptoms are headache, organ pain (mostly in the area of the stomach), eye ache (which results in an inability to see clearly), joint ache and tiredness. The less commonly reported somatic symptoms are vomiting, anorexia, tremors, asthma and paralysis. The psychological symptoms that are linked to the presence of the evil eye have been reported as anxiety, obsession, insomnia, persecutory fantasies, anger and hate, envy, pathological doubt, depression, extreme fear, hyperactivity and aggression (Campion and Bhugra 1997; Pfeifer 1994).

Following Blum and Blum (1970), it would be remiss to talk about the phenomenon of the evil eye without paying attention to the rituals deployed to cast it out from a sufferer. This section takes a wider view of the rituals for protection adopted globally in order to highlight similarities and variances. One of the most significant rituals comes from the Arbereshe culture, which states that individuals affected by the evil eye need to believe in order to be cured (Galt 1982). Arbereshe people introduce the element of belief into the healing process. They counterbalance belief in the evil eye with belief in goodness; they maintain that it is only through the sufferer's will to believe in the healing ritual that the healing process is actually activated. According to Migliore (1997), Arbereshe culture is the same as Greek culture in suggesting that religion plays an important role in the ritual of exorcising the evil eye. Papanikolas (2002) proposes that demonic powers find pathway through human jealousy in order to manifest themselves in our spiritual world. It is only through belief in the greater power of saints, Jesus, God or the Holy Spirit that the evil eye can be cast out of a person's body, and the transition from being possessed to being a healthy and spiritual individual facilitated (Quave and Pieroni 2005).

After his fieldwork in Mesopotamia, Thomsen (1992) revealed that in order to protect their babies from the evil eye, parents repeatedly spat on them, mumbling, '*Sj nu-i fie de deochiu*!' ('Let it not be a cause of casting the evil eye'). Mesopotamians also called their babies ugly as a way to protect them from fascination (ibid.). According to Mesopotamian and Greek tradition, it is commonly believed that babies have magical powers and are able to understand and spot the evil eye. Therefore, when they sense the evil eye, they start crying or become uneasy. Mesopotamians are very protective of their children, knowing that their purity and spirituality attract the evil eye; there is a strong positive correlation between spirituality and religiosity on the one hand and satanic phenomena and manifestations on the other. Albanians, conversely, ground their rituals against the evil eye in nature. They maintain that cows possessed with evil give bloodied milk, and they therefore spit on their children to protect them from the evil eye (Arensberg 1965; Garrison and Conrad 1976).

Another ritual related to the evil eye comes from Serbia, where mothers often wear a red thread on their middle finger during pregnancy in order to protect their baby from being possessed by the evil eye later on (Murgoci 1923). An alternative version of this ritual can be found in Macedonia, where individuals wear red and white threads around their necks or wrists. Similar beliefs can be found in China, where the colour red symbolises good luck (Simmons and Schindler 2003). Another tradition, similar to the Greek one, comes from Bangladesh, where for the first nine days after a baby's birth the mother stays at home to protect her child from the 'eyes' (one can also draw similarities to the Gaelic islanders' belief in the spiritual number nine and its power against fascination). The baby must not leave the house until the women have created charms with words from the Koran for protection against the evil eye. Most commonly, though, mothers place a black dot on their baby's forehead, which represents the '*kujul*' (the ultimate protection) (Lawn et al. 2004; Marsh et al. 2002; Winch et al. 2005). In traditional Anatolian folklore, mothers try to keep their neonates away from any strangers' view, believing that babies are subject to spiritual attack from evil through the possession of the evil eye until they adjust to their worldly reality, which takes place within ninety days. In most cultures, mothers argue that the evil eye can cause mental illness in later life.

In his extensive fieldwork in one of the Scottish Gaelic regions of Italian villages, Wirt (1982) discovered that old women who could exorcise the evil eye were producing oral charms while tying a red thread in a cross. Residents of villages in southern Italy believe that the red thread in a cross protects individuals and households from the evil eye and witchcraft. Wirt argues that the evil eye is strongly correlated with witchcraft in people's consciousness. However, it is argued that the unconscious belief in witchcraft makes individuals more vulnerable to the evil eye (Murgoci 1923; Wirt 1982). In addition to that belief, residents from southern Italy have developed a specific interest in numerology and its healing energy, which may be deployed against the evil eye. To be more precise, the spiritual numbers of three and nine (the trinity multiplied by itself) are powerful numbers against the evil eye; they therefore incorporate these numbers into their lives (Black 2007). However, the most complicated amulet against the evil eye to incorporate healing numbers comes from Pennsylvania. The number of the ingredients used for these protective amulets should be three, as this represents the spiritual number in numerology and the Holy Trinity. The ingredients can be garlic bulbs, salt and pepper grains, spring and autumn wheat, incense, bread crumbs or a child's caul (Gifford 1960).

In Central Europe, however, and more precisely in the Bukowina area of Poland, people tend to use rituals to create protective shields from the evil eye. Midwives here put up a red tassel, nailing it over the front door of the house where the newborn is to live. It is suggested that this keeps envious eyes away and shields the house from the evil eye (Thomsen 1992). Thomsen also observes that needles and red thread on the threshold are employed to protect a household from negative energy in general. Similarly, in Macedonia, twisted white and red threads are put onto a silver knife at the door to protect households and their members from the 'eye'. However, Murgoci (1923) clarifies that red and white threads in combination with a silver knife are not for protection against the evil eye specifically, but against any evil spirits. Another belief about the evil eye comes from the East, specifically from the Ottoman tradition, and supports the Eastern Christian belief regarding the phenomenon. Belief about the evil eye is strongly integrated into Turks' everyday lives and is associated with the negative influences of demonic spirits. They also believe that in order to be protected from the evil eye's powers, the use of blue amulets is necessary. They therefore suggest that people should wear something blue at all times, rather than red and white threads (Bettez 1995; Siebers 1983). In the former territories of the Ottoman Empire, people believe even today that praising someone can attract envy, and therefore that the *nazar* (evil eye) is cast. Ottoman tradition dictates that if a person praises someone else, they should also clearly state that they mean no harm. Therefore, most times they should repeat the word '*masallah*' ('may God protect you from the gaze') (Berger 2011; Rolleston et al. 1961). This defuses the negative influence that such admiration might cause to the praised individual and soothes the negative effect that the evil eye can have upon that person. Religious leaders play a significant role in protection against the evil eye in Muslim-Ottoman regions. People usually seek out religious leaders for protection and healing from the evil eye, who then pray for those who are suffering from it (Özden 1987; Yalin 1998). Yalin (1998) argues that those suffering from this condition turn to spiritual or religious healers rather than consulting the medical professions. In doing so they feel better understood and not dismissed, as Yalin and Özden suggest.

Another ritual used against the evil eye, common among Balkan villagers, is *kurşun dökme*: the pouring of water, ideally holy water, over the heads of those who suffer from the phenomenon. Such a ritual finds parallels in the Yugoslavs' *baba* (an old woman who is experienced and skilled in casting out the evil eye from a sufferer). The ritual that she follows involves putting charcoal into water while repeating prayers. If she cannot create a prayer, then she says the Lord's Prayer. She then pours the water on the sufferer's head (Bettez 1995; Berger 1997).

In Mehedinti, on the other hand, the person who can cast out the evil eye uses bread instead of charcoal, especially after the sacraments, as in Yugoslavia. The priest thus throws a crumb of bread, representing the body of Christ after the sacrament, into a glass of water. If the crumb stays on the surface, it is an indication that the sufferer will get better soon. If the crumb goes to the bottom, the sufferer no longer belongs to the world and the priest starts the death lament (Berger 2011; Reiter 1981). This tradition parallels the ritual followed by the *baba* in the Balkans. The healer puts two pieces of charcoal (life and death) into a bowl of water. If the piece representing life goes to the bottom, the sufferer will die soon, while if it stays on the top, the sufferer will be healed (Murgoci 1923; Dundes 1981). Berger (1977) also points out that in Mehedinti tradition, the wax ritual is also followed. The religious or spiritual healers warm up candles and then rapidly cool the wax. The wax then takes the human form. If the head is upwards, it is an indication that the evil eye is not fatal. If the head looks downwards, however, the person is about to die.

The above examples give significant information about the rituals of protection against the evil eye, and in doing so facilitate a better understanding of the phenomenon as it is observed in the field later on. More precisely, these examples give the reader a better understanding of the complexity of the phenomenon while at the same time providing an introduction for what follows in this book. The specific topics which have been analysed up to this point give an overview of the phenomenon of the evil eye as it has been observed in different geographical areas, and inform the research and its quest to link the phenomenon with the Greek Orthodox tradition – something that is actually rare in the existing literature. This provides context for the later sections, which will consider the evil eye in the geographical area of Corfu. The following section therefore engages with the Orthodox tradition even further in relation to the phenomenon of evil eye, making its primary focus the Greek Orthodox traditions and practices around protective rituals.

PROTECTIVE RITUALS FROM EVIL EYE IN THE GREEK TRADITIONS AND CUSTOMS

Greek tradition has developed many ways to protect individuals from the evil eye, such as spitting in the presence of those who possess it, or wearing protective amulets in the form of blue eyes, phalluses, and clothes of blue or red colour (Papanikolas 2002). The ritual that old women can follow includes olive oil and a small glass of water; the woman dips her index finger in the oil and then creates the sign of the cross on the forehead of the possessed individual, before dropping one drop of olive oil in the water. This process is repeated three times, moving on to the cheeks and then the chin of the possessed person. If the person is possessed by the evil eye, the oil drops take the form of an eye. Then the old woman starts saying prayers – which are kept secret – enabling the concentrated oil to be dispersed (Charles 1991). The Greek Church follows Jesus in his works against the power of the evil eye in his ministry. In the early years of the Greek Church, the prayers of exorcism against the evil eye were performed only by experienced and designated priests and exorcists. It is only recently that it has become acceptable for any priest to perform exorcism due to the order of his Ecclesiastical authority (Church of Greece 1999). These different means of protection against the evil eye appear to invoke the Latin phrase *similia similibus* ('like dissolves like' or 'likes are cured by likes'), which is the basic rule of witchcraft.

Based on Greek customs, parents pin blue eye amulets on their babies' clothes in order to protect them from the evil eye. Dinonisopoulos-Mass (1976) suggests that babies have the ability to cast away those who have the evil eye; when newborns sense someone with the intention of doing harm through the evil eye, they become uneasy or bite their mother during breastfeeding. It is common to see people on the streets secretly spitting as a way of protecting themselves or their loved ones from the evil eye, or making sexual gestures towards those who possess the evil eye (that is, touching their genitals).

Even today the belief persists in Greece that red and white threads around individuals' wrists are sufficient to protect them from the evil eye (Murgoci 1923; Zauberdiagnose and Schwarze 1992). According to Eastern Christian tradition, red represents blood, and more specifically Jesus' sacrificial blood. Red also represents the blood on the door that protected the Jews from the angel of death in the tenth plague. Based on Greek tradition, the blue beads are known as 'preventing stones', or stones that can prevent misfortune. In ancient Greece, blue was the colour used to prevent miscarriages (Zoysa et al. 1998). The colour has subsequently been used to prevent misfortune and the evil eye (Peabody 2006). However, during the pagan years, blue was attributed the power to counterbalance the dark phase of the moon. Thus, it was believed that blue shielded a person's body from the power of black magic, and therefore misfortune could not be caused to that person (ibid.).

The phenomenon endures as a powerful folk belief in Greece, and no one likes to talk about it or its manifestations, so as to protect themselves from it. It remains unspoken, and only within the Church can it be named and therefore treated. The Church recognises a wooden cross as a protective amulet against the evil eye. However, the wood should be taken from the trees of recognised monasteries or convents (Dionisopoulos-Mass 1976). Children cannot wear a cross until the day they are baptised; the Church suggests that a small icon, blessed by a priest, would be the appropriate way to protect unbaptised children from demonic powers. Finally, the Church proposes that drinking holy water *(ayiasmos, αγιασμός)* from the Epiphany celebration of the blessing of the waters can protect people from satanic manifestations. In addition, regular practice of the faith, confession and receiving Holy Communion are the best means to garner protection from the evil eye (ibid.). Due to the divergent historical influences, people from different Greek districts adopt different rituals to protect themselves from the evil eye.

The Church maintains that the first defence against demonic powers and the evil eye is the sacrament of baptism. Through baptism, the baby receives the first ritual of exorcism. This belief can also be found in works of fiction. Dante Aligheri, in his masterpiece *The Divine Comedy*, placed dead, unbaptised children in the first level of Hell, in front of Hell's gate. Through baptism, the baby is immersed in water, which symbolises life, as water is the major element of life and no one can survive without it. Water also symbolises fluidity and passage from death into life, and therefore symbolises purification and rebirth. The oil of chrism used during baptism brings healing and enlightenment, which introduces the baby to a full Christian and sacramental life (Schmemann 1974).

According to Greek Orthodox beliefs, Jesus is the incomparable exorcist. It is His name that priests use to cast demons out of human bodies and to empower themselves when facing demonic powers. Only under Jesus' name can the process of spiritual healing be accomplished (Papademetriou 1974). In terms of the *vaskania*, which is the worst type of evil eye, the Typikon suggests that the exorcist should start the procedure with the blessing, followed by Trisagion prayers; next, the exorcist says Psalms 142, 22, 26, 67 and 50, and then follows the hymn of the Canon of Supplication to our Lord Jesus Christ. Part of the healing ritual is the blessing of the oil, which is later used in exorcism. Finally, three prayers of exorcism by St Basil the Great and four prayers of St John Chrysostom are said to complete the ritual. However, according to the Typikon, the oil used in exorcism is blessed and given to the possessed person after the exorcism of the evil eye, as protection for the rest of their life. There is a tradition, especially in northern parts of Greece, which dictates that the oil used in the first exorcism of the evil eye is buried with the individual when they pass away (Dundes 1992b).

In Greek society individuals consult their priest rather than their doctor for spiritual issues (Peterson-Bidoshi 2006; Thomas 1971). The Greek Church approaches the phenomenon of the evil eye in its mild and moderate form in the simplest but most powerful way, namely the sacrament of the Holy Eucharist. Those who are possessed with the evil eye have only to prepare themselves to receive Holy Communion. The Holy Eucharist is the oldest liturgy in Greek Orthodoxy; it cannot be taught but is rather experienced (Schmemann 1997). Its origin goes back to the Last Supper that Jesus had with his disciples, where he gave clear instructions about the way to offer bread and wine as his flesh and blood in his memory. The Holy Eucharist is one of the most important liturgies due to the fact that the congregation and the clergy are united in the name of the same God. Through the Holy Eucharist the cosmic balance is restored by the celebration of both dead and living powers; it is the perfect integration of these polarised forces (Scotland

1989). The Holy Eucharist is offered through three different rituals of the Divine Liturgy: the liturgy of St John Chrysostom, the liturgy of St Basil the Great and the liturgy of St James. The first two saints and their teachings are used for exorcisms in severe cases of possession by the evil eye, as mentioned above. Holy Communion is therefore considered the most powerful way to protect against the evil eye (Schmemann 1997).

Some contemporary views regarding rituals against the evil eye come from different societies. In Lucanian societies, religious leaders pray three times and read prayers against the sufferer's evil eye. These leaders say that they pray three times while holding a cross or a saint's icon, as the number three symbolises the Holy Trinity and its power over Satan and his demons. Three is also a spiritual number in numerology, linked with healing power and purification. It is also argued that the prayers can be adjusted according to the sufferer's symptomatology. If the symptoms are persistent, the sufferer can only seek another's help after nine days have elapsed since the first exorcism; nine is three multiplied by itself (Bettez 1995).

Following this discussion on the evil eye and its symptomatology, it is important to examine whether the phenomenon has any connection to an individual's mental health. Such an investigation allows us to emphasise the connection that the phenomenon might have with the individuals' suffering. It also highlights the current research's interest in examining the connection not only between the evil eye and mental health, but also between both phenomena and Christian Orthodox tradition and beliefs. Therefore, the exploration of the evil eye and the protective rituals has paved the way for the question of whether the evil eye can in fact cause mental illnesses. However, before we explore such a correlation, we must understand the functioning of the mental health system in Greece. This is the main focus of what follows.

THE MENTAL HEALTH SYSTEM IN MODERN GREECE AND THE CORRELATION WITH THE EVIL EYE

The mental health system in Greece is still at a premature stage, and unfortunately it is developing very slowly. Mental illness carries stigma, and it is commonly accepted that Greeks do not speak about this topic, as it is something they are ashamed of and feel the need to keep secret (Douzenis 2007). After researching the Greek mental health system, Douzenis found that most of the time, individuals with mental health issues are forced to leave their homes and go into hospitals or asylums where they are compelled to rest in bed; at times they are restrained and receive hot and cold showers, among other things. Hartocollis (1966) recognises that the problems facing the mental health system in Greece emerge from folk beliefs, which are linked to primitive religious beliefs. Secrecy here becomes the catalyst for the deterioration of someone's mental health, something in which the current research is interested as well. However, I tend to see a further connection between the secrecy around mental health and the secrecy regarding suffering from the evil eye – a phenomenon which is discussed in the following pages.

In addition to the negative beliefs attached to mental illness, Bouhoutsos and Roe (1984) revealed that 98 per cent of mental health services are run by the Greek state-operated health service. They also point out that these services, which are run by the Greek government, provide only pharmacological intervention, stigmatising the individual who is then defined by the mental illness label assigned to them by doctors. The shame that is attached to seeking support for mental illness is so great that it can cause social isolation. Karastergiou et al. (2005) argue that mental health services have been centralised in the major urban centres, so that for those who live in villages or on islands it is almost impossible to obtain access to any mental health treatment unless they travel to city centres.

However, Law 1397 of 1983 introduced a starting point for reformation of the mental health system in Greece. The second event that contributed to this reformation and increased public awareness of the problem was Regulation 815/84, which was proposed by the European Economic Community (EEC) (Bellali and Kalafati 2006). Nevertheless, Karastergiou et al. (2005) believe that the most important event that positively affected mental health awareness in Greece was the investigation of the Greek mental health system by the British press in 1989. In that year, British journalists exposed unacceptable conditions at the lunatic asylum of Leros (Zissi and Barry 1997). This resulted in international outrage and forced the Greek government to start a campaign to change the mental health system. Subsequently, the Greek Orthodox Church became involved in the governmental reformation of the mental health system. However, although the government continues to seek reform, this campaign has since been abandoned by the Church (Avgoustidis 2001). As Madianos et al. (2000) show, the campaign involves the decentralisation of mental health centres. Long-term care in asylums is no longer offered, and new ways to treat those with mental health issues are being investigated. However, the pace of change in the system is so slow that the literature that has been published in regard to Greek mental health is unreliable (Marci 2001; Bellali and Kalafati 2006).

One might have already concluded that there is very little contemporary research into mental health in Greece. In my attempt to develop a better understanding of mental health, I was confronted with the difficult task of identifying any reliable source that might link mental health deterioration to the phenomenon of the evil eye in the Greek context. Therefore, I used universal literature in order to support my conjecture that mental illness is strongly linked to the evil eye. Even though some psychiatrists deny the evil eye's existence and concurrently the effect that it has on a person's mental health, the phenomenon recurs in psychiatric literature (Pereira et al. 1995). Priests of the Greek Orthodox Church, who are recognised as spiritual leaders and faith healers, quite often link the evil eye and demons to an individual's mental state or to mental disorders (Younis 2000).

Bayer and Shunaigat (2002) argue that those whose mental health is affected by belief in the evil eye tend to be from a low socio-economic background and are mostly unemployed males. This suggestion was supported by Dein et al. (2008) and Olusesi (2008), who argue that belief in the evil eye is reinforced by people from low socio-educational backgrounds. With regard to gender difference, there is currently debate as to whether males or females are more affected by the evil eye. Weatherhead and Daiches (2010) propose that there is a strong correlation between an individual's states of anxiety, distress and spiritual suffering. A person's mental health is therefore correlated with their link to God (Al-Krenawi and Graham 1999; Mohammad et al. 2014). Khalifa and Hardie (2005) make the link between the evil eye and demonic possession, and point out that these can both cause mental illness. They also suggest that individuals can experience a form of possession by evil spirits that is generated through overlook (Khalifa et al. 2011; Dein 1997). However, Dein et al. (2008) oppose this theory, suggesting that those suffering from the evil eye cannot be possessed by spirits because fascination is the human ability to cause harm through a malevolent stare; they regard the evil eye as a form of spirit possession.

Psychiatrists in the West today rarely acknowledge folk beliefs, and neither discuss them in terms of spiritual diagnosis nor explain mental disorders as manifestations of religious constructs. This means that they fail to understand the contribution of the evil eye to mental illness, while at the same time undermining the therapeutic value of folk belief to a person's well-being (Fabrega 2000). They also fail to understand the individual as a whole, as human beings are not purely networks of neurons and connections but are also spiritual beings. Fabrega (2000) maintains that because psychiatrists fail to see the individual as a spiritual being, they fail to come up with long-lasting treatment, leaving sufferers feeling disrespected. Cinnirella and Loewenthal (1999) maintain that sufferers do not trust their doctors and are less likely to share their spiritual suffering and symptoms with them. That mistrust, they add, comes from the fact that doctors appear to be ignorant of the religious aspects of their afflictions, and sufferers are afraid that they will be judged and misdiagnosed (Loewenthal 1995; Loewenthal et al. 2001). It was only recently that the American Psychiatric Association recognised religious belief as an important factor in mental health, adding these beliefs to the *Diagnostic Statistical Manual* V (DSM-V) in 2013. This addition signifies the importance of the cultural dimension of human disorders.

There is a strong link between religion-related disorders and dissociative symptomatology. Pereira et al. (1995) argue that such dissociations are manifested through various negative behaviours, which can be taken as psychotic symptoms. However, those who believe in the evil eye and possession experience bodily and mental dissociations. These dissociations exhibit symptomatology including somatisation, interpersonal conflict and sociocultural sanctions. The World Health Organization (2018) recognises possession and the symptoms that believers might attribute to the evil eye in the *International Classification of Diseases* (ICD-11, 6B63) The DSM-V (2013) recognises these in section 300.15. However, further research is required to identify the diagnostic criteria of the dissociative trance disorder which is strongly linked to the existence of the evil eye. Habimana and Masse (2000) argue that belief in the evil eye and its symptomatology is strongly correlated to personality disorder. It is also argued that the manifestations of the malevolent glance through the evil eye should be taken as cultural control of the individual bordering on general paranoia (Di Stasi 1981; Domash 1983; Machovec 1976; Madianos 1999; Stephenson 1979). Greek Orthodox priests argue that they have certain criteria with which they may diagnose a person's paranoia regarding possession of the evil eye; they then treat the condition with special readings from prayer books and with amulets and charms. The criteria are empirically defined and so differ according to each individual.

Hussein (1991), who comes from the Islamic tradition, maintains that faith healers use diagnostic names to describe anger, dissociation, envy or extremely painful mental states, while at the same time attributing these symptoms to the evil eye. It is believed that future mental illness can be caused by *göz değmesi*, *kötü göz* or *göze gelme* (names for the evil eye) in a person's life at their time of entering the earthly world (Özyazıcıoğlu and Polat 2004; Özkan and Khorshıd 1995; Zoysa et al. 1998).

Khalifa et al. (2011), in contrast to Bayer and Shunaigat (2002), argue that female Muslims in Britain are more likely to believe in black magic and the evil eye, which in turn affects their mental health. El-Islam (1995) suggests that most of those who believe that the evil eye can cause physical and mental harm also exhibit psychiatric symptomatology. However, Appel (1976) suggests that individuals in southern Italy believe that the evil eye can cause spirit possession, as sufferers act as if powerful negative forces are controlling them.

Migliore (1997), in his study on the evil eye in Arbëreshë, Albania and southern Italy, discovered that spiritual healers can identify twenty-one symptoms caused by the evil eye, including mastitis, infections, nosebleed, dermatitis, hepatitis and abdominal pain (De Martino 2000). Peterson-Bidoshi (2006), in her fieldwork studying the *dordolec* in Albania (the neighbouring country to Corfu), points out that according to Albanian tradition, the evil eye can cause sudden damage to property or cause serious spiritual harm to an individual, and that this can manifest as mental health issues. In southern Italy, which is also close to Corfu, it is argued that those who suffer from the evil eye can exhibit specific symptomatology, such as headaches, depression, tiredness, insomnia and hypochondria (Argyle and Cook 1976; Herzfeld 1981). Similar symptoms are described in the Arabic Middle Eastern regions. '*Ayn*' (evil eye) can cause symptoms such as drowsiness, dropping of eyelids, exhaustion, cramps and delusions (Patai 1976; Khan 1986; Marcais 1960). In Bedouin tradition, on the other hand, the evil eye is related to sex. It can thus cause sterility, a reduction of sexual activity, menstruation difficulties and problems in pregnancy (Levi 1987; Thomas 1971). Hussain (2002), similarly to Pieroni and Quave (2005), argues that in Asia, as in the Middle East, it is commonly accepted that the evil eye can cause mild-to-severe mental health issues, which are manifested through physical symptoms. Thus, sufferers who are possessed by evil spirits can develop depression and hallucinations which cause dissociation between their spirit and body (Al-Krenawi et al. 2000). In the Balkans, and more specifically in Romania, people share the same symptomatology that exists in southern Italy and among the Bedouins, but here, the evil eye can also cause digestive problems, severe depression and delusions if the spirit possesses the individual for a long time. In extreme cases, the evil eye can cause petrification and death (Murgoci 1923). Louis (1951) linked the evil eye to the wet and dry theory and stated that it can cause eating disorders as it dries up the individual from within.

CONCLUSION

This chapter has given an outline of what the evil eye is, according to Greek tradition and in relation to the Greek Orthodox Church. It has provided a general introduction to the evil eye and its links with envy and 'death', while also presenting the inner journey that the evil eye can facilitate in the quest of the self. Such a connection gives rise to many questions that appear to be fundamental to our understanding of the phenomenon and its influence on mental health. What does the evil eye mean to people today? Why is it so important and how is it linked with mental health? Why do psychiatrists tend to ignore its manifestations when assessing a person's mental health? Envy and the evil eye carry humanity beyond the boundaries of morality, beyond right and wrong, to the world of duality and survival versus destruction. We also know now that even this morality is arbitrary, because different cultures have different definitions of morality. However (and for the purposes of this chapter), envy, or the evil eye, is not a moral issue. An envious person cannot be punished for being envious; and, on the other hand, envy cannot be perceived as positive in any society.

To this extent, human beings can be protected from the evil eye only when they develop a spiritual way of living, which results in a relationship with God. Without this relationship there is a constant fear of death; the constant anxiety of being eliminated. This book tries to give answers to these questions and to develop a better understanding of the phenomenon of the evil eye. It focuses on the spiritual way of living that might deliver a person from suffering mental illness.

One of the persuasive elements of this study is that it promotes a multidisciplinary approach to the circuitous phenomenon of the evil eye and its relationship to the Greek Orthodox faith in the Corfu region. Many researchers have tried to explore this topic. However, there is a significant lacuna vis-à-vis the role of religion and mental health with regard to the phenomenon, not least in the Greek Orthodox faith. Despite the fact that many scholars have examined the phenomenon of the evil eye in different cultures, no one has yet examined it in the context of Greek Orthodoxy. The lack of such an examination might suggest that the subject is of no interest. However, this chapter argues that the evil eye is still a very vivid phenomenon, and one that has preoccupied many scholars from different disciplines for over a century. As such, it is a phenomenon that still requires further exploration.

Orthodoxy is the dominant religion among the Greek population, and as such, language can be a barrier preventing a researcher from thoroughly examining the phenomenon, since meaning might be lost in translation. As a researcher, I have the privilege of being Greek, which means that I have the advantage of understanding the language. At this point, it is important to give an account of who I am as a researcher and what has influenced me. Therefore, the following chapter engages with the methodological approach that I adopted, with the characteristics of the field, and also with my narrative, in order for the reader to build a picture of the research as a whole and the researcher's biases.

Chapter 1

The Selected Region, Informants' Demographics and Methodology

INTRODUCTION

At the outset of this study, I sought to identify the areas in Greece which exhibit a significant manifestation of the evil eye. This task was quite difficult and complicated, given that, at this early stage of research, what I was hoping to explore and discover through my fieldwork was as yet unclear. After discussions with a sufficient number of clergymen and academics, I became increasingly interested in examining a phenomenon that had not been influenced in any way by the Ottoman Empire. So far, the evil eye has been explored extensively in many geographical areas other than Greece. These areas have significant cultural influences from the Ottoman Empire. Therefore, many similarities regarding the phenomenon of the evil eye could be observed between Greece and Turkey. However, the Ionian Islands, and specifically Corfu, have never been investigated in this regard. It is therefore important to examine whether the phenomenon is understood differently due to the lack of Ottoman influence in this area. It is important to stress at this point that most parts of Greece and the Middle East except the Greek islands of the Ionian Sea were conquered by the Ottomans and occupied for hundreds of years. Among other things, I was interested in examining the differences and similarities regarding the various beliefs about the evil eye within a sociocultural milieu in Greece that has experienced strong Western influence. I therefore decided to investigate the evil eye in the Ionian Islands, and more specifically in Corfu.

GENERAL INFORMATION ABOUT THE HISTORY OF CORFU

In ancient times, Corfu, or Kerkyra, took its name from the nymph Korkira, the daughter of the river god Aesopos. Korkira was so beautiful that Posei-don fell in love with her, kidnapped her and brought her to live on the island later named Corfu. According to Homer, Corfu was the residence of the Phaeacians and the island where Odysseus found rest on his way back to Ithaca. Throughout history, Corfu has been a significant port with commercial interests due to its geographical position (Schroeder 1996). Its naval power extended to all parts of the Adriatic Sea; During the Peloponnesian war Corfu was well known for its navy and helped Athens to fight against Corinth. In 338 BCE, King Philip II conquered and occupied Corfu. During the Roman Empire, the island was permitted to keep its autonomy and independence in return for allowing Romans to use the port; thus, Corfu has been greatly influenced by Rome right up to the present day. Its architecture is also strongly influenced by the Romans. Jason and Sossipatros introduced Christianity to the island and built the first Christian church there in 40 CE (Kosmatou 2000). During medieval times, Corfu again united with the Romans to fight against attacks by barbarians and pirates (Luttwak 2009).

However, in 1267, Charles of Anjou, the French king of Sicily, conquered the island and tried to replace Orthodox Christianity with Catholicism. The Christian Orthodox population was persecuted and Orthodox churches were converted to Catholic places of worship. In 1386, Corfu was returned to Venetian rule for four centuries and enjoyed a time of prosperity. Following the Treaty of Campo Formio in 1797, Napoleon Bonaparte took control of the island (Schroeder 1996) and made it a French state. During that period, Corfu once again became a significant port in the Mediterranean. France also invested in education, and many academies were built during that period. Finally, in 1814, Great Britain took possession of the Ionian Islands, which were ruled under the United States of the Ionian Islands. During that time, in 1824, the first Greek university was established. On 21 May 1864, the British donated Corfu to the new king of Greece, and Corfu became part of the Greek territory (Baghdiantz-McCabe et al. 2005; Donald 1992; Kosmatou 2000; Luttwak 2009). This brief history shows that Corfu has been through many significant developmental stages before reaching its current form.

Corfu was chosen for the purposes of this study not only because of its important geographical location – situated as it is in the north-western part of Greece and having in addition strong influences from Italy – but also because of its history as a significant commercial port. Corfu has been influenced by many countries and has a multicultural orientation in its lifestyle. Even the Psalms are different in the Ionian Islands from any other part of Greece or the Middle East; they are more Westernised and have not been influenced by Byzantine church music, as the clergy tend to claim (Spinks 2010). However, the core religious beliefs appear to have strong roots in Eastern Orthodox Christianity. The majority of Corfu's population hold strong beliefs about the evil eye, and these beliefs govern their lives and their attitudes to mental health. In other words, the vast majority of the population of Corfu have experienced Western influences, maintained their Christian characteristics, and simultaneously hold strong beliefs regarding the evil eye, its manifestation and ways of healing. It is important to understand the role of the Greek Orthodox Church during the period of the economic crisis as an introduction to the field. Therefore, the following section aims to give an account of such matters.

ECONOMIC CRISIS AND THE GREEK ORTHODOX CHURCH

It is important to mention at this point the pivotal role that the Greek Orthodox Church plays in Greek society, and how the new role of the Church has been shaped by the emergence of the financial crises in 2009. Understanding the Church's role in Corfu provides the information necessary to better comprehend the phenomenon of evil eye and the influences that religion has on individuals' consciousness of it. The Metropolitanate of Corfu is one of the eighty-two Metropolitanates of the Greek Orthodox Church. Administrative, pastoral and spiritual work are under the care of the local Bishop of Corfu, who acts according to the norms and the direction dictated by the Hierarchy of the Holy Synod of the Greek Orthodox Church. The relationship between the local Church of Corfu and the Greek state, as well as the consequences and the impact of the financial crisis, are the same in Corfu as have been apparent in all the other Greek regions. Undoubtedly, the Church has enhanced its entwinement with Greek national identity in the wake of the economic crisis. In addition to its role and function as an ecclesiastical institution, the Church has since 2009 reinforced its nationalist characteristics, which are interconnected with the history of Greece. After the fall of Constantinople in 1453 and the collapse of the Byzantine Empire, and during the four hundred years of Ottoman rule, the Ecumenical Patriarchate of Constantinople acted as both the religious and civil authority for all Orthodox Christians (Makris and Bakridakis 2013). The Ecumenical Patriarchate performed and operated according to its double dimension for many years, and these two characteristics have deeply imprinted in the Hellenic consciousness. For this reason, the proclamation of the Autocephalous Greek Orthodox Church took a patriotic form, in parallel with the attempts of the citizens of the newly established Kingdom of Greece to maintain their national identity and fight for their rights and their existence as a Greek nation. With the establishment of the independent Kingdom of Greece in 1832, the Orthodox Church came under the authority of this Greek kingdom, and its important role continues to this day, especially since 2009 (Barth, 2001). Makris and Bakridakis (2013), in their attempts to better understand the role and the ecclesial affairs of the National Greek Church after the emergence of the financial crisis of 2009, reveal that for the last two centuries, the political elite in Greece has interfered with Church affairs, with the ultimate goal of controlling the Church and increasing state influence, control and power over it.

A closer look at the relationship between the Greek state and the Greek Orthodox Church after the economic crisis exposes the tendency of the state to rekindle the popular ideology of administration, developed during the Byzantine era, known as *synallilia (συναλληλία)*. This is an ideology promoting equality in power between the state and the ecclesiastical powers (Troianos 2013). After the economic crisis, the Greek Orthodox Church has succeeded in maintaining much of its power and influence within Greek society, particularly because it operates as an autocephalous ecclesial body independent from the Constantinopolitan Church – the Ecumenical Patriarchate, which is based in Turkey (Makris and Bakridakis 2013).

The turn of increasing numbers of individuals to the Church, in combination with the increased belief in the evil eye, necessitates a closer examination of the role of the Church after the financial crisis. It is important to briefly illustrate the profiles and characteristics of the leaders of the Greek Church during this period. Metropolitan Christodoulos Paraskevaides of Volos was elected as Archbishop of Athens and all Greece at the age of 59 and held the position from 1998 to 2008; ten years after his death, public opinion about the late Archbishop holds that he was one of the most charismatic Church leaders to have served the Holy Synod and acted as Archbishop of Athens. Among his many achievements were his successes in attracting the interest of social media and promoting the idea that the Greek Orthodox Church has been the historic carrier of the Hellenic-Christian identity, which is injected in the everyday life of the Greek Church. Archbishop Christodoulos thus began a new era for the role of the Church in which Greeks started to feel proud of their national identity, which comprised both Christian and Hellenic elements. After Christodoulos' sudden death in 2008, Metropolitan Ieronymos Liapis of Levadea became the new Archbishop of Athens at the age of 70. Ieronymos II, a low-profile clergyman, was elected by the members of the Holy Synod of the Greek Church because they preferred a less dynamic leader for the Church. Ieronymos II was known for the challenging relationship he had with his predecessor. Politicians and a few clergymen, as well as a significant proportion of the media, have criticised Archbishop Christodoulos for damaging the role and the identity of the Church due to his over-involvement and intervention in state affairs. Many bishops hoped that Ieronymos II – given his low profile – would bring peace in the Church and maintain a good relationship with the Greek government, enriching the pastoral and spiritual role of the Church and avoiding any involvement in politics. This change of the strategic plan that the Church adopted allowed a more subdued approach to the societal issues that the faithful were facing; this created anxiety in individuals, as the Church was not as present as before. Therefore, belief in folk rituals increased even more.

In 2009, and to a greater extent 2010, Greek society began to descend into its worst ever economic crisis, worse even than the post-war fallout of 1945. The country faced an emergency situation in which certainties and moral values were challenged and seriously shaken (Makris and Bakridakis 2013). Financial analysts maintained that the Greek crisis should not concern only Europe, but the whole Western market, as it highlighted a neoliberal move which in fact took advantage of the weaker economies. The Greek crisis has thus become a paradigm for the exploitative form of European financial capitalism. Greece therefore became one of the few member states of the Eurozone that exhibited structural and political inefficiencies, which caused its financial dysfunction and also the political and social fissures which placed it at the periphery of European financial activities (Troianos 2013).

Unfortunately, the economic crisis unveiled a rotten economic system and social structure which reached its nadir in 2009. The Greek economy and societal system evinced multifaceted corruption, chronic political incompetence and clientelism. All of this resulted in the denigration of the two major political parties, which had governed the country for over thirty years, and poisoned not only the political but also the social arena and the public services. Sadly, in 2009 and 2010 it was revealed that politicians, publishers, social media personas and churchmen had been involved in financial scandals that contributed to the economic crisis, and surprisingly, only a few have been brought to justice. Emblematic contemporary images in Greece, and particularly in the capital and Corfu, include people begging for money on the streets and looking in green and blue bins for food, and children fainting in schools due to malnourishment, while unemployment reached 50 per cent among the younger generations (Makris and Bakridakis 2013).

The next wave of the financial crisis, which aggravated the general population, came in 2010, with the deep cuts in pensions and wages leaving households with no money to support their everyday needs. These cuts were followed by austerity measures, which deeply affected Greek society. Professionals started living in constant fear of having no job or income to support their families. The realities of the wider socio-economic infrastructure became apparent, with shopkeepers closing their shops while wholesalers became more powerful, with the general public attacking bankers, with the lower social classes attacking the higher classes, and with ultra-nationalists attacking immigrants. All these reactions comprised the fallout of the financial crisis, which eventually took the form of extreme riots during which four people chose self-immolation in front of cameras as their only way out of their financial struggles. Finally, the austerity measures became even tighter in the following years; Greeks have lived under bank capital controls since 2015. Greece is now in a state of *bellum omnium contra omnes*, which increases the fear that extreme conditions might emerge in everyday life. People attack one another on the streets, tax evasion has started to surface, many individuals (especially from the private sector) avoid paying income tax, and extensive financial fraud and tax avoidance is committed by everyone, from doctors to house cleaners. Many health-service doctors will, for a fee, declare individuals disabled so that they can be eligible for disability allowance and benefits, and chemists have started selling health service-funded drugs on the black market. It must be stressed that the list of everyday financial frauds is not limited to the above, but extends to numerous professionals and households. In a society with a corrupt political system and a bankrupt economy, which operates on fear and anger, the beneficiaries alone are not enough to manage the situation. With the financial crisis reaching its peak by 2013, a large number of individuals who were not frequent churchgoers before the crisis turned to the Church in order to find security for the future; at the same time, folk beliefs are becoming more popular than ever. It appears that individuals have started to engage with folk beliefs in an attempt to control the fear of the unknown future. It is at this point that beliefs and rituals involving the evil eye become more popular than ever.

It would be wrong, however, to conclude that corruption is omnipresent in Greece. Individuals are more inclined to comply with austerity measures when they feel that they are respected and in receipt of good public services. In Greece, however, this is not the case, especially since 2009. Greece therefore faces its worst structural crisis, one which threatens the population's morals and national identity. The moral challenges are mostly related to the immorality that stems from the capitalist system, which takes the form of neoliberalism in Greece, and its attendant kleptocracy: the corrupt governmental leadership and system which abuse power to exploit individuals and resources for personal benefits (Bauman 2008).

These are the conditions and circumstances amid which Archbishop Ieronymos II was called to serve as the leader of the Greek Church. There was no space for him to maintain his low profile in the face of the current status quo, as that would be taken as madness; however, for the new Archbishop to decide to become vocal and oppose the status quo would be equally difficult, especially in the wake of his predecessor Chrystodoulos, under whom the image of the Greek Orthodox Church had been tarnished. Ieronymos II therefore had to very carefully position the Church in relation to the challenges of the economic crisis that was 'killing' Greece. As such, immediately after his election he disbanded the Allilengii (Solidarity) NGO that Chrystodoulos established during his office, because extensive fraud had been conducted in its name. In order to replace the work of Allilengii, Ieronymos established another NGO, Apostoli (Mission), the main focuses of which were rehabilitation, ecology and charitable activities. In addition, Ieronymos re-established a relationship with the Ecumenical Patriarchate, after a long and challenging period between the Greek Church and the Church of Constantinople under Christodoulos' leadership.

It became apparent early in Ieronymos II's presidency of the Holy Synod of the Greek Church that he did not want to be overly involved in political matters. Therefore, he reacted in a completely different manner than his predecessor to the difficulties that he faced as the leader of the Church, chiefly the high taxation of the Church and the changes within the Ministry of Education that decreased the teaching hours of religious education at all educational levels, in addition to other religious public affairs. He approached all the above issues from a spiritual and pastoral perspective, making appropriate decisions without however causing further frictions between the state and the Church. However, on 5 October 2010, amid the Greek government's request for support from the International Monetary Fund (IMF) and a heated discussion regarding Greece leaving the Eurozone, the Holy Synod of the Greek Church discussed the Church's position vis-à-vis the economic crisis for the first time. Ieronymos II's speech and the discussion among the members of the Synod that followed became part of the Encyclical No. 2894, entitled *A Theological Conception of the Economic Crisis*, in March 2010. It was read instead of a sermon on the following Sunday across all churches in Greece and was well received by the faithful. For the first time, the Church made a public declaration about its position regarding the economic crisis. The declaration starts with a strong statement that Greece is no longer free but rather enslaved to its creditors, and continues by attacking the politicians who brought the country to its knees. For the first time, the Church used the emotionally charged words 'foreign occupation', which refer to the Nazi occupation and were chosen to incite believers to react to the status quo and resist the austerity measurements (Makris and Bakridakis 2013). As a result, the ultra-right party received more votes in the 2012 elections, and the Greeks developed a strong sense of national identity and began reacting aggressively to anything that threatened that identity. From the outset, the Church adopted an anti-Memorandum position.

Having so far examined the implications of the financial crisis in Greek society, it is important at this stage of the study to illustrate the demographic characteristics of the selected informants.

INFORMANTS' DEMOGRAPHIC CHARACTERISTICS

Corfu has undergone many changes and transformations in order to reach its current social configuration. According to the last census by the Hellenic Statistical Authority in 2011, the overall population of Corfu is 104,371 people. The graphs below give a thorough breakdown of the population according to their education (Figure 1.1), employability (Figure 1.2), gender (Figure 1.3) and population and occupation distribution (Figure 1.4).

It can be observed from Figure 1.1 that 20,304 males have graduated from higher education or completed compulsory education, and that 20,593 females have done so too. On the other hand, 30,449 males have completed only primary school or have abandoned education, with 3,128 not being able to read or write; 33,025 females are in this group, with 2,881 unable to read or write. From Figure 1.2, it can be concluded that 36,477 individuals are employed, with 8,267 unemployed and 59,609 financially inactive, as a consequence of the financial crisis.

Members of the chosen groups of informants had Greek Christian Orthodox backgrounds and were over the age of eighteen. Both males and females were recruited, and the target groups for interviews and observations were as follows: laypeople, clergymen, folk healers and mental health professionals.

It is important now to take a closer look at the actual demographics of the informants.

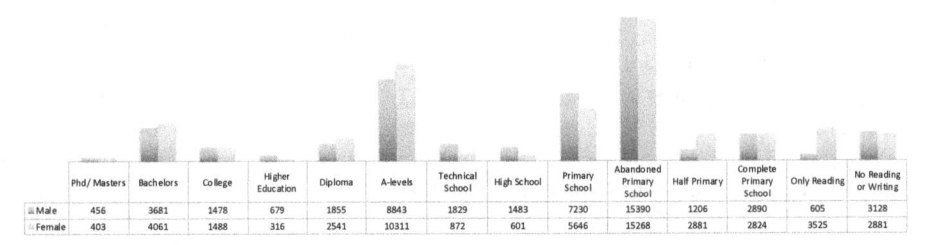

	Phd/ Masters	Bachelors	College	Higher Education	Diploma	A-levels	Technical School	High School	Primary School	Abandoned Primary School	Half Primary	Complete Primary School	Only Reading	No Reading or Writing
Male	456	3681	1478	679	1855	8843	1829	1483	7230	15390	1206	2890	605	3128
Female	403	4061	1488	316	2541	10311	872	601	5646	15268	2881	2824	3525	2881

Figure 1.1. Informants' education. Graph by Nikolaos Souvlakis.

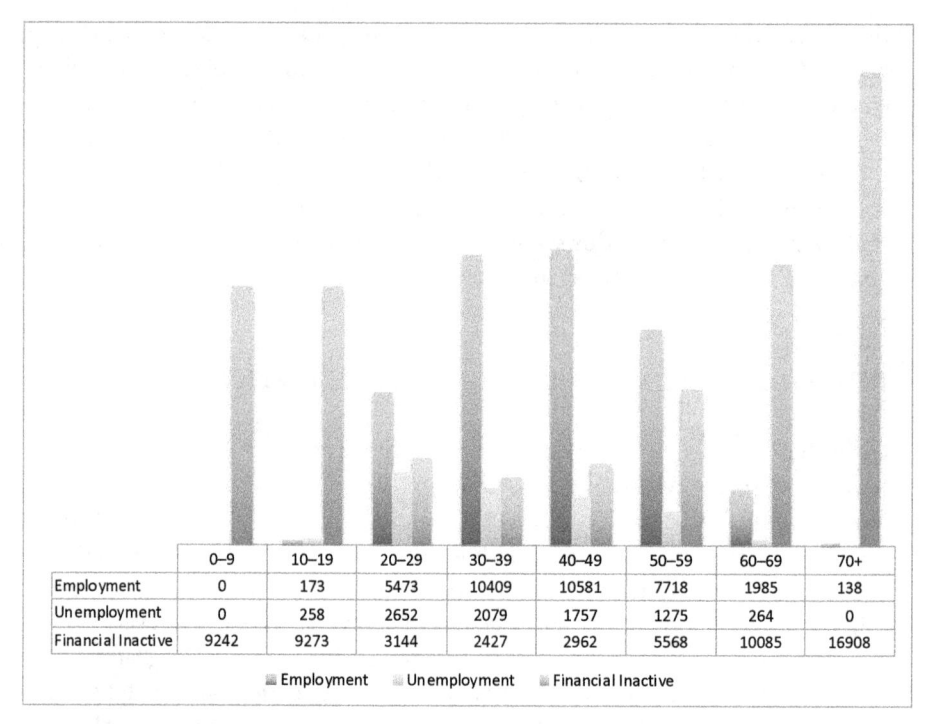

	0–9	10–19	20–29	30–39	40–49	50–59	60–69	70+
Employment	0	173	5473	10409	10581	7718	1985	138
Unemployment	0	258	2652	2079	1757	1275	264	0
Financial Inactive	9242	9273	3144	2427	2962	5568	10085	16908

■ Employment   ■ Unemployment   ■ Financial Inactive

Figure 1.2. Age and employability. Graph by Nikolaos Souvlakis.

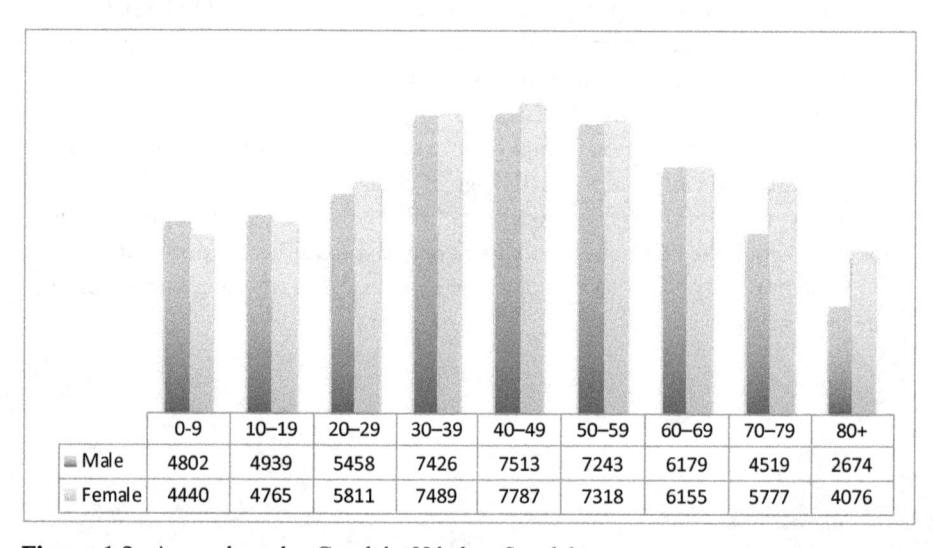

	0-9	10–19	20–29	30–39	40–49	50–59	60–69	70–79	80+
■ Male	4802	4939	5458	7426	7513	7243	6179	4519	2674
■ Female	4440	4765	5811	7489	7787	7318	6155	5777	4076

Figure 1.3. Age and gender. Graph by Nikolaos Souvlakis.

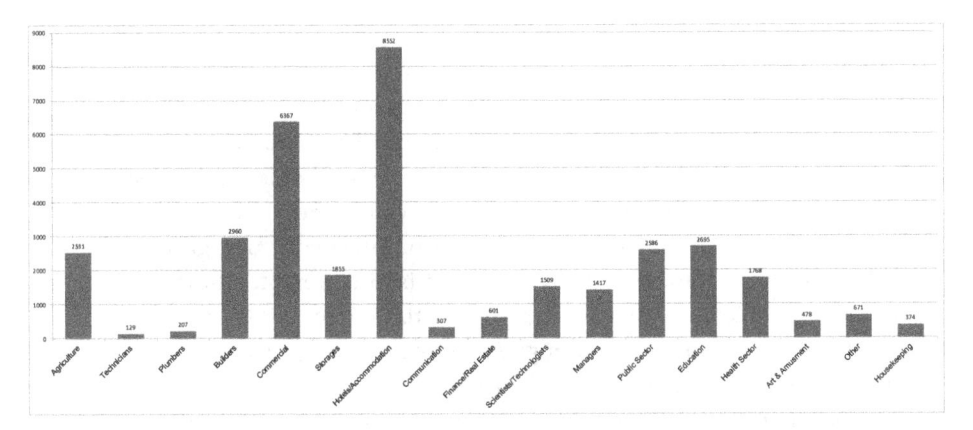

Figure 1.4. Occupational and population distribution. Graph by Nikolaos Souvlakis.

LAYPEOPLE

The total number of lay informants that gave testimonies in one-to-one discussions was 231 (130 females and 101 males), 186 of whom held higher education degrees and forty-five of whom left education after high school. They were all employed in either part- or full-time jobs; 152 were married, forty-seven were single and thirty-two had lost their partners. Ninety-two informants were between 18 and 29, 105 informants were between 30 and 49 and the remaining thirty-four informants were 50 or above. The lay informants' demographics do not overlap with those of the other three groups.

It is clear from the previous chapter that the evil eye finds fruitful ground in people from various socio-economic groups, but mostly among those from a low socio-economic background. Therefore, laypeople were the major source for gathering data. It is these people who are most affected, not only physically but also mentally. Their views regarding the evil eye were vital to accurately understanding the phenomenon and its manifestations. The census revealed that laypeople were greatly affected by the financial crisis and the recession in Greece, and this caused a surge towards tradition and increased people's territorial feelings and religious beliefs. Laypeople thus give life to the phenomenon of the evil eye; ethnography is nothing without informants, and the evil eye is nothing without individuals. Simply put, research on the evil eye would not have been appropriate or valid without consideration of their views.

CLERGYMEN

According to the Hellenic Statistical Authority's census of 2011, the major religion in Corfu is Orthodox Christianity. The Archbishop governs the clergy on the island and on the neighbouring islands, and priests are allocated to the major towns and villages, while others are sent to serve smaller villages and parishes. The number of informants that gave further testimonies in a group or one-to-one setting is ninety-eight; all males, sixty-nine had completed higher education and the remaining twenty-nine had completed local seminary training. Twenty-seven were between 18 and 29, forty-five between 30 and 49, and the remaining twenty-six were 50 or above.

The phenomenon under investigation is strongly related to religious beliefs and the conflict between God and evil, so it was important for me to gain access to the clergy's view of these issues. Priests are perceived as significant leaders and exceptional individuals within society, and as wielding not only power over religious matters, but also political influence (Prince 1995; Harris 2007). Considering the power and social status of priests in Greek society, and more specifically in Corfu, it was important to consider their views with regard to the evil eye, as their input was fundamental to an understanding of how the Church approaches the phenomenon. It was also important to consider the priests' views on the rituals for casting out the evil eye from possessed individuals, and on the evil eye's effect on a person's mental health. Priests are a significant group when examining this phenomenon, given that they deal with possession by the evil eye as part of their clerical duties.

FOLK HEALERS

Folk healers hold a particular place in Corfiot culture, and it seems that they play a particular role in regards to the phenomenon of the evil eye. Despite their sociocultural status, they are well-respected members of society. Informants sought the support of folk healers not only because of their healing powers in relation to the evil eye, but also for any spiritual or psychological matters. Ninety-six folk healers engaged in further discussion as informants in either one-to-one or group settings; thirty-nine were males and fifty-seven females. The majority of the folk healers had completed higher education and were employed (n = 68); the remainder (n = 28) left school after high school.

Folk healers were observed in order to reach an understanding of the evil eye from a different perspective. The majority of them were women from all age groups; male folk healers were from younger generations, and were mostly trained by women. The feeling is that women folk healers are more trustworthy in their rituals to cast the evil eye out from sufferers. The younger generation of folk healers – regardless of their gender – were mostly asked to offer their services among their friends and peers, and in cases where the effects of the evil eye were weak, while the older generation of healers were called to cast out the evil eye when its effects were persistent and powerful. There was a dynamic associated with the age of folk healers as well as with their religiosity. The elderly folk healers – who had achieved more experience and regularly attended church – seemed to be more powerful than others. In addition, there was a link between the methods of the rituals used to cast the evil eye out and the power of the folk healers. During the fieldwork, I observed that those folk healers who used rituals and amulets relevant to Greek Orthodox tradition were called to offer their services mostly in cases related to powerful evil eye symptomatology. This study recruited, observed and conducted follow-up interviews with the majority of known folk healers in Corfu. The results were inconclusive regarding their education and social class.

MENTAL HEALTH PROFESSIONALS

There was a limited number of mental health professionals engaged in the field: fifty-six in total. Thirty were females and twenty-six males. All had completed medical degrees. Two were 50 or above, and the others between 30 and 49.

The literature covered in the previous chapter revealed that the evil eye affects a person's mental and physical health in multiple ways. Even though mental health professionals belong to the upper-middle social class and are sceptical of the phenomenon of the evil eye, according to the literature, they nevertheless deal with evil eye symptomatology, and it was therefore important to investigate their views about the phenomenon, especially since the evil eye is such a controversial phenomenon and one which has existed for years. It was important to understand how science, in this case the mental health profession, understands the phenomenon, its symptomatology and the healing process. It was also important to understand the views of those who do not believe in the evil eye and to see what they make of the symptomatology, which could prove difficult to explain scientifically.

Thus far, I have outlined my position within my chosen ethnographic field, and the importance of examining the four informant groups mentioned. These four particular groups arose from the fieldwork as the major groups that treat the phenomenon fundamentally differently, but also with many similarities. Therefore, it is important to examine these groups and their attitudes in more depth in order to understand better the phenomenon of evil eye.

Corfu has an interesting geographical position that has over the years attracted political and religious interest, as discussed above. In addition, this chapter has explored the demographics of the four particular informant groups, whose members each share specific characteristics as described above. Besides the demographic nuances of the region under study, it is also important to understand the methodology adopted in order to gain access to the data, which is presented in detail in the next section. The next section also engages with my own influences and life narrative.

METHODOLOGY

Having examined historically the phenomenon of the evil eye as it occurs globally, as well as in the Mediterranean and specifically in the region of Corfu; having highlighted the relations between the evil eye and Greek Orthodoxy and tradition; and having presented the informants' demographic characteristics, I embark in this section upon an examination of my rationale in regard to the chosen methodology, and conclude by outlining the attendant ethical considerations.

THE RESEARCHER'S INFLUENCES

It is important to develop a common understanding and language when referring to psychological ethnography, and to clarify which concepts are of interest to me while investigating and observing the fieldwork. According to Kohut (1971), ethnography focuses on the investigation of the heuristic role of linguistic and non-linguistic cultural forms in formations, which then allow the later development of one's personality and social persona. However, Kohut misses one of the most fundamental elements of psychological, and more specifically psychoanalytic, ethnography, which is the relational aspect. LeVine (1982) later articulates that psychoanalytic ethnography is about developing an understanding of the hermeneutic relationships between subjects and society in an imaginative and symbolic interplay in which society and culture co-exist in constant interaction with the individual's levels of consciousness. However, both psychology and ethnography have been subject to many changes over the years, in response to the challenges faced by both fields. The two fields developed simultaneously, and this engendered common preoccupations (Kracke and Herdt 1987); scholars in both fields try to comprehend and construct a deep understanding of their observations, whether this is the informant's psychical conflict or a social phenomenon. In addition, both fields see the subject as a conduit for the recording of the other's narration (Sperber 1985; Marcus and Cushman 1986. It is important for ethnographers who work on psychoanalytic concepts to remember that psychical processes are internal, but take place within a historical and cultural context; it is necessary, therefore, to overcome the tendency to pathologise either cultures or individuals (Obeyesekere 1981).

However, over the years, similar approaches have emerged regarding fieldwork in both disciplines. The first fundamental similarity resides in developing insight and understanding about the individual (LeVine 1982; Weinstein 1991). LeVine (1982) initiated the personal ethnography approach, but did not push this development any further; Marcus and Cushman (1986), therefore, in their attempt to exemplify LeVine's approach of personal ethnography, suggested that psychoanalytic ethnographers should develop relationships with their informants in a similar, but not identical, manner to the rapport that they create in their clinical work. However, this definition lacked the level of professionalism required to prevent ethnographers from simply interpreting data through their psychopathological and societal norms.

In the interdisciplinary dialogue between psychology and anthropologically informed ethnography, a new field emerged within the spectrum of anthropological studies, which brought psychologists and ethnographers into close working proximity. At the same time, psychoanalytic ethnography received growing attention within the wider field of anthropological studies (Hasse 2012). Given the common interests that ethnography and psychology bring to investigating a particular phenomenon, the current study pays specific attention to the psychoanalytic branch of psychological ethnography in the process of analysing the collected data. I have thus been influenced by Hollan (2016), who argues that psychoanalytic concepts contribute to enhance anthropological and ethnographic symbolism and sensibilities. In addition, he points out that psychoanalytic concepts within ethnographic studies bring to the fore specific interpretations of the data collected from the field and particular aspects of the informants' existence that would have been ignored otherwise. Denham (2015) and Leary and Tangney (2014) illustrate through their work on psychoanalytic ethnography the significance that psychoanalytic concepts play in enriching ethnographic fieldwork.

Psychoanalytic ethnography illustrates elements that any other anthropological branch would find it impossible to engage with. It engages with complex issues of personhood, which Hollan (2016) defines as the narratives that individuals adopt to describe their everyday challenges. It tries to comprehend the complexity of the phenomenon as it is manifested in individuals' narratives, and as expressed in their immediate reality and their unconscious imagination. Levy and Hollan (1998) approach complex personhood in a more holistic way, describing it as the common behaviour of a group of people that at times passionately disagree with each other, but also cause harm to each other. Mindful of the significant contributions of psychoanalytic ethnography, the current study applies this methodology in an attempt to identify and examine the complex phenomenon of personhood as it is manifested within the evil eye. Particular attention is therefore given to the collective unconscious of the participants, and to how the evil eye is manifested within society and how it interacts with the formation of personhood. The application of the psychoanalytic ethnographic methodology in this study enables me to better understand the individual's reality and imagination when it comes to the phenomenon of the evil eye.

I am therefore advocating the ethnographic understanding of personhood that is informed by anthropological studies and indebted to the psychoanalytic ethnography scholars' attempts to engage with the elements that can be observed anthropologically. Nonetheless, I attempt at the same time to interpret psychoanalytic concepts and theories through anthropologically informed ethnographic investigative strategies. However, combining psychoanalytic concepts with anthropologically informed ethnography is rather challenging, as the two disciplines require different sets of skills for the interpretation of social phenomena (Hollan 2014). Instead of engaging with the challenges here, I will discuss some of the methodological and theoretical issues which arise from the application of psychoanalytic and anthropologically informed ethnography.

Various psychoanalytic concepts can be applied to illuminate the data from the fieldwork. Bregnbæk, as described in Hollan (2014), refers to the cultural constitution of the defence mechanism and the oedipal complex in evidence during her anthropological research in the New Flower Church in China. Susan Isaac's theory of fantasy has also been used by Gammeltoft (2017) to further examine contemporary Vietnamese families, in Isaac's attempt to understand distress and domination through her fieldwork. Lacan's theory of the Real was also applied by Mikkelsen (2016) in his fieldwork in Denmark. Mikkelsen explains the unthinkable solitude in Danish society through the Lacanian Real: the mystic realm of informants that represents the linguistic limitation within an individual's narrative. And Segal (1986) applies the theory of melancholia to better understand the dark mood associated with loss among Palestinians grappling with statehood's failure to ensure national security. However, the current study follows Hollan's (2016) psychoanalytic concept of complex personhood and Kakar's (2012) concept of mother–child dependency. Kakar was eager to investigate the guru-and-seeker relationship in India and determine how such a relationship forms self-agency. It is obvious that the current study is influenced by Kakar and Holland's psychoanalytic concepts, which are applied via anthropological strategies to interpret the data from the field. To be more precise, this study has been influenced by adult transference syndrome (whereby individuals transfer emotional states to external animate or inanimate objects or ideas), which reflects the mother–child symbiotic state and is expressed in the guru-and-seeker relationship as described in Kakar's field data from India (Kakar and Kakar 2007; Kakar 2012). In addition, the study investigates the roots of the attitudes around the phenomenon of the evil eye, which affects individuals' sense of personhood through their relationship with the other's eye; at this point, it is Kakar and Kakar's (2007) theories again that influence my techniques for interpreting the data from my fieldwork. Similarities to Kakar's work can be deciphered in Steffen's research (2016) when the latter adopts the object-relationship concept of projective identification to capture the complexity of the relationship between clairvoyants and seekers in Danish society. Steffen describes projective identification as a defence through which individuals depart from things that they do not want to face or engage with, while at the same time communicating to others that these unwanted things make them feel as if they are in touch with unwanted elements of the self. The current study is also influenced by Steffen's work in the attempt to understand the internal dynamics that force an individual to cast the evil eye upon others. However, Mitchell (2000), a non-Kleinian analyst, is less apt to agree with the idea of projection identification where the other is the receptor and identifier of the projective feelings. Mitchell instead argues that if an individual identifies with the projections of another individual, these projections as a result constitute the intersubjective space which is influenced by both the projector and the identifier's developmental history and narratives.

One of the main reasons that I chose anthropologically informed ethnographic methods to examine the phenomenon of the evil eye is the fact that anthropology is a biosocial discipline that examines humans and social phenomena in totality and in their natural setting. Mindful of the cultural dimension of human existence, the current study deepens our understanding of the phenomenon of the evil eye and its purpose through history; the comparative applicability that the study adopts allows me to examine transhistorically the evil eye's development in Corfu. The application of such comparative methods enables me to compare different social groups selected from the wider society of the region in question, in order to identify similarities and differences in regard to the phenomenon under investigation. From the description of psychoanalytic ethnography, it becomes apparent that there is a cross-cultural applicability of the specific psychoanalytic theories that the current study is influenced by. The main focus of psychoanalytic theories rests on the human being (the participants) and how they develop a relationship with the self and the community, which is actually the key concern of this study.

For this reason, Kracke and Herdt (1987) suggest that psychoanalytic ethnographers should develop a certain self-awareness in order to always be aware of the transferential and counter-transferential communication that they bring to their fieldwork. Kracke and Herdt's suggestion brings to the fore the most fundamental commonality between ethnographers and psychoanalysts: the interpretation of symbols. The psychoanalytic ethnographer should always be aware of the symbolography of their field and develop interpretive techniques similar to those used in their clinical work (Ricoeur 1981; Sperber 1985; Muensterberger 1996).

Winnicott (1971), on the other hand, suggests that the psychoanalytic ethnographer should always be mindful that symbols or rituals can sometimes be the individual's transitional object, stemming from an early psychical developmental fixation or the need to perpetuate an early damaging attachment; while the transitional object would allow smooth transition from fantasy to reality. Grolnick (1987), following Lacan, Gill and Spencer, argues that the psychoanalytic aspect within ethnography and anthropology is problematic because it cannot reach beyond symbols. She argues that psychoanalysts do not have a good grasp of the theoretical background of their activities, due to the fact that they mostly rely on the subjective reality as expressed by their informants (Gill 1982; Schaefer 1976; Gedo 1979). However, Grolnick appears to be influenced by older ethnographers, and fails to adjust to the implications and requirements of the new digital age. Ricoeur (1981), in a criticism of ethnographic anthropology, states that ethnography is not a scientific discipline, but rather a hermeneutic one. He goes further, stating that the hermeneutic is the aspect in which ethnographic studies examine individuals' needs and desires within a system. However, ethnographers and anthropologists can work well together, informing each other and giving a thorough account of the field observed.

Psychoanalytic, anthropologically informed ethnography appears to be a valuable approach when it comes to examining societal phenomena such as the evil eye. It gives ethnographers the chance to understand some of the fundamental internal conflicts and the effect that these have on mental health; it also allows for observation of the phenomenon in its raw version without any beautification, which can happen when quantitative methods are applied. Following Ricoeur (1981) and Grolnick (1987), anthropologically informed ethnography looks not only at the psychical manifestations and conflicts stemming from early relationships – which find expression through belief in the evil eye – but also acknowledges and investigates expression of the phenomenon in a person's present circumstances and its effect on their mental state. Butler (1997) and Hunt (1989) would both argue that the subjectivities of individuals are formed by the psychical defending mechanisms of the society around them. However, Cohler (1992) and Bowman (1994) point out that such a view is informative but also limited; it gives insight into subjective societal defences, but ignores wider cultural and historical influences. Even though psychoanalytic ethnography provides insight into the individual's interpretation of the psychical processes of the group in which they live, it pays little attention to the aspects that allow them to maintain these cultural defences (Halliday 1978; Hinshelwood 1987; Rustin 1991; Spiro 1965). Heald and Deluz (1994), however, argue that psychoanalytic anthropology can fall into the trap of pathologising informants; it creates difficulties for the researcher who is attempting to blend in, as they also take on an authoritative role. Stein (1981) expresses a different view, stating that psychoanalytic knowledge provides a significant toolkit which gives the ethnographic researcher a wide spectrum of interpretations in order to give an in-depth analysis of the human states within a given cultural and historical context (Kracke and Herdt 1987).

The question this raises is how the researcher's background knowledge and research approach fits within the psychoanalytic ethnographic field; at this stage it is therefore pertinent to introduce myself. It is already clear that I have chosen the field of psychoanalytic, anthropologically informed ethnography, but it will be helpful to understand why this approach is important for me. As psychological ethnography engages with symbols, it is imperative to explore that element of the field before I introduce myself as part of the field.

ETHNOGRAPHIC VIEWS OF SYMBOLISM

When engaging with psychological ethnographic methodology, it is important for the researcher to be aware of symbolic meanings and references, and of how symbolism is related to the findings as derived from the fieldwork.

Deacon (2011) describes symbolic ethnography as the words' manifestation into ideas and physical referents. In other words, I am paying attention to the informants' linguistic symbolism, comparing it with their physical and behavioural manifestations. In addition, I investigate not only the linguistic utterances as expressed by informants, but also the culturally generated attitudes used to represent the phenomenon of the evil eye. The evil eye is thus approached as a cultural phenomenon which is characterised not only by elements such as linguistic narratives, but also by behaviours expressed through interaction within the social setting, ritual performances and religious artefacts.

McGee and Warms (2004) maintain that symbolism under anthropologically informed ethnographic analysis is characterised by two elements: the iconic and the indexical. The iconic element, they argue, refers to the phenomenon under investigation as evidenced in the behaviour(s) and expressions articulated through rituals and art. On the other hand, the indexical element refers to symbols as expressed through innate forms of expressions and communication, such as language and facial expressions. It is therefore imperative for the researcher to apply different techniques for collecting data from the field in order to enhance the ethnographic reliability and validity as expressed through symbolic meanings and rituals, both internal and external. Deacon's (2011) contribution on this matter is vitally important. He advances that symbolic reference has an arbitrary nature that can only confuse the researcher if the symbolic nature of the phenomenon has not been learned through actively living in and engaging with the field; otherwise, it would lack comprehensive trans-generational reference, which has an important impact on the researcher's ability to precisely interpret the symbols attached to the phenomenon under study.

Consequently, I am interested in investigating the phenomenon of the evil eye through the two separate systems of symbolism which are associated with it. The interpretation and the role of symbols is thus approached through their mechanics and the logic that shapes the physical references to the evil eye, and associates them with the existing societal marks and rules found within the region of Corfu. The other approach that I adopt in relation to the importance of symbolism in ethnographic approaches and analysis stems from Deacon's (2011) definition of symbols. During his attempts to negotiate the purpose of symbolic anthropology, Deacon states that symbols are elements of linguistic codes that are expressed unconsciously through the everyday language of behavioural patterns.

Now that the symbolic engagement and the methodology I adopted in order to approach the fieldwork has been discussed, it is important to introduce myself; this is the aim of the next section.

THE RESEARCHER'S NARRATIVE

I grew up in a traditional, conservative Greek village, the second-born of a poor but well-respected family. Secrets in my family were part of my cultural upbringing, and I therefore learned to respect them from a very young age. I also learned the importance that culture plays in personhood, and to fear deviating from my cultural tradition. From an early age, I learned about the fear of being cast with the evil eye – something I am now coming to understand better. During my childhood and adolescence, I found that I was afraid of the evil eye, and I governed my life based on the traditions which offered protection from it. However, I managed to distance myself from this lifestyle after becoming disappointed and angry with the clergy and with God. I tried to explain my existence from a more philosophical and existential point of view, rejecting any input from religion, and during my years away from faith I found myself in a quest for meaning. However, the more I looked, the more puzzled I was by the meaninglessness of my existence, and I therefore revisited religion and faith after some years, on a personal journey in which I came to terms with my own disappointment and anger, which I had earlier projected onto God and the clergy. I now approach the phenomenon with my own biases, which at times come from an agnostic point of view and at times from scepticism. However, it is not appropriate to deny my cultural background, which includes a deep respect for and acceptance of the supernatural and a belief in the existence of good and evil in the world through a Christological point of view. Finally, as a result of my personal journey, I can identify my biases and be aware of them, especially when encountering them during fieldwork.

Professionally, I have a psychoanalytic background, which influences my approach to fieldwork. When I started this research, I was anxious and apprehensive because I could not place myself in the ethnographic research, having found it difficult to define my role and my approach. I knew from the beginning that I did not identify with any known ethnographic research, because what defines me professionally is psychology and psychoanalysis. I therefore had to find a way to place myself within ethnographic borders, and the breakthrough came through my encounter with the paper by Georgina Born (1998) in which she talks about psychoanalytic anthropology. Reflecting on her work, I was able to draw many similarities between anthropologically informed ethnographic fieldwork and psychoanalysis. What was prominent within psychological ethnography, and what was familiar to me, was the use of transference and counter-transference as a way not only to understand the field but also to interpret the data. Briefly, transference and counter-transference take place in practice in every interaction that we have with one another. Transference refers to the unconscious behaviours that we have when interacting with one another, based on our previous relationships with significant others. Counter-transference is the reaction and the role that the other takes based on our transferential communication (Born 1998; Jung 2006; Racker 2001; Etchegoyen 2005).

I was strongly influenced by my psychoanalytic journey as a patient, but also as a clinician. I was deeply influenced in particular by Freud and his conceptualisation of the phenomenon of splitting. Analysts base most of their theories on this phenomenon, which is one of the primitive defences against anxiety. Splitting is the process in which an individual experiences a fragmented reality through the experience of splitting the self/object into bad and good. The two psychical objects are separate and antagonise each other, with the good object being idealised and becoming a persecutory refuge. The bad object, on the other hand, is a frightening object driven by a destructive drive (Thanatos) with persecutory elements in order to find life (Segal 1979). Denial and omnipotence are the two sophisticated defences that are strongly related to splitting. As a researcher, I was influenced by the theory of denial as the omnipotent internal destruction of perception conceptualising a bad object without a reality check. This process results in individuals operating from a developmental position that adopts a more deductive way of thinking, where everything is either bad or good. In other words, the object/other cannot be perceived as whole or as united because the individual's perception of personhood is fragmented, and the individual feels an internal void. Such fragmentation creates the persecutory fear or anxiety that the bad object could destroy the good one and, ultimately, the self (Mitchell 2000). Segal (1982) maintains that anxiety and fear of persecution stem from the murderous aspects of the self. In turn, we project these destructive aspects onto the bad object, which, through splitting, remains internal or is displaced through projection onto others. However, Segal suggests that if the individual is caught up in the fantasy of anger and terror, the persecution becomes irrelevant.

Psychologists suggest that the cultural and societal context in which an individual experiences their reality feeds their splitting. Thus, pain and suffering, or uncertainty, worsen an individual's tendency to experience the object as fragmented. It is argued that through this process, the individual loses the boundaries between the 'person' and the 'other', and comes to feel as if the 'other' is under their control (Segal 1982). One of the reasons that I as the researcher am placing myself in the field of psychoanalytic anthropology, and more specifically that of psychological anthropology, is because it centres textuality and methodology within the general area of ethnographic methodology, but in an anthropologically informed manner. Since the beginning of psychoanalytic thinking, it has been believed that theory should be embodied within clinical work. Psychoanalysis was developed from observation, which is at the core of fieldwork in anthropological and ethnographic studies. Post-psychologists and psychoanalysts offer to oppose pure theoretical exegesis, proposing that the richness of experience and understanding of the human being is accessed through shared intersubjective space. As a relational psychoanalyst, I identify myself as a psychological ethnographer, within the broader field of ethnography and anthropology.

I will consider the role of defences and various positions (paranoid-schizoid) in combination with attachment theories and transitional objects, and I will examine the phenomenon of the evil eye from a psychical point of view in order to gain an in-depth understanding of it, along with the triggers and needs of those who believe in it. In accordance with psychoanalytic anthropology, I will therefore examine the power of the evil eye and its effects on one's personhood and mental health. This school also provides tools to identify the healing or integrative process which allows individuals to heal from internal suffering: this process can find physical manifestations through belief in the evil eye.

Having examined the ethnographic field in which I am placing myself, and having analysed the fundamental elements of the chosen field, it is important to identify the characteristics of the informants. The next section gives a thorough analysis of the actual fieldwork and the importance of choosing the specific field site in relation to the subject matter.

THE FIELDWORK

In this section, an explanation of the fieldwork research and its challenges is presented. Rossman and Rallis (2011) point out that when observers are in a fieldwork situation, they can play several roles. In addition, they argue that it is immensely important for the field researcher to participate in what they are investigating; otherwise, they would not be able to gain in-depth insight into the phenomenon. In this way, the field researcher allows the informants to understand that they are a member of their society, and any negative connotation attached to the role of researcher becomes less significant (Rossman and Rallis 2011). The researcher thus starts to blend in with the observed group, and becomes a member of the observed society. However, this raises an ethical issue which is still debated among ethnographers.

How ethical is it to deceive informants into thinking that you are part of their society? It is argued that no researcher deceives informants out of malevolent intentions (Shaffir and Stebbins 1991), and Shaffir and Stebbins also argue that deception in order to gather important data and be trusted might be necessary when the field researcher cannot genuinely be part of the group under investigation. Morgan et al. (1993) add that if people know they are being observed, this can alter their behaviour; therefore, some sort of deception is necessary in order for the field researcher to gather data as objectively as possible. On the other hand, Gubrium and Holstein (1997) suggest that if the researcher becomes one with the group, they lose the objectivity that allows them to take the observer's position and distance themselves so as to analyse the phenomenon. In light of these factors, I planned to participate fully during fieldwork in the lives of the informants. There would not be any deception of the informants, as I would explain my background and the nature of my presence in the community. However, I had to make it clear that at the same time, I was undertaking research on the evil eye, and also make clear my role as a researcher. At that time I had yet to decide how long I would stay in the field, although it would be for a minimum of three months. Ryan (2005) suggests that the social constructive roles or the framework of a setting start to lose their power when a relationship between two individuals is present. I therefore planned to fully participate in the field, allowing time for informants to trust me and welcome me into their everyday rituals. Marshall and Rossman (2010) suggest that the field researcher should be fully and not sporadically present. In my case, this was because the phenomenon under study is rather sensitive and not easily disclosed; I thus needed to establish myself in the cultural group and the communities that were under investigation. Only through full participation would I be able to gain access to data.

My primary aim was to use ethnographic fieldwork techniques to collect data and find contradictions between behaviours and linguistic representations concerning the evil eye. The fieldwork would enrich the research with valuable data. However, in order to produce strong arguments about the phenomenon, its symptomatology, its spiritual aspects and its healing process, I needed to use different qualitative techniques in order to examine the four target groups mentioned previously. Thus, I employed the following qualitative methods: interviews, observations and focus groups. The methodology posed significant ethical issues that needed to be considered. The next section gives an account of the ethical considerations that I negotiated as part of the methodology.

ETHICAL CONSIDERATIONS

Doing fieldwork raises significant ethical concerns that need to be addressed in advance. At each stage of the fieldwork it is important to show respect and professionalism to informants. I examined the phenomenon of the evil eye and its manifestations in relation to individuals' well-being. I planned to participate fully in the community, which I was to join in order to better understand the phenomenon. A field researcher often encounters unusual ethical dilemmas; to begin with, the nature of the fieldwork presents a challenge due to the strong relationships between the researcher and the informants that can be developed. For instance, it has been reported that field researchers sometimes feel a sense of betrayal when they have to leave the field (Belensky et al. 1997). In addition, the field researcher might also be accused of using the informants for their own academic development. Mindful of these cautionary tales, I was in constant touch with my supervisors during the fieldwork in order to be able to debrief, and to mitigate and defuse any such feelings. It was and is my intention to keep in touch with the informants after leaving the field, and to feed the data back to them in order to correct any misrepresentations on my part.

Another ethical dilemma that required attention stems from Fine's (1993) argument that ethnographic studies do not follow the same idealistic research ethics encountered in other qualitative and quantitative approaches. Fine goes further, stating that such approaches originated in the post-positivism epistemologies that have been applied during the last few decades. I most definitely would encounter evidence of Fine's propositions throughout the fieldwork, and I might appear not to have been as ethical as a quantitative or qualitative researcher might have been. While there is no international research ethics framework for ethnographic studies, most researchers look to the American Anthropological Association (AAA) for research guidelines, and I adopted these guidelines for the current research. However, before I went into the field, I followed all the processes to acquire ethical approval from the Department of Theology and Religion at the University of Durham. When approval for the research was granted, I contacted the Archdiocese of Corfu in order to be granted access to the parishes. By the time I went into the field, all the necessary ethical approvals had been granted.

According to these ethical guidelines, I needed to be clear about my role in the community, ideally for the duration of my presence. It was also important to debrief and to provide psychological help to those who might feel any discomfort during the interviews. Debriefing those who might feel worried about my presence was also a concern; this was mitigated by liaising with a local counselling centre which agreed to provide support to informants should they ask for it. Another ethical dilemma was the consent form. Generally speaking, it is appropriate for a researcher to gain written consent from all informants, wherein they state that they would like to participate in the study. Due to the nature of my fieldwork, however, there were times when obtaining written consent from all the participants was difficult, and it is not always possible to ask for written consent when making observations. A solution to this problem comes from the guidelines supplied by the AAA, which states that due to the nature of fieldwork, verbal consent is adequate to give permission to conduct research. In addition, informants were assured that their identity and sensitive data would be kept anonymous, unless they gave permission for such data to be shared and made available to the public. What follows is a detailed description of the design of the methodology used, starting with the procedures adopted.

PROCEDURES

What follows are the steps that I adopted before I began my fieldwork and after I received the University's ethical approval, starting with my first interaction with the ecclesiastical authorities. Firstly, I submitted a proposal to the Archbishop regarding the areas I wished to investigate in order to gain permission from the ecclesiastical authorities to access monasteries and parishes. With his approval, Greek Orthodox places of worship (parishes, churches and monasteries) were contacted so as to gain access to individuals who suffer from possession by the evil eye. I then made contact with the parish priests and the abbots of the monasteries to introduce myself and develop relationships with them. In addition, I asked the archdiocesan staff to introduce me to the priests. As I was a stranger, this maximised my opportunities to meet religious leaders and increased my chances of getting to know them. The most important procedural aspect was word-of-mouth encouragement to participate in the study from the priests to their parishioners. I was to be established among the parish communities, and would start to build relationships with laypeople in order to observe the phenomenon and be allowed to enter their houses. I was clear about my role in the community and the purpose of the study. Later, I approached individuals who had experienced the evil eye in order to gain verbal consent to observe or interview them. I would also follow up with participants who had been healed, in order to identify the effect that it had had on their mental health. It was my aim to visit and take part in healing rituals by lay healers with regard to the evil eye. Places of worship and healers' houses are the places that provide support for those afflicted by the evil eye and its demonic manifestations. People tend to visit these centres to seek help in order to improve their mental health and receive spiritual healing. In addition, monks, among others, are considered religious healers and can be found in monasteries or spiritual centres. I also planned to take temporary and repeated short breaks (of about thirty to forty-five minutes) from the fieldwork in order to look after myself, as there was a potential risk that I might be overwhelmed by the material and data to which I was to be exposed. These breaks were to enable better focus on the research. In anthropological research, it is important to know how the fieldwork will be recorded, in order to observe as much data as possible. What follows is an account of my preparation before I entered the fieldwork and my engagement prior to my departure.

PREPARATION FOR THE FIELDWORK

Even though I had been a member of Greek society for about thirty years, and even though I grew up in a cultural environment where the evil eye had a dominant societal role, I approached the phenomenon with a scepticism which needed to be explored further and then put aside. I did believe in the evil eye, but later life, education and experience led me to doubt the phenomenon. That said, I tried to keep an open mind, as it appears clear that the evil eye significantly affects individuals' everyday lives. I was also missing important elements, such as the philosophy of worship in the Greek Orthodox religion. I had been approaching the phenomenon with the belief that religion is a manipulative institution which takes advantage of people's fear of being possessed by the evil eye. Part of my journey was to open up the subject matter to specific groups for criticism and discussion, and so I discussed the phenomenon with friends and academics. To my surprise, I realised that they were more passionate than I was myself about the phenomenon of the evil eye; this was the triggering factor that made me reflect in retrospect that I needed to understand this blockage of not wanting to engage with the phenomenon. I realised that I had been guarding myself, and had not allowed myself to connect with the subject because I was lost and scared. I had been warned that I would not be accepted by religious groups in Greece because I was considered an atheist (the priests' term after I challenged them).

After several discussions with priests, as well as interaction with the literature, I came to the conclusion that for years, I had been prejudiced against religion and had not been able to see past its institutionalised forms;

I was therefore seeing only its negative aspects. However, during discussion with clergy and individuals from my own birthplace, I realised that religion plays a dominant role in their well-being and everyday life; this was especially important to them after the trauma of the financial crisis in Greece. I got in touch with my core religious belief, which I had never forgotten, but which had been clouded by negative experiences due to the maleficent behaviour of some priests. As someone who has personally suffered from the evil eye, I myself know that there is something beyond my spectrum of understanding, and it is that something that I was trying to observe and assess. Therefore, before attempting the fieldwork, I read more about the phenomenon, and this led to many interesting observations about what I was soon to investigate. These experiences not only confronted my scepticism about the phenomenon, but also broadened my mind with regard to its theoretical manifestations. I came to an understanding that the phenomenon reaches the sphere of physics, as well as the psychological, philosophical and religious spheres. I therefore found myself increasingly interested in investigating the phenomenon, and began corresponding with the clergy and other social groups in order to understand its religious and experiential aspects. The next question was how to establish myself within these different groups, which did not share the same social characteristics. The answer came from the methodology that I was adopting; I therefore proceeded to focus groups in order not only to examine the different social groups and how their members interact with each other, but also to gather data on the same phenomenon from different sources. However, before I engage with these questions, it is important to share my experience of how the journey in the field started.

After being away for many years from Greece and from the Orthodox tradition as it is manifested in the country, I finally arrived in Corfu in April 2015. It was a lovely sunny day, and my immediate reaction was a sigh of relief, which could be witnessed in my breathing. Somehow I felt like I was at home, a feeling that I cannot necessarily describe; if I attempt to do so, it might lose its significance. I can only express that feeling through its manifestations in my body. I caught myself thinking how blessed I was to encounter this journey, a thought which immediately gave way to an overwhelming feeling of fear. This fear stemmed from my past experiences and the upcoming unknown. I am not the most socially driven person, and at times, I prefer my own company to being around others, so the fieldwork brought to the fore a situation with which I do not actually feel comfortable: to be sociable. The thought that I would have to be a member of a community was thus rather terrifying.

The priest who was waiting for me at the airport came as a gift, as he distracted me from my thoughts. After some pleasantries, we started discussing religious matters, and it felt like he was testing my faith. It appeared that I passed his 'test', which allowed him to act with more warmth, and we developed a more relaxed dialogue. On arriving at the Church accommodation, and after being introduced to the staff, both lay and clergy, I went to my room and lay down, looking the ceiling. A strange sense of lostness was now my predominant feeling; this was exhilarating one moment and paralysing the next. I did not know how to start my journey, or what it meant to conduct fieldwork. I retreated to what I know best, which is to isolate myself in books. I therefore started writing my fieldwork diary, using it as an excuse not to go out and meet with others. My first days in the field found me following those who offered me accommodation and introduced me to different individuals. During these first days of the journey, I was experiencing a paradoxical situation, as I thought that I was focused on my studies, but at the same time, I was lost because I did not know what I was actually doing.

Two days passed and Sunday arrived: my first encounter with the congregation. It was the first time after my arrival in the field that I felt energised and pleased to be attending liturgy. People were welcoming me and showed an interest in getting to know me better, expressing their queries about the purpose of my arrival. Some were sceptical of the subject that I was investigating, while others appeared to be very friendly and wanted to help me navigate the field. The village I was staying at was about five miles from Corfu city centre. It was a small village with few permanent residents. The architecture of most of the small buildings in the village followed a traditional Venetian architectural style which recalled another time. Only the existence of the cars on the narrowed roads reminded me that we were living in a technological era. On my first visits to the field, I had noticed that there were no children playing in the street, and it appeared that the village was primarily occupied by the older generation. There were only a few children visiting the church and attending Sunday services while visiting their grandparents.

Attending church services allowed me to start getting to know people. After the services, we used to arrange meetings at the church to discuss matters that people wanted to share with me. The development of these types of relations slowly led us to discuss aspects of the evil eye. It took me by surprise that my middle-aged informants were the most reluctant to talk about the phenomenon. Younger and older informants were more open with their encounters with the evil eye, positive or negative. However, mental health professionals approached me with scepticism and criticism, despite their age range. At times, it seemed as if they were a kind of a cult, and that only members could interact with each other or take part in their rituals. Then I realised that it was simply how the social norms were playing out; doctors and mental health professionals are busy and highly respected, and do not want to be bothered with daily worries. On the other hand, I received a lot of help from the clergymen, despite the authoritarian role that they adopted at times when interacting with me because of their position and rank.

Almost two months further down the line from my arrival, the weather was getting better and better, and I started meeting informants from different villages to share significant stories about the evil eye. In the closed communities of Corfu, I came to realise the meaning of the idea that 'your reputation precedes you'; people respected me because I was a 'researcher', and it took me a while to shake off that title so that they could see me as a human being and feel free to talk to me genuinely, and not based on what they thought I wanted to hear or what was appropriate. It was then that I started having in-depth and genuine conversations with individuals about the evil eye. I stayed in the field for two years, and after the sixth month I felt established; I was still scared, but also open to whatever the field was about to reveal. During my research fieldwork, I met diverse individuals – young, old, conservative and liberal – but despite their different characteristics, they most definitely left their mark not only on the development of the argument about evil eye, but on me as well. They helped me not only to understand the phenomenon even better, but also to develop an existential understanding of the existential being, which, it later became apparent, was linked to the evil eye. In addition to meeting the informants individually, I was confronted with the difficult task of systematically approaching them. The next section is therefore my attempt to explain how I collected data from different sources in order to increase the reliability and validity of my study.

FOCUS GROUPS

The phenomenon of the evil eye is surrounded by individuals' preconceptions of bad luck, and this could have led to suspicion towards anyone investigating the phenomenon and reluctance to speak of it. In addition, priests may have found it difficult to talk to me about the phenomenon on a one-to-one basis. In order to overcome these potential difficulties, but also to increase the reliability and validity of the research by using the triangulation method, I made use of focus groups as a means of collecting data. My role was to facilitate and stimulate group members to participate in the group discussion and later interact with each other, generating in-depth discussions and new thinking. Not only did I facilitate the discussions, I also observed their intensity and the behavioural changes of the members. Even though the group members were aware that they were being observed and monitored, after a while, they tended to forget this and behave as they would in everyday life; this is another fundamental benefit of the focus group. One criticism of the method is that a group can be dominated by one or two strong characters; however, my psychoanalytic background and the approach that I adopted equipped me with the knowledge and clinical skills to address these issues and draw others into the discussion (Creswell 1998; Fern 2001; Krueger and Casey 2000).

According to Nachmais and Nachmais (2008), focus groups can be seen as groups of informants that share certain characteristics in relation to the phenomenon under investigation. In order to increase the reliability and validity of the themes and results emerging from the focus groups, I conducted group interviews several times with similar informants, so as to identify trends and themes, as well as behaviours and patterns, in regard to the evil eye. I was not simply interested in the informants' narratives, but also in their natural interaction with each other. Finally, I was also interested in informants' non-verbal communication and reaction to others' narratives, and how they influenced one another. As well as the focus groups, I was also interested in collecting data from individuals via one-to-one discussions.

ONE-TO-ONE DISCUSSIONS

In addition to visiting the selected field for observation, the study also included face-to-face follow-up discussions. These could only be successful if I could first build relationships with the community and the individuals involved. This done, I could observe the phenomenon and start asking questions. I found myself mostly siding with Silverman's (2004) suggestion that semi-structured interviews are more appropriate for field research than surveys. Silverman also suggests that field interviews are more interactive and fluid. Kvale (1996) adds that surveys or prepared interviews are too restrictive to encompass the complexity of a phenomenon as observed in the field. I therefore took an active role within the group under observation, which facilitated better engagement and enabled me to build trust and provide a sense of security so that informants could speak freely about the evil eye. Through face-to-face discussions, I aimed to gain insight into what participants had experienced, what they believed about the evil eye and how it affected their mental health and well-being. Therefore, semi-structured interviews were designed.

I also adopted Gillman's (2000) and Ritchie and Lewis's (2003) suggestions that face-to-face discussions are the most suitable method for subjects where depth of meaning is required. The research therefore began by recognising the immense significance of the subject matter and its context. However, there is debate in relation to Gillman's and Ritchie and Lewis's views about face-to-face interviews regarding realist versus constructivist perspectives (Banfield 2004). Semi-structured discussions seem to follow both emancipatory and participatory models. One of the fundamental criticisms, however, of semi-structured discussions is that the informants respond differently to the researcher based on how they perceive the latter, and also based on what they think the researcher wants to hear (Denscombe 2007; Gomm 2004). I therefore worked to achieve a balance of data collection methods, and attempted to minimise informants' attempts to manipulate the data through my third qualitative technique: observation in the field.

OBSERVATIONS

One of the fundamental strengths of observations conducted in the field is that they provide a vivid and honest account of the social phenomenon being investigated (Stigler 1992). Observations do not rely on self-reportage through interviews, which means that the phenomenon is recorded in a true and unbiased form. Observations also provided me with a wide range of diversity and applicability; they can be either informal or formal, structured or unstructured, and the researcher is able to adjust to any social environment and observe the phenomenon in its true form (Moore and Notz 2006). This meant I was able to observe any contradictions between behaviour and individuals' narratives.

Participating as an observer enabled me to gain deep knowledge about the intricacies and internal dynamics of the phenomenon that could not be acquired from the literature. In addition, through the observations, I collected detailed information that participants would not have been able to state directly, as the words are bound and limited by cultural and social constructs (Turkle 1992; Lacan and Fink 2007). I therefore kept a journal of observations created through observing the participants, who were active members of a religious community, and of interactions with the members of particular religious groups. As such, I was able to gauge the difference between experience and language: between what participants usually do and the exact words they say.

In addition, I was able to observe several situations and social constructs relating to the evil eye. Lofland and Lofland (1995) maintain that researchers who conduct fieldwork can collect data which would not otherwise be possible to gather. To be more precise, I could observe the different behaviours of individuals who jointly belong to the particular cultural group under observation. I also collected data by observing each moment that the evil eye was manifested during the period in which I lived among my informants. Lofland and Lofland also assert that fieldwork informs the researcher about the social interaction between two or more informants. Through such encounters, I was able to identify whether the social construct of the evil eye in Corfu was affecting the manifestation of the phenomenon. This study therefore identified the positions and roles of the people within society in relation to the evil eye. I was also able to observe the ways that society is organised around the phenomenon, and to see how social groups have been developed and how they interact. I also gathered data regarding the conservative social groups that have developed concerning the phenomenon, and the constitution of the boundaries of these groups, in order to further enhance my understanding.

Having engaged with the methods of data collection, it is important to understand how I recorded the field; this is the focus of the next section.

RECORDING THE FIELD

Gubrium and Holstein (1997) mention that one of the most important aspects of conducting fieldwork is that the researcher is present to capture every moment of the phenomenon; no camera can capture the rich material that can be gathered through a researcher's first-hand experience. It was therefore important for me to keep notes while investigating the phenomenon. Empirical observation of the phenomenon as it was experienced was also recorded in terms of 'what I think has taken place'. I aimed to make clear in the notes when I was writing from a subjective point of view. Lofland and Lofland (1995) suggest that a field researcher can anticipate behaviours and prepare a standardised recording form. However, in this study I chose not to do this; I wished to enter the field as ignorant of the phenomenon as possible, in view of the fact that I was entering the field with my own biased thoughts and beliefs. Creating a standardised recording form would have reduced the chances of observing the phenomenon as it happened and reinforced my existing biases.

I used different methods of note-taking and coding for my observations during the fieldwork and also kept chronological notes and maps. It was also useful for later analysis to create charts regarding the observed phenomenon. A two-stage coding system was used, as proposed by Hay (2005). The first stage was to identify the basic themes arising from the data, and the second stage was to move to secondary coding, which allowed exploration of the interpretive in-depth codes for identifying specific behaviours, beliefs and patterns.

The next important phase in any research is the analysis of the data in order to produce results. The next section explains my methods of analysis.

ANALYSIS

The data from the fieldwork consists of in-depth interviews, transcripts, observations and field notes. The field notes were written during or after the observation of participants. In addition, textual documents and notes relating to the procedure of conducting the fieldwork were gathered, and the analysis included careful and repeated interplay with the data. This data produced the themes that I was able to define and analyse. In addition, it was important to pay attention to the analytic thoughts that emerged during my engagement with the data. The ethnographic analysis adopted is not a periodical analysis, but rather a process that started when the first data became available and continued until the end of data collection.

The research was likely to produce vast amounts of non-numerical data, which can easily be overwhelming and difficult to manage. However, this apparent challenge actually proved beneficial. In tandem with the feeling of being overwhelmed by such a large amount of data, there came a need to listen to my inner voice in order to gauge whether some symbolic meaning might be attached to it and to better understand the data. Retrospective consideration of what the data might mean for me shed light on what it reveals about the subject under investigation. It was also important to actively listen to the narrative of the data: what stories emerged from the narrative? How did they inform the subject under investigation?

Ethnographic researchers examine the way in which individuals interpret a phenomenon in a specific context (Smith et al. 1999, 2009; Smith 2007; Heron 1996). Anthropologically informed ethnographic analysis is a bottom-up process through which the researcher generates codes (themes) from the data (Smith 2007; Reid et al. 2005; Larkin et al. 2006). The importance of such an analysis is to preclude the researcher from approaching the data with set ideas about the phenomenon obtained from reading the existing literature. Ethnographic analysis is not used to test hypotheses or theories, but rather to add to existing theories and facilitate the healthy development of the field (Larkin et al. 2006; Flowers et al. 1997). After the data transcription was completed, I worked closely and intensively with the produced text in order to gain further insight into the informants' narrations. In this way and through knowledge garnered from observations, I began to gain an understanding of my informants' world, and I tried to balance the phenomenological descriptions with in-depth interpretations based on informants' accounts. However, due to the nature of the investigation, preparation was necessary in order not only to protect myself as the researcher, but also to equip me with some awareness of the fieldwork and the subject matter. Therefore, certain themes were starting to emerge from the analysis.

The aim of obtaining themes in a research study is to identify emerging topics from the data. In order to identify these specific themes, I applied certain techniques. The most important of these is coding the data. Coding is the process of identifying key words stemming from the data, but also meaningful attitudes and narratives as observed in the field. Therefore, the whole analysis and process of obtaining themes begins with open coding. At that stage, codes are emerging from the data without any particular direction or limitation. Open coding involves identifying nuggets of meaning across all the collected data. Through this process I attempted to categorise the phenomenon and attribute labels to the codes. The comparative method used in open coding allows the researcher to constantly compare the data with existing codes in order to achieve theoretical saturation – the point at which the researcher is unable to develop further codes.

Following on from open coding, I utilised memoing. During this stage, I was constantly attaching theoretical notes to the established codes. I was also able to revisit the codes and re-examine them, allowing for concepts to emerge. The creation of action notes to be attached to my codes, with the view to arriving at a cohesive understanding of the collected data, was therefore necessary. Another significant aspect of the data analysis after coding and memoing was the identification of categories. As such, the codes were categorised based on their commonalities, and core and sub-categories were identified across the themes.

Within the analysis that was adopted, there were certain challenges in regard to reliability and validity; these are dealt with in the next section.

RELIABILITY AND VALIDITY: AN ETHNOGRAPHIC CHALLENGE

When examining phenomena in an ethnographic manner, I considered two basic but very important elements: the first was that the phenomenon under investigation was observed in its natural setting, and the second was related to the comprehensive understanding of the phenomenon by me as the researcher, as well as how it was perceived and interpreted by the informants. The application of anthropologically informed ethnographic methodology relies on the data collected by the researcher, which stems from observations of social interactions and the ways in which the phenomenon under investigation is acted out in the informants' lives and reflected in their narratives. In addition, the ethnographic methodology also relies on direct interaction and interviews between the researcher and the informants. An important aspect of research into a specific phenomenon is the holistic approach to the data that attempts to develop a deeper understanding of the phenomenon under investigation. What characterises ethnographic studies is the fact that researchers do not formulate a hypothetical scenario before the fieldwork; in fact, the hypothesis emerges during data collection (Nurani 2008). This methodology has one major drawback, namely the question of its reliability.

Eisinga et al. (2013) describe reliability as the researcher's ability to reproduce the procedures and findings of their research. They continue by suggesting that reliability upholds two assumptions: the first suggests that a research study should be repeated using the same procedures, and the second that the interpretation of the data should be consistent in using the same methodology; there is thus external and internal reliability. In order to increase its reliability, the current research used repeated interviews with and observations of the same informants for the duration of the fieldwork. However, the challenge for ethnographic research lies in its particular circumstances; the natural setting, the differentiation of the informants and the background social setting change every time the researcher tries to replicate the procedure (Nurani 2008). Burns (1994) therefore concluded that reliability in ethnographic studies is compromised, because a phenomenon is observed in its natural setting and logically the natural setting cannot be replicated.

Another challenge that ethnographic studies, and especially anthropologically informed ones, face in relation to statistical reliability is the fact that the researcher's agreement is needed in order to replicate findings (Burns 1994). Burns claims that reliability should not be considered in ethnographic studies, due to the fact that a phenomenon under investigation changes organically as a society and its people change, and therefore its accurate description changes accordingly. The description of a phenomenon under investigation might differ because of the researchers' various approaches and interpretations, as their description is based on interpretation of the data collected from the field. However, Gall et al. (2005) propose that ethnographic research should investigate a phenomenon and identify the source of its descriptive disagreements, in order to develop a dialogue between these disagreements in an attempt to resolve them. Another solution to the challenge that researchers face in regard to the reliability of a study is the attempt to describe the applied methodology of a particular study as comprehensively as possible, in order to provide clear guidance to the next researcher on constructing their approach identically to the original methodological strategies (Nurani 2008).

The strength of research derives not only from its reliability but also from its validity. According to Burns (1994), validity is related to the researcher's ability to draw cohesive and generalised results with confidence. When the research procedure lacks clear methodological strategies, the researcher's ability to draw results with confidence is affected and the study lacks internal validity. On the other hand, when the researcher cannot generalise the results across groups, the external validity of the study is weak. Unlike other methodological designs, where the external variables are controlled, ethnographic research lacks the ability to control extraneous variables, as the phenomenon under investigation is studied in its natural setting. In addition, ethnographic studies last longer: the data is collected over a long period of study in the phenomenon's natural setting (Gall et al. 2005). However, the counterargument regarding the longevity of ethnographic studies comes from Burns (1994). He argues that longevity allows ethnographers to draw their results with confidence, as they constantly compare and analyse their data in order to ensure the relationship between reality and scientific categories as derived from the field. In addition, he maintains that anthropologically informed ethnographic studies attain better validity because the observation of a phenomenon is conducted in its natural setting rather than in an *in-vitro* setting.

Mindful of the challenges of internal validity, in the present study I used triangulation, the combination of different data collection methods, as proposed by Burns (1994) and Nurani (2008). This technique consists of constant verification and validation of the qualitative analysis. In this way, I constantly assessed the sufficiency of the collected data. To this end the data was examined again and again in relation to the tentatively formed hypothesis; if it was not consistent, the suspicion was raised that it was insufficient. Triangulation therefore allows researchers to increase internal validity by collecting data through different methods, such as observations, interviews, group interviews and so on.

Another important aspect of ethnographic research is the fact that researchers face the challenge not only of internal but also of external validity. External validity refers to the generalisation or applicability of results across groups. The results of ethnographic research are based on the natural setting and its context, and the researcher therefore needs to specify the conditions of the field in order to be able to generalise the results. Burns (1994) proposes that external validity exists if the phenomenon is consistent through a number of studies. The current study succeeded in increasing its external validity by adopting a methodological strategy that included different methods (interviews, group interviews, observations and so on) for examining the context within which the phenomenon took place (Nurani 2008).

Despite the challenges that ethnographic studies face in regard to reliability and validity, their primary advantage resides in the methodological techniques that allow the researcher to observe a phenomenon as it occurs in its natural setting. In addition, ethnographic studies allow researchers to unveil the intra-structures of a phenomenon in a community setting. However, no research methods are without their particular strengths and limitations. What follows is a discussion of both the importance of and the difficulties presented by the adopted methodological approach.

STRENGTHS AND LIMITATIONS OF THE METHODOLOGICAL APPROACH

One of the strengths of the research was that I shared a common sociocultural background, religious background and language with the participants. This meant that I was able to understand all the idiosyncratic customs, as well as the jargon and idioms, used in certain areas of Greece. In addition, people feel more comfortable when they interact with a clinician who shares their cultural background (Souvlakis and Cross 2008). Finally, the fact that I am Greek gave me permission to enter healers' houses, something that would not otherwise have been possible. I am from a small island where folklore, magic, God and evil are dominant elements in peoples' everyday lives. I was thus entering the field with a deep experiential understanding of the phenomenon of the evil eye. However, there would still be potential obstacles to recruiting participants, because the evil eye is still a taboo subject in Greece.

Greek people do not like to talk about evil and demons because they are afraid of the bad luck that accompanies such discussions. Resistance to co-operation was also likely to come from the priests, because of reluctance due to their belief system to examine their ways of dealing with the evil eye. From my experiential knowledge of the field, to examine such things is blasphemy.

CONCLUSION

In this chapter I elucidated the methodological approach of the present anthropologically informed ethnographic study, exploring the meaning of psychological ethnography and exposing my position and biases as researcher. My narrative was discussed in order to shed light on my own views and influences when it comes to the interpretation of the phenomenon under study. A discussion followed of the processes that I adopted to analyse the data in my attempt to obtain as much information about the phenomenon as possible. This chapter also analysed the applied methodological approach and gave an illustration of the research questions that were posed during interactions with informants. In addition, I gave a short description of the four different categories of informants: laypeople, priests, mental health professionals and folk healers. The four categories are examined in depth in the following chapter, which elaborates further the results as they stem from the data and are attributable to each category. Finally, this chapter explored my own limitations and strengths as a researcher, taking into account the fact that I was living and interacting in a field in which I was well known, and highlighting the ethical considerations that were adopted from the American Anthropological Association (AAA). With an understanding of all the methodological steps that the research adopted, we now proceed to the analysis of the collected data, starting with the different attitudes that the four major groups exhibited in the field.

Chapter 2

Informants' Different Attitudes and Understandings Regarding the Evil Eye

INTRODUCTION

Having examined in the previous chapter the participants' specific characteristics, the field's demographics and the methodological approach adopted to collect data from the field, this chapter aims to provide evidence of the phenomenon of the evil eye as it is perceived and interpreted through the eyes of Greek Orthodox individuals from the four preselected groups of participants (laypeople, clergymen, folk healers and mental health professionals) in the region of Corfu. The belief that a maleficent eye is capable of inflicting pain and misfortune from a distance is what this chapter aims to explore, through the informants' engagement with the phenomenon. The terms used in this chapter are thus a true reflection of the informants' narrative and wording. The question of whether there is an innate human belief that the eye – and in our case the evil eye – encompasses malevolent forces is assumed to remain unanswerable and unanswered, being beyond cognitive comprehension. The analysis of the data, however, showed that this question may be partly answered by the evidence provided: there was a plethora of amulets hung around people's necks and wrists or worn under cloths to protect the wearer or loved ones from unseen powers. Pagan ideology seems to be inflected by religious leaders' interpretation of the phenomenon of the evil eye. It is important at this point to comprehend the general view of the Greek Orthodox Church regarding the evil eye. Is it real or just a folk belief? The answer appears fairly emphatic, as most of the priests I spoke to during my fieldwork were firmly entrenched in their position on this matter.

In the previous chapter, I described the importance that the Greek Orthodox Church plays in contemporary Greek life and culture. The most important public holidays are in fact the days when the Church celebrates religious feasts, and the majority of the population adheres to the prevailing national religion. Christian Orthodoxy still plays a fundamental role in promoting and maintaining Greek identity and ethics. The Orthodox Church is also the established state church in Greece, and it plays a significant role within civic and governmental affairs. Religion is also highly present in all matters of everyday life, starting from the education system, in which Orthodox Christianity is a compulsory module and students are engaged in short morning prayers before the beginning of classes. People are also prone to make the sign of the cross when passing in front of a church. Despite the rapid growth and influence of Westernisation and globalisation, Greece remains a deeply religious country.

LAYPEOPLE'S ATTITUDES TOWARDS THE EVIL EYE

This section aims to give a thorough account of the themes that the collected data from the fieldwork, as well as my personal observations and diary, revealed about the evil eye. This part of the analysis seeks to provide information about the various attitudes exhibited by informants towards the phenomenon. The present chapter is therefore arranged based on the themes that certain demographics exhibited, starting with laypeople.

SOMA AND PSYCHE IN RELATION TO THE EVIL EYE

It was towards the end of my anthropologically informed ethnographic research, while I was trying to deal with my grief over leaving Corfu, that I had a significant experience which led to a discussion about the evil eye. On one of my walks around the old town of Corfu, I witnessed something that my mind failed to comprehend, despite my attempts to rationalise it. I was sitting on a bench opposite a very old church, the Church of St Gerasimos. It was a warm summer day. A woman in late pregnancy (so it seemed) walked in front of me. When she passed in front of the church door, her stomach muscles and skin were relaxed to the point of being loose. As a result, the stomach area, which held the baby, stretched and expanded until it reached the woman's feet. Out of fear, and without really knowing what was going on, I went over to check if everything was all right. The young woman was accompanied by an elderly lady who appeared to be her grandmother.

In a state of shock, the young woman sat on the bench where I was sitting, and her grandmother started praying. I exchanged numbers with the elderly lady and asked her whether I could visit them the following day to check how the pregnant woman was feeling. A couple of days later, I visited them at the pregnant woman's house, where her grandmother welcomed me. She admitted that when they returned home they had been very shocked, and she had started praying when she realised that her granddaughter had not been in the church for a long time. In addition, the grandmother realised that the pregnant woman was not wearing the protection that she had been given for her wrist. She told me that the baby was fine, and that they had visited the doctor on the day of the event. According to her grandmother, a pregnant woman should always wear a protective amulet, because they are subject to the negative energy of other people, especially other women. Later on, Maria, the pregnant woman, told me that she felt as if she had dreamed the incident, and that it was only through the discussion with her grandmother and me that she realised that the event had actually happened. Maria also told me that every time she encountered an evil spirit, she felt it in her body, as her body reacts 'strangely'. Maria told me:

> I am not sure what is going on, Nikos, with my body but I can tell you that it does not feel right. It is like my body becomes a separate entity, which I have no control over. Most of the time I am scared when that happens, thank God it does not happen often but when it happens it is scary. It feels like my body tries to tell me something when I have the evil eye, like it tries to communicate with me and I am failing to listen to it. It is scary when that happens I am telling you. However, when I gain control of my body I go to church and I pray and light a candle and then I have the feeling that something is restored, like I feel whole again.

Maria came from a privileged upper-class family and had a good educational background. She was in her mid-twenties when I met her and was married to a man that she had fallen in love with a year before. Her husband was a well-respected individual in his early thirties, with a good position in the political landscape of Corfu.

It was through my discussion with them both, and later with many other individuals, that it became apparent that individuals are believed to be able to cast the evil eye on others when they are carrying malice in their soul. This communication and transmission occurs through the sensory paths. Gossiping, gazing, handshakes or any other bodily engagement while interacting with others can transmit the evil eye. In the majority of cases, the evil eye is manifested through somatic distress and creates a triangular suffering, as the shield (body) has been penetrated. This is why I call Maria's experience a triangulation of suffering; it starts with the body, but the suffering of the body is related to and communicates suffering to the spirit and the soul. It seemed that people in Corfu were engaging with the evil eye and were therefore activating it, whether consciously or unconsciously. It was clear from my interaction with Maria that many individuals tend to embody the evil eye, which then works towards the breakdown of the boundaries between beliefs and perception. In other words, the evil eye brings together a triangular interaction of the body, soul and spirit.

In my quest to further understand the phenomenon of evil eye as a triangulation of suffering, outside my own thread of thoughts, I came across Paul's Epistle to the Thessalonians, where he refers to the interconnection between soma, spirit and soul in order to reach internal and external peace (1 Thess. 5:23). In Corfu, people are mostly influenced by the Greek Orthodox Fathers' view of the threefold manifestation of a human being, as conceived by Paul. Soma is thus the material manifestation of a human being; psyche refers to the energy with which the body acts, through feelings or cognition; and soul is the entity or force by which a person comes into touch with the transcendent or with God.

My informants, however, appeared not to be aware of this tripartite structure of a human being, and they often confused psyche and spirit, referring to the two interchangeably. Others approached psyche and spirit as distinct and split parts within a person's body. In this view, the psyche is the regulator of the emotions, and the spirit manages and defines spiritual and mental intelligence, while the body becomes the shelter of these functions. These informants also stated that through its manifestations, the body is the receiver of transcendental communication; this does not always relate to God, and at times creates confusion and guilt. The informants revealed that the evil eye is a demonic energy that seeks to control the psychical or spiritual functioning of a human being. In order to get full access to it, however, the body needs to be weakened; as Maria said, 'It is like my body becomes a separate entity which I have no control over'. Demons gain access to the body through the evil eye and try to weaken it from the inside. Therefore, the evil eye is nothing more than a means through which evil entities obtain access to an individual's soma to control their spirit. Tonia, an informant in her late fifties, said:

> My body is in pain every time I suffer from the evil eye. It is not like the pain that we know, though, it is different. I am not sure if you can understand me, Nikos. It feels like I am losing access to it and I am scared that I might do something

weird. During the event I feel like nothing matters, as if I am entering a dark hole that absorbs me and I do not matter. It feels like I am eaten alive and I lose purpose, or worse, I do not matter. The worst thing though is not the part where I lose control of my body, but afterwards, when I recover from that experience I feel so ashamed and embarrassed that it takes me a long time to recover from it. The pain that comes from the feeling of me not mattering is in fact excruciating, but is a different suffering, it is more a spiritual suffering. It feels like my body is weakened and taken control of by different powers that I do not want even to imagine, Nikos.

Tonia was a devout Christian who practised her faith regularly. She was well educated, but had never been given the chance to receive higher education. Within the triangulation of suffering, the evil eye becomes a form of possession. Maria and Tonia gave an account of their suffering, and their narratives described some form of possession that included initial disembodied manifestations. Therefore, in what follows, I engage with the phenomenon as a form of possession, as revealed in the data.

LAYPEOPLE'S UNDERSTANDING OF THE EVIL EYE AS POSSESSION BY THE DEVIL

The evil eye is considered an evil energy, and this finds support in the preaching of many clergymen within the Greek Orthodox Church. This demonic energy is associated with internalised evil, which can cause serious physical and psychic damage to individuals. One of the informants, a man in his mid-forties, mentioned that:

> [the] evil eye has to do with the Devil; otherwise priests or prayers would not have any power over it. Every time that I have the evil eye it is like I am possessed, I have irrational bodily pains that if I ignore it feels like they eat my spirit. I start doubting my faith, I stop going to church or praying and one of the worst feelings is that feeling of absolute desperation, as if there is no hope for tomorrow. When I have the evil eye and I ignore it, most often I end up sitting with friends and not being able to recognise them, not cognitively of course, but it is that feeling of 'what am I doing here'; a question that leads me to a very dark place. Most of the time, and especially when I am spiritually energised, the evil eye strikes me and weakens that energy by disease affecting my relationship with my body. When I lose that connection my relationship with myself and God is shaken and that scares me the most.

Believers and those who practise Christian Orthodoxy do have a certain resilience to this evil energy. There was a certain fear associated with the evil eye and its manifestation as '*vaskania*'. Through the fieldwork and the informants' testimonies, a split within the phenomenon could be determined. This split was with reference to doctrinal and practical religion: the phenomenon of the evil eye is part of the lived religion, while '*matiasma*' (the action through which someone suffers from the evil eye) belongs to the doctrinal teachings of the religion. However, in everyday life, these two parts are interwoven, making the split in the phenomenon almost impossible to detect without deeper analysis, as both are considered to be a form of possession.

Like Maria, some people believe that the evil eye is a demonic force through which the Devil captures and possesses a person's body. An informant in her late forties stated that:

> Any manifestation of evil, such as the evil eye, within the Orthodox territory is considered the Devil's power. It is satanic energy that provokes damage through vaskania; it is most certainly Satan's work. I have plenty of examples from my family that can support that statement. Talking about myself, I was possessed with the evil eye, but also I caused to someone the evil eye at times when I was not in touch with myself but close to God. I know it sounds contradictory, as one would expect that being close to God increases self-awareness. I can argue the contrary though. I have learned from my family that I need to surrender to God in order to be saved from my sins. However, the surrender was to suppress my dark and negative feelings, which then became the fuel that enabled Satan to possess me through the evil eye. Surrender to God without being aware of who I am does not help me at all, in fact it fuels satanic powers, enabling them to intervene and gain control of me through that 'surrender'. The first step by which they can gain control of me is through the evil eye.

This informant was a devout Christian, and was married with four children. She had received a good education but never managed to enter higher education. However, that did not prevent her from pursuing her dream to be a successful professional. What was highlighted in her narrative was the phenomenon of split and suppression. Individuals, both the above informant and others from the field, were in agreement that according to the Greek Orthodox tradition, they suppressed their dark thoughts and emotions in the name of God. However, this attitude did not in fact bring them closer to God, but rather distanced them, as the difficult emotions still existed and they simply ignored them. Thus, the informants' self-blindness appeared to be as honey to the bee that is satanic powers, and these powers would try to gain control of someone initially through their body. The vehicle to do this is the evil eye. As many informants argued, the Devil declares his presence by using the '*vaskania*' form to possess people and cause them to stray from God. Many of the Devil's followers in the lower order of demons try to take advantage of human beings through the evil eye, but it is only the Devil's manifestation through the evil eye that can steal people's souls.

Other informants, and especially those from the younger generation, opposed the idea that the Devil steals souls through the evil eye. They made it clear that it is indeed the Devil's power that takes the form of the evil eye, but claimed that it works in different ways. They believe that they are safe so long as their body and psyche remain fit. Further exploration revealed that in using the word 'fit' they were referring to the spiritual connection with the transcendent. Some believed that such a connection could only be achieved through God's representatives – priests – in specific holy places like churches and monasteries. Others believed that the connection could be achieved anywhere and at any time, as long as they were open to receive 'spiritual messages'. Up to this point, the data analysis has revealed the connection between the evil eye and the soma, but also the ways in which the evil eye can be the means of possession when individuals are not in touch with themselves; however, nothing has yet been mentioned about the energy that the body upholds or how this might be related to the evil eye. Thus, in what follows I examine and analyse the relation between energy and the evil eye in form of possession.

Dimitris, who is in his twenties, expressed some ambiguity about the evil eye:

> The evil eye is like possession. We get mentally and physically ill without any physical cause, for some other reasons that I fail to understand, or by these energies that we emit as human beings, if we focus on something. I believe that our minds have the capacity to emit energy and change the status quo of many things, even to cause harm to others by possessive negative energies that direct someone away from his own spiritual purpose.

Dimitris clearly maintained a bipolar position regarding the definition of the evil eye. It is religious possession, but it might also be a consequence of a human being's transmission of energy. The significance of what Dimitris is saying is that the evil eye can be seen as possession originating from humans rather than demons. Such a view was validated by many other informants, confirming that possession is caused by other people when they emit some maleficent energy.

Through energy transmission when the evil eye is involved, individuals can feel whether a person has bad intentions and may feel threatened by being close to them. When they maintain contact with that person, they start experiencing 'weird' things, such as bad luck, moodiness, lack of motivation or loss of body functions (for instance sex drive). Sofia is a woman in her fifties who feels as if her body is raided by a negative energy which affects her bodily and psychically. She mentioned that this bodily channelling happens when she is in close proximity to malevolent individuals: 'it feels as if I absorb their negative energy'. Sofia's words seem to echo the truth about the evil eye for the majority of the informants with whom I interacted. Further support for this idea came from Kerkira, a young woman in her twenties, who stated:

> I fear thinking negatively about others, especially my exes. Every time that I have wished for someone to have a bad time, or something bad to happen to them, it returned back to me as if it were me inflicting pain on myself. Hence, I avoid having negative thoughts about others. I must be very bad at manipulating my bad energy, and therefore I try to suppress it out of fear of hurting myself.

Kerkira was talking about energy and how to channel or suppress it. However, her experience was different to the common definition of channelling, as described by Brown (1976): the alteration of a deeper level of consciousness in order to communicate, or even channel through one's body, spirits or spiritual energies from different dimensions. According to the informants' accounts, there is an exchange of radiances within the evil eye's field that is constituted through the sufferers' bodily channelling. They were talking about networks of invisible energy, which intercommunicate with each other and trigger the '*matiasma*'. Sofia, like many other Corfiots, was open to the notion that the evil eye is an exchange of energy and is part of the human spiritual dimension. This belief was mostly supported by individuals in their early twenties, and those who are considered to have a middle-class education; however, it also found strong support among older women who were greatly devoted to the practice of Christian Orthodoxy. There is a constant electromagnetic exchange that affects another person's mental status, through which the evil eye weakens both soma and psyche.

Martha was a very devout woman in her seventies; she was ignorant about spirituality, but nevertheless was a very spiritual person, who stated that:

> [the] evil eye cannot exist without channelling; it is the only way to maintain sanity and integrate what has been ripped off from us with the introduction of technology and Western views. The broadcasting of the evil eye allows us to keep open the spiritual doors, bringing together reason and intuition, body and psyche. The evil eye can affect us all and has both satanic and human attributes.

Despite the fact that the evil eye appears to be seen as possession by the Devil, it was also observed to be a phenomenon that works through the individual's body and allows them to be in touch with the supernatural. The following section analyses this observation further.

THE EVIL EYE AND DIRECT CONTACT WITH
THE SUPERNATURAL THROUGH THE SOMA

It was before the Easter celebration that I visited Spyros in his office. He had invited me for the purpose of interviewing him about the evil eye. He talked about the evil eye as something extraterrestrial: a supernatural phenomenon that expands to the supernatural realm. At the same time, he made a connection with religion, and more specifically the battle between God and Satan. Spyros therefore associated the evil eye with the supernatural, which he believed to be beyond the limits of human cognition, as we cannot understand things that the eye cannot see. He also understood the evil eye to be a power rather than energy: a supernatural power that he himself failed to understand. It was then that he started talking about the evil eye as a mystical experience, belonging not to the natural (physical) realm but rather to the spiritual. Spyros talked about personal experiences of the spiritual, which led to the conclusion that there was a strong connection between the evil eye and the spirits of the dead. He was referring to some sort of spiritism, which stemmed from the spirit of the dead and direct contact with him through the evil eye.

In many cases during my fieldwork in Corfu, it was reported that a direct contact with the dead had taken place, without any specific medium being present, but instead through the informants' body via the evil eye. There was thus something natural about the channelling of the (dead) spirit and its communication with the informants. Through these observations and the informants' narratives, a paradox was born, suggesting that even though the evil eye is placed in the realm of the supernatural, its manifestations are natural and include physical attunement and awareness. Thus, the following question was raised by Alexandra:

> I am not really sure what the evil eye is; does it belong to natural or supernatural realms? Most of the time when I have the evil eye it is like a strange uneasiness in me, it is like I am restless. The more I stay in that state of evil eye possession, the more it feels it is not me who is talking but something else that tries to talk to me through all these manifestations. It sounds crazy, I know, but it feels like that and I am scared when it happens; that is why I have a very close friend who is a clairvoyant and who helps me to cast it out.

Thus, a rather different set of boundaries had to be drawn with regard to the phenomenon. As the evil eye is perceived through its physicality, and as a real entity, it should be considered natural and not supernatural. Kostas said: 'The evil eye generates a web in which a person's body senses it'. Giannis, meanwhile, stated that:

the body should have some sort of memory or intelligence, as we are picking up evil eye transmissions to communicate with what it is out there: good or bad. Most of the time there are evil manifestations, but I am not sure if it is Satan or other entities around us. Clearly, if our mind has a certain intelligence to understand things and interpret reality, our body should have some sort of intelligence to interpret things as well. What if our body is our medium to communicate with the spiritual world? I have heard in church about many spiritual experiences in which people felt the presence of God initially through their bodies, and then they started making sense of the experience. I have had some of this type of experience myself. What I am trying to say really is that clearly, our body can be unconsciously a medium to perceive things that the mind initially fails to comprehend, and I believe that the evil eye is some kind of manifestation of spiritual power that tries to say something to us.

Giannis was in his early thirties, and as a devout Christian, he linked the evil eye with bodily intelligence and spiritual powers. He stated what appeared to be a common view among Corfiots: that the evil eye is a phenomenon that is not empirically based, and therefore scientists dismiss it, but that it is nevertheless a powerful phenomenon. Later, through the fieldwork, I met Anna, who brought up the idea that the evil eye is indeed a supernatural phenomenon, but one that is also in our memory. Through the evil eye we utilise parts of our body which have been long forgotten. We open doors that have long been shut. She then added that the evil eye reminds us through its natural manifestation of the existence of another dimension; this is a dimension that our brain cannot comprehend, and it is only through the body and emotions that we can perceive it and attempt to understand it. The evil eye, therefore, became for Anna a real declaration of the spiritual dimension; she and many other informants argued that the evil eye is part of the spiritual life, discerned through sensory experience.

Ria, a clairvoyant who is in support of Anna's belief about the evil eye, stated that the phenomenon is not a form of spiritual possession, but rather a spiritual power which is manifested through humans and mostly interacts with their bodies; this is why people can become possessed by it and lose control of their bodies – or as Ria proposed, 'when the evil eye hits someone, the sufferer becomes diseased because they start being possessed by the caster's eye, which creates a sense of disembodied agency'. She also stated that the evil eye can be healed, because it is a spiritual power that is imposed on one's body from the outside. Scientifically oriented minds, she added, find it impossible to understand the nature of the evil eye, as it falls outside their way of thinking; the evil eye is therefore dismissed as an objective sensory perception. She stated:

It is a difficult subject to talk about, as it has received many controversial opinions within the Christian Orthodox tradition. Personally I am a very devout Christian; however, when it comes to the evil eye I strongly believe that it is a spiritual power that links the spiritual realm with the real one. Some might say that there are spirits which try to communicate with us, not necessarily to possess us but to try to teach us something, if I may say that. Sometimes these spirits might be linked with religion and be seen as evil, but I am not sure if in fact they are. The simple truth is that I do not know. According to my experience of being possessed with the evil eye, it is not a nice experience, but most of the time it leads me to some realisation about myself.

Stamatis, a young man in his early twenties, took a step further than Ria's account of the evil eye and highlighted the similarities between evil eye energy and radiation. He said that we listen to the radio and watch television without questioning the energy that comes into our houses: this is radiation that we cannot see, yet we nevertheless accept it because it creates comfort for us. The evil eye is no different to this kind of energy; it is radiation that we cannot see because it takes place in a realm that the human eye cannot perceive; however, it can be felt through sensory experience. In the same way that radiation can be perceived through the radio or television receiver, the evil eye can declare its existence and be experienced through the body. However, the majority of informants stated that the evil eye is not inhibited by scientific schemata, but is more a psychically dynamic phenomenon. This means that it travels intersubjectively and interculturally, transcending biological and physical representations. Petros mentioned that the evil eye is an energy that travels freely above and beyond the suppositions of science, but always within the boundaries of everyday spiritual life. The supernatural and possession-based understanding of the evil eye leads us to a significant attitude about the phenomenon which brings to the forefront the individual as a sufferer and as a caster through the process of empathy. Empathic responses to the evil eye are therefore the main focus of the next section.

EVIL EYE POSSESSION AS A FORM OF EMPATHIC RESPONSE TO SUFFERING

Among informants, there was a certain emphasis on the intensity that is witnessed and experienced in relation to the existence of the evil eye. One of the informants told me:

> It is like a foreign power controlling my body, my spirit and my whole existence. When I suffer from the evil eye I lose control of who I am and I do things that

I cannot recognise, I behave as if it is not me, and then I am embarrassed. Needless to say, the body malfunction that I experience goes through different manifestations, from headaches to digestive problems, etc. It is like I am a different person. Oh yes! The way that I relate is affected as well. It is like I do not want to know anyone, it is a very claustrophobic and isolated experience.

The power that takes over a person's being affects not only the body but also the emotional, cognitive and behavioural aspects of the individual. Martha stated:

What scares me is that the evil eye is like something penetrating my body and I have no control over it. It penetrates my whole existence, and most of the time I am not aware that it is happening in order to protect myself. I feel helpless when it comes to the evil eye. Yes, I have been wearing religious amulets, and not all the time, but it seems that nothing is happening, and I am not protected. It might be my fault that they cannot work, or so I am starting to believe. The amount of emotional suffering that I experience is indescribable and often there is no particular reason for me to feel that pain. There is something, though, that comes when I call on my mother to cast evil out or when I ask the priest to read me a prayer. Most of the time the person that cast the evil eye on me comes into my mind, sometimes I know the person, or some other times a face that I cannot recognise comes into my mind.

This view was shared by many Corfiots, who stated that it felt as though they were carrying someone else's negative energy. It was concluded, therefore, that Corfiots believe that the evil eye is a form of energy through which they can assist someone through their suffering. To be more precise, they stated that when the evil eye penetrates the bodily frame, they feel pain and do suffer, but the suffering is not theirs. Thus, they argued, they are carrying the suffering of another person. In other words, the evil eye is the medium through which a caster seeks help for their suffering. It appears to be an empathic means through which an individual can feel the internal emotional turmoil of the caster due to the lack of external mirroring.

Many informants also described feeling as if they left their bodies and lost their sense of time; it was as if they were not present. They also felt out of sync with their reality, as though they did not belong to it. They described a space of absence, like a black hole where nothing matters; like a spiritual isolation. They became 'empty vessels'. Many spoke about *kommara* (stemming from the Greek word κόβω, to cut). Those suffering from the evil eye did indeed experience an internal and external disconnection, at an individual and social level. Stefanos stated that he felt like his soul was becoming heavy, after which he would lose the sense of its existence. Then his body would try to reach a new homeostatic state, and he would experience headaches, body pain, dizziness and stomach upsets (the stomach is considered by many Corfiots to be the place where the soul is hosted in the body).

Many Corfiots are opposed to the idea that the Devil is stealing their soul in an attempt to lure them away from God. They believe instead that it is the suffering of another human being that is projected onto them and makes them suffer. In support of this notion, Stamos says that '[the] evil eye feels like our psyche is possessed by someone else'. In a way, they maintain that the evil eye is a form of spiritual communication between one suffering soul and another, in an attempt to seek help. On many occasions, the informants had known through the experience of their symptoms who had cast the evil eye on them. They were thus becoming stronger vessels for the caster and sufferer to overcome their spiritual pain through the healing rituals. Here it seems that the evil eye is a means of communication which forces the sufferer to feel the caster's emotional state, but also their existential struggles. As such, there is a strong link between the evil eye and empathy, as it becomes a form of empathic response to the caster's suffering. However, it initially has a negative impact on the sufferer. So far, nothing has been said about the origin of the need to cast the evil eye as a means of communication from the caster's point of view. The question therefore remains as to what forces individuals to cast the evil eye in order to communicate their own suffering. The following section – including the account of Ioli, a Corfiot with a long history of experiencing and witnessing the evil eye – may shed some light on this question.

THE NARCISSISTICALLY INJURED AND THE EVIL EYE

Ioli, a Corfiot in her late eighties, invited me into her house to discuss my interest in the evil eye. She welcomed me and offered me dinner, stating that there is nothing better than a discussion over dinner and a good glass of wine. She then started questioning my beliefs about the evil eye and asking what I made of it. When I attempted to generate a discussion about the phenomenon, Ioli started laughing, to the point that I became irritated. When I explained this to her, she told me how wrong I was about my research, and that I had missed the basics, that is, the origin of the evil eye. She then took me on her historical journey, revealing a rather interesting aspect of the evil eye. Ioli stated that:

> The evil eye is nothing more than a profound need to relate to someone or something. I strongly believe that the evil eye is nothing more than a desperate

cry to be seen. Everything starts with the lack of mirrors since we are young. I have sadly observed this with my kids. When they were young, I was so preoccupied with my business that I was not there for them, especially in their attempts to define themselves through my eyes as their primary source. Their omnipotence needs to be seen ... I failed to meet it. As a result, later on they developed that weird need to want to go above and beyond to be noticed, to the point that it attracted negative comments that affected them in all sorts of ways, mostly psychologically. I came to this conclusion through my own experience, Nikos, and through my observations that the evil eye is nothing else but a reparative attempt to redress the early narcissistic needs to be seen that we acknowledge we cause to our children or to ourselves. However, the evil eye becomes complicated, because it is mixed with our adult needs and fears.

Ioli and other informants discussed how the evil eye stems from a Venetian tradition, according to which it is the infant's failed attempt to understand their caregivers, who hold the vital power to keep them alive. These informants also maintained that infants depend on their caregivers and therefore want to possess them; thus, the infants try to mirror their caregivers as a way of understanding themselves. The reflection that infants receive from those that they think hold the power to keep them alive (their carers) is therefore the beginning of their personhood. Ioli linked this to the notion of captivation, and was laughing at my ignorant assumption that the evil eye is purely a phenomenon of misfortune rather than a form of making sense through captivation. Ioli practised Christianity, but was rather confused about how a phenomenon such as the evil eye was attached by Christian Orthodox priests to demonology, giving it such a damaging meaning.

It was mentioned that the evil eye does indeed contain a notion of anger, as the psychical structure re-enacts the primal failure of the infant to possess its carer as an attempt to understand the world. Thus, the evil eye's association with anger can affect and psychologically damage other people or objects. However, according to some Corfiots, this destructive power comes from the human need to be seen at an internal psychical level. George posed a question about this internal meaning: 'I am not sure that I understand; not the phenomenon, which I cannot [understand] anyway, but its motives. What is going on with me that I want to destroy what I do not possess?' Following this, I embarked upon a series of discussions with the informants to try to make sense of what these people meant when they related the evil eye to an internal need to be seen and to interact with the 'other'. Michalis, in his late fifties, argued that he did not know how to perceive the evil eye, but he had noticed that when he emitted the evil eye to someone, he was usually aware of it. He also stated that most of the time, he felt angry about a quality or object that he did not possess, and could also witness this in others.

Some of the informants described an internal schism, which made them feel like two different people and occurred when they observed something that they liked but did not have. They felt angry that they did not have it, but not necessarily envious. The anger could be so strong that they felt it destroyed them from within; therefore, they emitted it to the person who held that quality, hoping to destroy the cause of the internal turmoil. There is thus an automatic need to use aggression and destruction to protect oneself. In a similar way, Hara stated that 'the evil eye is our inability to sustain loss, and we use anger through the evil eye to destroy anything that reminds us of what we do not have but want to have'. Something primal manifests itself when people are denied something they need, yet see it exhibited by others. The evil eye, therefore, is people's inability to admire in others what they desire; it is manifested through the hate and anger of internal conflict. Hara expressed it well when he said that 'We are too proud to admit that we like what we see, because it is too painful for us, and hence we want to destroy it because it reminds us of our internal pain'. Hara also said, 'I feel humiliated to see in others what I really want to possess' and 'my instant reaction is to hate and want to destroy it'. Litsa said: 'The need to destroy through the evil eye appears to be the individual's need to counter-attack, in their initial psychical attack, the presence of an 'object' that they do not possess'.

Many informants associated the evil eye with psychical attacks that can cause mental illness, or as they described it, 'madness'. They were referring to the evil eye as something strong that inflicts the weak. Within the notion of strong and weak, it is believed that the evil eye is an internalised power that transmits evil energy through the eye and causes mental distress and misfortune. Georgia described the human body as a vessel in which a certain amount of strength or energy can be stored. However, it was clear from the findings of the fieldwork that the amount of energy an individual can store in their bodies varies from person to person. Under certain everyday circumstances, the storage is in equilibrium with the individual's psychical homeostatic state.

It was argued that the homeostatic state is disturbed by internal or external emotionally charged situations or traumatic experiences. The internal energy storage has certain upper and lower thresholds. Sofia said:

> When the energy exceeds a certain threshold, or drops below it, then the individual can cause or be afflicted by the evil eye. This means that a negative thought, or just a gaze, can cause damage to someone, as the person who emits that energy is highly emotionally charged.

Despite the damage that the evil eye can cause, it is an attempt by the individual who causes the damage to reach their homeostatic state. One informant stated:

> It is like having a fire in me; I do not want to cause harm or distress, but I cannot control it. When I feel the fire inside me and I think about someone, then that person starts to feel weird. I have caused distress to my own children at times.

Due to this internal 'fire', individuals appear to operate like an overcharged battery that needs to be defused before it explodes. The evil eye, therefore, is like an explosion, damaging anyone or anything around it. Most of the time, a person does not know they can harm another until they do so, and so the damage is unintentional.

In a state of disequilibrium, a person can emit or be susceptible to the evil eye, which is a means of restoring homeostasis. The informants also suggested that those who are suffering from physical or mental distress are more likely to be affected by the evil eye, as they are already in disequilibrium. It was believed that individuals who have weak ego structures to protect themselves from the energy of the evil eye are like empty vessels in which the evil eye stores itself. When that happens, they start suffering from nightmares, irrational fears and anxiety. Other symptoms can take between a couple of minutes and a couple of days to appear, and may include muscle tension, mental distress, confusion, feeling internally empty and headaches.

So far, we have explored laypeople's attitudes towards the evil eye. It is important now to investigate the clergy's attitudes to the phenomenon, as it is linked to Christian thinking.

CLERGYMEN

The majority of priests in the Orthodox Church seem disposed to condemn any witchcraft – a category to which the phenomenon of the evil eye does not belong, according to my informants. Priests deem anyone who deals with the evil eye outside the realms of the Church a charlatan. Psychologists, psychotherapists and any folk healers are thus seen as a real threat. At the same time, there is confusion as to what these 'charlatans' do; do they offer a real cure from the evil eye, or just an illusion of getting better – a placebo that instils false beliefs in individuals? At times, there have been certain hostile attitudes among clergymen reminiscent of the Roman Empire; an enmity towards an incomprehensible phenomenon deemed to be magic.

These beliefs have been influenced by noetic science, which suggests that the mind can overcome the laws of nature simply by utilising brain energy. By developing a better and deeper understanding of their consciousness, an individual can gain access to a better and expanded understanding of reality, finding that physical boundaries might take on different forms and lead to a constant communication with the inner and outer space of one's body (De Quincey 2005).

One can legitimately conclude that the attitude of Christian Orthodox priests is rather dubious when it comes to the evil eye. Even though they accept the misfortune that the evil eye can cause, they tend to believe that those with virtue and fortune should be afraid of transcendental forces that inflict pain and misfortune through the use of the eye. The position they hold with regard to the evil eye is thus heavily influenced by pagan philosophy, and its teaching that humans are capable of bending the laws of nature, rather than by the Scriptures. For this reason, priests try to qualify their beliefs and their expressions in order to make them religiously acceptable.

In attempting to understand the evil eye from the clerical perspective, I came to the belief that the phenomenon is living proof of humanity's deficit before God. The materialistic and psychological scarcity which precipitates the phenomenon is a reminder of human nature; it is a reminder that people can try to look like God but can never exceed His grace. It is also an admission of the potential of human beings to be destructive. It was therefore suggested that the evil eye is a deadly sin which gives insight into how evil arrives in the world. The evil eye, therefore, becomes a reality onto which humans project their sinful guilt. However, people fail to acknowledge that the evil eye, which originates with human beings, can overwhelm and corrupt. Therefore, it became apparent that in fact, no humans inaugurate evil through the evil eye. Evil already exists on earth, and people simply experience the feeling of belonging to the transhistorical evil presence.

The physicality of the evil eye can be recognised by the calamities that it causes. However, there is another layer in its functionality, that of punishment. This is noticeable through the psychical suffering that it causes, and this functionality was described as the sickness that was once outside, but is now inside, working its contentious ways against the body. This leads to the conclusion that mental suffering and death are manifestations of the punishment of the evil eye. Father Andreas stated that

> The evil eye is part of the first sin, when humans felt impotent against the great power. Throughout history, as a way of allaying the sense of internal helplessness, people have resorted to religious beliefs, within which the evil eye belongs. Religion was a way for humans to find a place in the cosmic

functioning, rather than being at its mercy. However, the purpose of the evil eye has been attributed to God. Genesis 2 and 3 exemplify this, where God curses the serpent and creates enmity between him and his seed. Thus, the serpent/evil eye has always been the divine instrument of God. It was the envy of the serpent towards God that allowed the evil eye to be present through Eve. Hence, if God created everything, ipso facto, God created the phenomenon of the evil eye and only God or his representatives can cast it away.

The evil eye is seen as a transgression of theological morals and norms. At times it has thus been compared to sin, and individuals who cast the evil eye are seen as having failed to obey the will of the higher power. Acting against the will of God is a matter of self-centredness, and therefore casting the evil eye is a narcissistic act – an act that demands attention, which cannot but bring malady to those who are surrounded by such energy. Father Andreas also stated that the evil eye was present throughout the history of Christianity, and cautioned that it should be approached very carefully. After all, in the book of the Wisdom of King Solomon, it is mentioned that the Devil envied the heaven above and wanted to destroy what God had created: 'By the envy of the Devil death entered into the world' (Wisd. 2:24), as Father Andreas also said. The evil eye therefore became a phenomenon that everyone fears due to its deceptive nature. In addition, the evil eye became one of the deadly sins in the eyes of the clergy, as it is humanity's urge to turn life into death. As Father Andreas stated:

> There is a paradox here: the cause of the sin is unhappiness at another's good fortune; yet the sin is actually based on something good having happened. It is difficult for some to admit this, and can lead to the desire to possess that goodness. There is within human beings a certain demonic tendency that weakens them.

The observation that the clergy sees the evil eye as a phenomenon with demonic tendencies was unavoidable. These tendencies are therefore explored in the following section, which starts with a personal experience.

DEMONIC TENDENCY AND ITS RELATION TO THE EVIL EYE

It was Saturday night, and I was doing my habitual walk around the port in the city centre when I came across a man who was wearing an amulet in the shape of a phallus. Out of curiosity, I greeted him; he replied, and we ended up at the local coffee shop discussing the amulet. The informant, in his forties, said that it was part of his family tradition to wear the amulet for protection. Further exploration led to a discussion of his view that the phallus is the ultimate protection against demons. He shared an experience from a couple of years earlier, when he had forgotten to wear his amulet; when he went to work, he felt as if a shadow was taking over him, making him a completely different person. He associated the shadow with heaviness, anxiety and demons:

> A shadow is the first sign that a demon has entered someone's body, my grandmother used to say. I remember when I was going to work that day that I forgot to wear my amulet. I could feel my body becoming heavy. It was a strange feeling, as I could sense the coldness from within. It was a moment when I was driving to work that morning when this darkness – it was like a dark veil that was dropping all over my body from head to toe, and I could not escape, no matter what. I felt paralysed even though I could move. It was like someone or something else was controlling me.

Notably, a shadow is always attached to the physical body, and sometimes can be seen but at others times cannot. The informant, named Costas, correlated this with 'blindness' and the evil eye.

When I discussed the above narrative with Father Charalambos, it was clear that the evil eye in Costas' case had become a passive process by which a demon enters a person's body through another's eyes. Demons play a significant role in Corfiots' everyday lives, even though they try not to think about them, as they believe that doing so attracts them; the demons are thought to float around people, observing them and waiting for the right time to strike. The evil eye is the process through which demons pollute one's body and soul. The evil eye is thus seen as an attempt by a demon to possess individuals and lead them astray from their godly-oriented minds. Father Charalambos gave a somewhat demonological explanation of the evil eye taking away the conscious or unconscious control of an individual who was aggressive towards another person, without however taking away moral responsibility for such action. He also stated that even though the evil eye is caused by demonic power, it requires a relational structure from the person who was instrumental in bringing it about. Through this relational structure, the individual does not simply become a devil's pawn. Accordingly, Father Charalambos suggested that the evil eye has no power and cannot emit negative energy on its own. It stimulates negative energy, but it needs an agent; it cannot affect anyone unless it is used by demonic powers, which possess individuals through the shadow of the psychic or demon. The evil eye therefore has an eschatological dimension according to some priests, since it goes against God's image and human attempts at redemption. In other words, the evil eye is perceived as seductive energy which leads human beings away from the 'truth'; it is the demon's attempt to pervert innocent minds. A demon, then, is the director of the evil eye, which causes sufferers to confuse true and false, right and wrong. But what are the mechanics of evil eye possession? What follows is an attempt to answer this question.

THE CASTER, THE SUFFERER AND THE MECHANICS OF POSSESSION

Even though one can see evidence from pagan philosophy in the priests' attitudes towards the evil eye, it can also be argued that this influence is not as strong today as it was in antiquity. Notwithstanding, it is believed that those who cast the evil eye on someone are doing more damage to themselves than to others. Some priests, probably under the influence of the teachings of St Basil, argued that is nothing but a scary folk tale to suppose that envy can cause harm and suffering to others through the exclusive agency of the eye, since no one has such power. In fact, some of the priests affirmed that the evil eye should be approached as a form of possession. They stated that it is not the person to whom the evil eye is directed that suffers, but the person who inflicts it. In their view, demons live among us and watch everything; they remain uninvolved in human affairs until they see an opportunity and then seize it. Thus, those demons that are hungry for hate find individuals who share the same hatred and employ them through possession to serve their own will. In other words, demons possess the individual, who momentarily shares their hatred, so as to fulfil their own deeds through the individual's eye – the evil eye. These individuals become slaves to the demons, and at the same time, they oppose the will of God. One might wonder whether such an attitude towards the evil eye is an authentic one, without any influence from antiquity. The answer might come from 'De invidia et odio', as described by Plutarch while he was outlining the paradox of Narcissus. Therefore, it appears that attitudes towards the evil eye in the twenty-first century still remain strongly influenced by ancient beliefs.

The Orthodox priests that took part in the field research argued that the evil eye is the initial stage, and that if this stage lasts long enough, it can lead to possession. They maintained that this stage is characterised by bodily dysfunction and disorientation. An individual who has lost their connection with the transcendent is more likely to become a vessel for demons. Those with 'no God' in their lives become weak and susceptible to envy and jealousy, through which they inflict harm. The timescale during which a person can move from pre-possession to possession varies, according to the priests; it could be hours or months, during which time the individual slowly loses their consciousness and completely surrenders to the will of the evil powers. During the pre-possession stage, the caster of the evil eye suffers more greatly than the person upon whom it is inflicted. The priests suggested that the caster experiences nightmares and therefore sleepless nights, and as a result starts to develop anxiety stemming from persecutory fantasies, which can then take the form of paranoia. They start believing that something is working against them, but they do not know what. The priests also proposed that only an experienced eye – an eye close to God – would be able to identify the symptoms and save the caster. The same, however, appears to be the case for the sufferer of the evil eye. There is a danger that those who suffer from the evil eye can be possessed by evil spirits if it remains undetected for too long. However, the sufferers face different symptomatology to the casters; they begin to lose bodily functions and their interest in living, and start having depressive symptoms, rather than the anxiety experienced by the casters.

Finally, I understood from my interactions with the clergy that there was a belief that the eye can cast harmful energies. In fact, they went further, linking these energies with fire and burning. Referring to the eye, which burns, they described the withering event of possession. The perplexity that arose from linking the evil eye to possession was later clarified by the data associating possession with fear of the divine. In other words, when the clergy referred to the evil eye as a form of possession, they were referring to a state of mind which they called *deisidaimonia* (δεισιδαιμονία): the aberrant terror of both divine and demonic in one place. At this point, my engagement in the field led me to wonder whether the evil eye was not entirely demonically driven. What if it was something different? Many priests had wondered this as well, and this is the focus of the following section.

THE EVIL EYE: THE MEDIUM OF THE OPPOSITION

It was one of the hottest days of the summer, and I was following the daily routine I had established for my fieldwork. I was about to go for my Sunday morning coffee, and was reading my paper and observing people passing by. I was interested to see people wearing all types of amulets to protect against bad energy. That morning, something striking occurred; around noon, a priest came for coffee after completing his Sunday church duties. He was wearing a rather interesting amulet, which was not a crucifix or a rosary, as could have been expected. Instead, it was a rather intriguing symbol, which, I later discovered, had its origin in Venice. Out of curiosity, I started talking to him. He was aged 56 and was celibate, having served the Christian Orthodox

Church for many years, and he was surprised by my interest in his amulet. After a while, he began to share some very interesting stories about the evil eye. There was sadness in his voice while he explained to me that Christians sometimes stray from their path, interpreting the evil eye as the intentions of the Devil and his hatred for the goodness in the world. The priest believed that the evil eye is instead a tool that God uses to judge those who rise above themselves. Thus, the Devil uses it to destroy goodness, and God uses it to make an example of the arrogant. In other words, the evil eye serves two opposite functions: fear and hatred, and love through punishment.

The priest shared a particular story to support his view about the evil eye. As a child, he had grown up in a very traditional family. His mother was very religious, and he was very beautiful and much loved by everyone in his family. However, he ended up being sick all the time. His family could not understand the reason for his sickness, and they therefore made a bargain with God: if he were to get better, then he would become a priest and serve God. After that, his parents started taking him to Sunday school, while at the same time attending most church services. However, the most interesting thing was that they stopped dressing him in beautiful clothes. They once told him that he needed to hide his beauty so that he did not invite the Devil's eye, and that he should move away from the pride he might take in his appearance, as this would attract God's wrath. Therefore, he started wearing humble clothes, and gradually there were no more compliments about what a beautiful child he was. Since that time, he had been devoted to God. He tried to be as humble as possible out of fear that either God or the Devil would punish him.

Such fear appeared to be the norm in clerical circles. The priests understand the evil eye as God's punishment for egocentrism, or as envy of others' 'goods' that comes from the Devil. These assumptions indicate that not only is the evil eye the dispirited outcome of praise, giving humans the power to cast it, but that it also creates confusion as to the intentions of the God of love. This interpretation of the evil eye creates the assumption that punishment is acceptable if a person's intention is love. Even though the evil eye has a similar effect on individuals, regardless of its interpretation, it is more acceptable when it is seen as God's wrath than when it is the Devil's hatred. This leads one to ask to what extent the opposing powers are different. The Orthodox priests stated that it is naïve to think that God and the Devil can be one. However, in the priests' own narrative about the evil eye, God's power and the Devil's seem to be one. To conclude, it was obvious from our discussion that the priest in the café condemned those who used or blamed God or the Devil for their own wrongdoings, since this removed any power that God or the Devil might have over people.

So far, we have explored the different attitudes and interpretations that clergymen attribute to the evil eye as possession. However, nothing has been mentioned of the fear that the evil eye instils regarding the absence of an agent. Therefore, what follows negotiates this issue, as discernible from the clergy's narratives.

INDIVIDUALS' FEAR OF ABSENCE AS RELATED TO THE EVIL EYE

One of the complexities of investigating the evil eye and the Christian Orthodox clergy's attitudes towards it stems from the multifaceted nature of the phenomenon. My results forced me to take a step back and look more closely at what it was that the clergy meant when they spoke about the evil eye. The data highlights the fact that the term cannot simply be used to describe attributions of the evil eye that have nothing in common. However, there is a strong acceptance within the system that the phenomenon exists and that it absorbs energy. The clergy stressed that there are challenges with the phenomenon, even within a system of beliefs. Be that as it may, it became apparent that the clergy attributed fear to the evil eye, or *vaskania* as it is better known. The fear did not stem from the sufferers of the evil eye, but from the construction of the phenomenon. The data collected from the clergy reveals that there does not appear to be a fixed or secure identity within which the evil eye takes place, but an identity in flux with no particular traits. In addition to the unknown or unpredictable identity of the phenomenon, the fear attached to it reflected a deep fear of 'non-existing'; it is the sufferer's fear of non-real identity that is cast out through the evil eye. The fear of non-existing, or other feelings of 'loss', take the form of envy within this phenomenon. Looking at envy and the evil eye in the abstract led to the possibility that envy is a shadow feeling of the fear of absence. The evil eye has a particular identity with which individuals can be associated, and it is easier for the clergy to control the phenomenon and its absence if envy is attached to it.

It appears that this fear has been cast upon human beings by God, the Devil or a malign supernatural entity. Named by an old priest as *Phthonos* (Φθόνος), it can be viewed as the personification of jealousy and envy. The fieldwork revealed that the phenomenon took the form of an entity with specific narration, boundaries and life expansion. Further exploration of the clergy's need to attribute human characteristic to the evil eye prompted a deeper understanding of the initial fear attached to it. The ambiguous identity allows for confusion and the absence of boundaries within the phenomenon. The priests often mentioned that such fear appears to have no particular focal point, and causes a sense of apprehension. Due to this confusion, the accounts they gave of misfortune following the evil eye have been equally confusing and intangible. In their attempts to understand and falsely control the phenomenon, they have ascribed to it a combination of forces, such as demons working through envious beings, or God trying to rectify the disastrous effect of *Phthonos*.

An important finding comes from the north of Corfu. Within the constellation of beliefs and attitudes around the evil eye, a little-known facet of the phenomenon is singled out here, arising from the deep-rooted sentiment that goodness attracts opposition through the supernatural forces of meanness and hostility. Clergymen from this area found it hard to accept the fact that human beings could inflict harm from afar. However, it was easier for them to accept this if the humans were simply being used as vessels by non-human entities which cast hate from the eye(s). The intervention of a transcendental entity, either God or the Devil, could bend the laws of nature and create abnormalities in someone's life.

Similarly, the existential phenomenology of the evil eye and its unlimited variations has an impact on the clergymen's attitudes towards it; they attribute fear to it as a way to distance themselves from it. The clergy's need to make sense of the phenomenon leads to the manifestation of another attitude towards the evil eye. It came as a surprise to me that the more educated clergymen approached the phenomenon with a smile at the irony that their brothers subscribed to a belief to which many have given their allegiance. It would be naïve, however, to criticise this expression of disdain and suggest that educated priests were condescending about the evil eye – or perhaps that they were embarrassed to admit to their own attitudes. Even so, such attitudes towards the evil eye constitute evidence that the phenomenon encounters some resistance within the clergy. In the quest to identify this resistance that was present within the educated circles of the clergy, it became apparent that there was a strong sense of inadequacy. The absence of clear attributes applicable to the evil eye has made the clergy feel that their theoretical religious understanding has failed to explain the phenomenon. Following this realisation, resistance emerges. It is encountered not as failure but rather as a fear of allowing themselves to relate to the phenomenon experientially rather than cognitively. There is a certain fear that if they related to the evil eye through the emotional part of their being, the priests would then lose themselves and their faith within the unfathomable nature of the phenomenon. For instance, Archimandrite Doctor Andrew stated that there are times when priests cannot escape from their human nature, and fear the absence of identity caused by the evil eye;

they seek to escape it by scorning it. This feeling of absence wells up into their consciousness through their emotions, which they try to resist. These results show that the evil eye is a phenomenon that highlights the absence of identity through which individuals maintain a position of free-floating anxiety. A sufferer feels that the negative emotions are directed to this feeling of loss of identity. In other words, the evil eye echoes the finite nature of our existence. It relates therefore to the existential element of a person's identity. It is important, however, to examine in more detail how the phenomenon of the evil eye relates to someone's subjectivity as it is manifested in the materialistic environment that sufferers and casters live in.

THE EVIL EYE'S SUBJECTIVITY AND MATERIALISM

During Great Lent, while Christians in Corfu were preparing for Holy Week, I had the chance to visit a monastery and to meet one of the monks, who was well known for his experience of the evil eye. He was the abbot of the monastery and was in his late sixties, and he welcomed me to his humble cell. A peaceful character with wild physical characteristics, he introduced me to his experiences of the evil eye. Although his account focused on the phenomenon itself, it also appeared to offer significant and compelling evidence that shed light upon the existential subjectivity of the suffering caused by the evil eye, and clerical attitudes towards it.

From the abbot's narratives it was concluded that the evil eye is a phenomenon that incorporates not only physical but also psychical experiences. An extensive system of beliefs is connected through the emission of the evil eye, undeterred by significant individual ramifications. It has been argued that the evil eye does not operate within the timeframe known to humanity as the present, but in a time-free and boundary-less structure. Within that structure, the evil eye is a form of connection with gendered historical manifestations. To be more precise, the fieldwork revealed that women adopted more extroverted communicative rituals, while men appeared to operate from the other end of the spectrum, and were more introverted in their rituals for dealing with the evil eye. To sum up, the evil eye is not simply idiosyncratic or even passive predestinarianism; it is rather the opposite. It is a systemic complexity encircling social aesthetics, social ethics and poetics of local historicisation.

The interaction with the clergy led to a deeper understanding of their perception of the phenomenon. The evil eye was understood elementarily as 'fire': a powerful psychical fire which melts the subject from within. An alchemical metaphor, it is the fire which liquefies the psychical self from within, leaving only dry land. The somatisation of the evil eye thus exemplifies such liquefaction and the inner pain. This metaphor brings to the forefront the question of a special manifestation of one's psyche. The melting of a suffering psyche caused by the evil eye provokes a split between spirit and body. This split, emanating from the sufferers of the evil eye, puts at risk the fundamental givenness of space created by the integration of spirit and body; therefore, the recuperation of the shared material is now at risk. The psychical storage is abandoned, leaving the sufferer confused and unsure about the definition of the storage materials. The absence of storage thus leaves the individual in a state of anxiety, unable to recognise the artefacts that now float in their psychical space. Consequently, the evil eye becomes a historical component embedded in historic human consciousness, replicating itself within time and space through its commensal conduct and ethics.

It was midday, and by that time many monks had joined the discussion I was having with the abbot. The aesthetics of the phenomenon were discussed, leading to the conclusion that the evil eye appears to be a transcultural vehicle for actualising consciousness and somatic metaphorisation for its sufferers. However, regardless of those suffering from it, the metaphorisation has become a homeostatic energy in Greek mnemonic processes. The evil eye therefore conjures up an afferent dimension of disunity within the transcultural context in which it takes place. It blends the somatic and psychical suffering and leads to a spiritual maturation, the abbot said:

> It is God's hand that allows suffering, because people would otherwise not listen, and they are moving away from Him. The evil eye therefore becomes God's tool through which spiritual experience emerges. It is like the evil eye is used for individuals to suffer, with the aim being that they see themselves and their actions, and therefore understand themselves better, their nature as God's creations, and become closer to Him spiritually. Besides, a deeper level of spirituality emerges from a deeper level of consciousness. In my experience the evil eye, through the plethora of symptoms, invites us all to introspection and better self-understanding.

My interaction with the monks deepened my awareness of the bifurcation of the evil eye in the society under investigation. On one hand, it showed the fear of the widespread functioning of the phenomenon, and on the other, its transcultural and metaphorical paradigm. The latter was not just a paradigm from pre-modern society; it asserts its existence in urban cosmopolitan societies today, in attempts to find meaning in everyday life experiences.

In the next section, I examine the priests' understanding of the evil eye within the area of gender, and specifically how they believe the phenomenon is related to womanhood.

WOMEN AND THEIR BODIES AS SEEN THROUGH THE PHENOMENON OF THE EVIL EYE

During my fieldwork, I recalled the short rituals that I had long forgotten but that now appeared immensely significant for my understanding of the evil eye. To enable better comprehension of later descriptions of the phenomenon, it is important to give a clearer image of these rituals here. Orthodox Christian places of worship have an aisle in the middle, which divides the nave into two areas; the left side is where women sit during church services, and the right side is where men sit. Father Andreas, who serves in one of the northern villages of Corfu, told me that it is important that men and women should not mix during the liturgy. They need to be separated in order to avoid causing any temptation to each other. In the beginning, it was Eve who gave the apple to Adam; women are thus more prone to evil temptation than men. For this reason, men sit on the right side of the church, and are therefore closer to God. A priest in his late sixties stated that:

> the other men [i.e. homosexuals] as well as being abnormal are closer to the female attributes and therefore closer to the Devil. These men are more powerful than women because they choose to be like men and act like women and, therefore, they can cause not only misfortune but also death by casting the evil eye to someone.

In the wake of the recent dialogue between Church and state about separation of the Church from the state, conservative priests have been forced to take dramatic actions that reinforce superstitions. During my fieldwork, it was observed that women from the city and surrounding areas wore trousers more often than the women in the villages. Many women, however, disclosed that priests have reprimanded them for inappropriate dress, calling them 'dirty creatures'. It was more common for priests to admonish young girls, rather than older women, for inappropriate dress. It was still a common embedded belief that menstruation causes dirtiness in a woman's body, and many women were not allowed to receive Holy Communion or even venerate an icon during their periods. Father Nikolaos gave me an example of the link between such embodiment and the evil eye through an experience he had had with his daughter, Despoina, a young lady in her late thirties. She was a devoted Christian, and spoke of her difficulties with the evil eye and what she had experienced. As a young girl, she always wanted to know how to cast out the evil eye (*xematiasei*, or ξεματιάσει). However, it was her grandmother who had to teach her, because of a requirement that this knowledge be passed on by every second generation. Her grandmother kept postponing this, until Despoina forced her to teach her at the age of 17; at this point, however, her grandmother told her that she would never be able to learn the healing process because she had become a woman, as she had begun menstruating.

Despoina's story piqued my interest in the formalities of the healing prayers in the eyes of the clergy. It was commonly accepted that women can use prayers to cast out the evil eye, but that the most powerful prayer comes only from the priests. 'Nothing can be compared to the power of the prayer that comes from priests', Father George told me. 'The prayers are not to be revealed to women, and if a woman healer needs to tell it to another woman, they always need a male mediator'. This triangular process of female–male–female was necessary for the prayer to have power, and to allow the transmission of its energy from one woman to another. Once triangulation takes place, women would no longer be subjected to Eve (evil), and they would not present any further spiritual danger. However, because Despoina had become a fully embodied self in the image of Eve, she was no longer allowed to learn the spiritual healing process, because she was now closer to evil. 'It is the church's responsibility to protect its body from impurity. Women are only "dirty" when they have periods; hence, their activities in the church should be limited', Father Sotirios told me.

It was obvious that the older generation of clergy shared the belief that women are unclean while they are having periods and therefore pose a certain danger of casting misfortune to others, because during that time they are closer to the Devil. In addition, it was a shared attitude that during their periods, women become spiritually dangerous to others, as they are prone to cast the evil eye to others, and also have the utmost power during that time. There was, however, a split in the beliefs of the clergy as to whether women pose such a threat out of malice (because during menstruation they are closer to the Devil), or because they are simply more powerful during that period. For the older clergymen, the evil eye appears to be attributed to the female gender. However, there was a contrary position emerging from the younger generation of clergy, who stated that the female body can be a spiritual vessel. It is women who can cast out the evil eye, and not men, despite the triangular relationship; and it is women who protect the household from negative energy. Father Nikolaos shared an experience of a woman who had used her body to create a sacred shelter in order to make a refuge; it was hard for him to get access to her during the rituals of casting out the evil eye. The woman was casting the evil eye out from a young boy, and her body became spiritually active, allowing the somatisation of the evil eye. In a way, she was allowing the evil eye to enter her body and to leave the sufferer alone; and in her body (soma), she processed and metabolised the negative energy. The majority of the younger generation of clergy argued that the phenomenon is genderless, and that both males and females play a significant role within it. Their powers come from their everyday interaction with their own spiritual selves and the phenomenon, and it is their responsibility to look after their individual cosmos; to allow themselves to become that vessel as the soma internalises the evil eye in order to metabolise it.

Attitudes towards the evil eye have now been explored from the perspectives of laypeople and the clergy. However, the demographics in Corfu highlighted another important social group which adopts different attitudes and which requires further exploration. Therefore, the next section engages with Orthodox folk healers and their views towards the evil eye.

CHRISTIAN ORTHODOX FOLK HEALERS

In line with Greek tradition, folk healers have developed their rituals not only from one generation to the next, but also through their interaction with the Church: 'I believe that the more I read the prayers and go to church, the more powerful and protected I become when I am about to cast out the evil eye from someone', Maria stated. However, there were some folk healers who expressed a desire for the Church to be more open and accepting of their practices, since they are based on prayers that have been passed down to them from previous generations. In fact, Katerina mentioned that:

> There are times that I would want to discuss evil eye rituals with my parish priest, but I am scared, as I know that he thinks all these are heretical and only a priest can cast the evil eye out. The strange thing is that I call upon God and Jesus to help me with the evil eye, but I cannot discuss my ritual in God's house the church.

Folk healer informants unanimously agreed that their power is positively associated with their years of practice and their knowledge of Christian Orthodox prayers, which allow them to be strong when confronted with the evil eye and its symptomatology. However, despite their educational and social status, there was only one informant from the group of folk healers who expressed some awareness of psychiatric disorders. Interestingly, the folk healers related how they started to develop a certain awareness of the evil eye's somatic and psychological symptomatology from the sufferers. The sufferers felt comfortable revealing these symptoms to them rather than to mental health professionals, due to a fear of being misunderstood and judged by the latter group.

The older folk healers expressed specific interest in the psychical representation of the evil eye. They disclosed that when they are dealing with such possession, it requires them to draw on their own internal faith and relationship with God in order to protect themselves from being exposed to their own vulnerabilities. In addition, when referring to the evil eye, they did not make any association with evil or any demonic powers; in fact, they argued that the evil eye is generated, and in fact born, in interaction between two individuals. Furthermore, it was concluded by the folk healers that the psychosomatic symptoms – such as dysphoria, low energy and motivation, and at times paralysis, but also anorexia, sexual dysfunction, obsession, depressive symptoms, anxiety and extreme fear – are anchored in the evil eye. Some folk healers stated that on rare occasions, sufferers experienced uncontrolled bodily reactions, and at times, 'something like seizures'. Finally, there was no distinct association between evil eye symptomatology and psychiatric disorder classification.

According to the folk healers, they approach the phenomenon of the evil eye separately from any psychiatric disorder, and treat it as a completely spiritual disturbance that requires addressing through faith. They also said that the most commonly anticipated treatment and rituals of healing are found in Christian Orthodox prayers and empowerment of the faith. In other words, the evil eye requires specific rituals, in agreement with the cultural hermeneutics which are rooted in the Christian Orthodox tradition and faith. Finally, the folk healers did not support the use of second-generation psychotropic drugs, stating that:

> The drugs create a blockage from which sufferers cannot overcome the psychical suffering. It imprisons and disables them from overcoming the suffering, as what they face is not neurological but spiritual. The more I talk with other healers, the more I start believing that medication might not be the only way of healing. We need to consider what is spiritual and what is physical healing. How can a medication heal spiritual suffering? To be honest I do not know, but I doubt that it can. It is not a disorder, I do not understand why we need to put it in that category, it feels disrespectful to the sufferer. I also believe that clinicians, especially in Corfu, fail to listen to their clients, and because they know that they cannot do anything for the sufferers' spiritual pain, they provide them with the easy treatment, which is medication.

But if medication is not the appropriate form of alleviating the sufferers' pain, then what might the correct healing process be? What follows is an account of the folk healers' views on healing rituals as related to the evil eye.

HEALING RITUALS

In an attempt to understand the healing rituals followed by folk tradition, I initially fell into the trap of interpreting the evil eye from a functional and structural paradigm, failing to identify its symbolic components and its significance to the restoration of one's happiness. Kluckhohn (1970), echoing Foster (1965), argues that phenomena such as the evil eye are easily misinterpreted due to their complexity. The ethnographers interested in the phenomenon and its structure therefore started to develop a normative egalitarian approach, and failed to comprehend the deeper meanings that the evil eye holds for the individual. Within that egalitarianism, and in order to avoid falling into the same pattern, Roussou (2005) and Galt (1982) describe the evil eye as the individual fear of absence and false superiority that threatens the spiritual health of the collective life. I therefore took a step back from the data and tried to understand it in accordance with the real significance that the evil eye holds for the folk healers, and in fact for people in general. In this section, then, I have drawn on ethnographic examples of the healing rituals that are associated with the ecology in which the evil eye is manifested. To be more precise, I have emphasised the ways in which folk healers in the region of Corfu heal and restore what links a person's body with the mediating object that the evil eye targets, in order to separate the soma from the perceived material object which defines one's selfhood. Therefore, the section starts with a case study inspired by observations in the field, and concludes with a discussion about the evil eye and soma as seen by folk healers.

CASE STUDY

During a Sunday service, George complained to Maria that he was tired and was experiencing constant headaches. Maria was 59 years old, a mother of three and a widow. At that time she did not say anything to him, but she was paying attention to what he was saying about his tiredness and headaches, from which he had suffered for a couple of days. The following Sunday, while they were both attending the Sunday liturgy, George was not behaving as usual. Maria was watching him, and suddenly she exclaimed, 'Είσαι ματιασμένος' ('You are *matiasmenos* [evil eye]'). She then invited him to come to her house a couple of hours later to discuss matters, and I was invited to observe this meeting. George visited Maria in the afternoon, and by the time he entered the house, Maria was already in the kitchen. She was making some noises, and when George was settled in the living room, Maria appeared from the kitchen armed with a bowl of water and a small glass of olive oil. Then she asked George to focus on the cross on the wall, and she started the ritual by making the sign of the cross three times above the bowl of water. At the same time, she was muttering a prayer that no one could hear. At that point, she dipped her index finger into the glass of olive oil and dropped three drops into the bowl of water. The interesting thing was that the oil drops, instead of merging into one pool of oil floating on the water, remained as individual drops, and then dissolved in the water. According to Maria, this was strong evidence that George was suffering from a very powerful manifestation of the evil eye. Maria then continued to mutter some more prayers, and asked George to give her something belonging to him. She continued to drop three drops of olive oil at a time into the water until they stopped dissolving. After a couple of hours, George was not feeling any tiredness or headaches.

Maria later told me that she had learned her rituals from her grandmother. Her grandmother believed that the prayers could not be shared orally, but rather should be passed to the next generation in writing, and only on Holy Saturday. Her grandmother, therefore, had passed the prayers to her on a Holy Saturday when Maria was 21 years old. Maria also told me that she learned the ritual with the oil because it is one of the most powerful rituals besides the priests' prayers. The olive oil and its consistency, according to her and her grandmother, represent Jesus' blood. When the oil dissolves in the water it means that the evil eye is very powerful, and that the sufferer is losing faith. The ritual allows the sufferer to experience Jesus' presence and see themselves within that interaction.

Maria's case is one of many that were observed in the field. Many observations of the evil eye and its rituals were presented in the literature review (Dionisopoulos-Mass 1976; Herzfeld 1986; Roussou 2011a; Veikou 1998; Rouvelas 1993). The folk healers in Corfu revealed many more rituals concerned with the evil eye. At times contradictory, they were however mostly shaped by the influences they had received – whether from the Venetian or British Empires, from previous generations or from their religious and family belief systems. Within the observations, however, there were significant overlaps, and these were always related to the importance of the self in the processes and its relationship with Jesus' image. It was also notable that all the folk healers referred to the evil eye as *kako mati* (bad eye) instead of 'the evil eye'. In fact, there was no reference to evil in their narratives. Their approach contradicts what has been heretofore established, as the evil eye in other parts of Greece is associated with the Devil (*kako mati*) (Dionisopoulos-Mass 1976; Roussou 2011b; Veikou 1998).

A few of the folk healers suggested that the evil eye and its rituals should be seen as part of the Christian spiritual world. Notwithstanding, the majority suggested that the phenomenon is an 'internal crisis from which the weak souls cannot escape'. Further elaboration led them to the statement that the evil eye might initially appear as negative energy transmitted from one person to another, but that it 'belongs to the collective'; the phenomenon is some kind of a mirror in which we see a part of the self that we are scared of witnessing. The symptoms appear as part of our avoidance strategy in facing and dealing with what might emerge' as the majority of the folk healers stated.

Reflecting upon the different, nuanced understandings of the evil eye in the field, one thing is undeniably certain: that it arises from within and upholds existential truths. Despite traditional theories that interpret the evil eye as a dangerous attack upon things that have enviable or admirable qualities, it is something more than that. 'It might be manifested through envy, but it is the envy that fills the internal gap that we feel when we are seen', a folk healer in her late forties stated. According to the folk healers, what makes an individual more susceptible to the evil eye is their unconscious experience of their own liminality.

The folk healers have developed a diagnostic understanding of the evil eye based on its manifestations. They unanimously stated that, on one level, the evil eye can be detected in headaches, appetite loss, loss of sex drive, fatigue, weeping or even constant yawning. They also said that the evil eye manifests differently in infants, who exhibit unsettling behaviour through crying, fussiness and unfocused pain. In rare circumstances, they talked about death. In addition, it was mentioned that things can break into pieces or get out of order.

When someone was believed to have the evil eye, folk healers were called in order to perform the ritual of *xematiasma* (ξεμάτιασμα: un-eyeing the conditions). The majority of folk healers were women, though there were also some men who were well respected in the community. In fact, it was suggested that the rituals should be passed from generation to generation, as in the case of Maria, from females to males and vice versa. In his work on the evil eye and possession in Africa, Hardie (1981) argues that folk healings are more powerful when they are performed by one gender on another, and by an older generation on a younger one. In addition, the instructions for the ritual should not be spoken aloud; they are written on a piece of paper, which is destroyed once they are properly learned.

In Corfu, it is believed that what makes the folk healers effective is their ability to materialise their soma as a mirror to absorb the disturbed image of the sufferer and neutralise it. It has also been argued that the physical body of the folk healer absorbs the negative energy in order to comprehend it. It is said that experienced healers can identify the nature of the evil eye and discern the way in which it might have been cast. One of the most commonly used healing rituals is the one Maria adopted. As reported by many healers, the water used in the ritual should be observed in silence. This αμίλητο νερό (unspoken water) is an important element for ensuring the ritual's success, due to the fact that silence envelops the purifying ability of the water. The oil used in the ritual is not just any olive oil kept by the family; rather, it needs to come from the oil lamp from the iconostasis. The ritual always starts with the healer offering the Orthodox blessing, praying silently over the objects to be used for the ritual, while making the sign of the cross three times as a powerful shield over themselves and the sufferer. The Orthodox blessing is repeated three times: 'In the name of the Father and the Son and the Holy Spirit, this ritual is for [the name of the sufferer]'. When the healer starts yawning, this is a clear indication that the sufferer has been cast with the evil eye. Finally, some folk healers advise the sufferers to sit in a quiet area with a relaxed posture to wait for the blessing to act upon them.

Following the first stage of the ritual, the drops are placed. The folk healer – in the case described above, Maria – drops three drops of olive oil into the water. As the drops touch the water's surface, the folk healer waits to observe one of two reactions: the first is that the oil creates a separate layer from the water, or that the drops merge together, as one might expect, since oil is hydrophobic. The other reaction is that the oil disperses and dissolves in the water. According to the informants, if the first of these happens, then there is no case of the evil eye. However, if confronted with the latter, then the evil eye is present, and its power is determined through the dissolving process. If the oil disperses into smaller amounts, then the evil eye is not strong; if it dissolves completely, then the folk healer is dealing with a severe case of evil eye symptomatology. If this persists, even after the folk healer's prayers, then they begin the process of spitting three times while making the sign of the cross on the edges of the bowl, while simultaneously saying Orthodox prayers and marking the sufferer's forehead with the sign of the cross made by the oil. An alternative to that version observed in older healers was to use charcoal instead of oil. Three pieces of charcoal are chosen and dropped in the water; if they dissolve and sink, then the evil eye is present.

During lunch one day, a young healer, Katerina, described to me another way of casting out the evil eye. She stated that one method is to say the Lord's Prayer three times while thinking intensely about the sufferer. At that point, her body becomes a vessel to accommodate the suffering of the other person, and she tries to understand where the suffering comes from and what it means. In this way, Katerina relies on her own body in order to cast out the evil eye. This ritual suggested by Katerina highlighted the importance of bearing the person in mind; it was agreed by other healers that holding someone in one's mind bears healing powers. This was elaborated to show that a significant aspect of the ritual is 'becoming the other person'; 'allowing our body to experience the fear and anxiety of the other person', which creates a space where they (healer and sufferer) meet; and, 'it feels as if we can see the sufferer as a true being and unwrap the layers that society wants him to develop to hide'.

> The rituals expose me to the other person – when I focus on the other person from whom I am trying to cast out the evil eye, I feel as if the person exists in my mind, the moment is like magic, the connection between the two of us is pure, and as if we are washed with something holy, which I think is the healing part of the rituals.

The healers create an intersubjective space through the rituals, where both experience each other in their true form. Many of them mentioned that through that space, it feels as if they are 'reborn'. Such a connection allows them to be in communication through distance. All of those interviewed disclosed that they do not need to be in verbal communication to know what the sufferer might be thinking or feeling, and in fact they can understand this through the manifestation of the evil eye.

I often caught myself asking the healers what they thought were the causes of these psychological disturbances and psychosomatic effects, and what they thought facilitated a healing process. The responses I received were interesting, and they all expressed the view that the cause of the disturbances must stem from the potent elements of the relationship. It seems that the mental representation of the sufferer in the healer's mind is for them fundamental to the ritual's efficacy; empirically, this appears to be the source of evil eye symptomatology. The space where both healer and sufferer meet consists of conscious and unconscious elements from which one's inner life is organised. Before proceeding to further exploration, it is important to try to understand what defines that space. All healers agreed that such a space is where all experiences, feelings and cognition are stored, and that individuals have access to them both consciously and unconsciously. Relational and Intersubjective Systems Theory would support this view, as it brings to forefront the importance of the mutual dynamic between two individuals, even when interacting at a distance (Atwood 2011). Within that dynamic mutuality, the subjective becomes intersubjective within the intra-psychical space. Thus, while the psychosomatic is an isolated product of a static mental representation, since the social configuration of the mind demands the origin, it remains, however, within the intersubjective webs (Atwood 2011; Maduro 2013; Orange 2011; Stolorow et al. 2002). The healers of the evil eye, therefore, suggest that the rituals foster an intersubjective environment where individuals start to encounter a holistic experience of their being; it is more than just a 'mere collection of unrelated symptoms'. There is an internal process from which the mind starts to develop a sense of being. It is only through relationships that the mind can understand its existence, and individuals start to become beings through relationships with others in the intersubjective space (Winnicott 1960). In a way, the healers embodied this, as they shared the sufferer's pain, and then adapted to their needs by providing psychical 'holding' through the rituals and the mind representation of the sufferer.

The healers suggested that charms and architectural thresholds (transitional spaces) play a very significant role in the process of healing and rituals, to the extent that architecture and orientation become imperative elements for the healers to adopt while treating the evil eye. The healers talked about some popular incantations in the Corfiot tradition of evil eye treatment by highlighting the tension between the internal and the external, and the 'in' and the 'out'. For example, the water used in the rituals must be thrown outside the house through the front door or the window. There is a vertical parameter in treating the evil eye, so that the good comes in and the bad goes out. This positioning is in combination with some specific prayers: 'to the deepest of the seas ... far away to the wildest mountains', indicating the power of transferability of the 'eye'. It was commonly accepted that amulets such as horseshoes, phallic symbols and blue beads work as destructors of the evil eye's intention to strike an individual, and it has been pointed out that amulets ingest its inertia. Healers spoke not only about the function of the evil eye within a social context, but also of its symbolic meaning.

Folk healers also related the evil eye to spiritual processes and considered the ritual for casting it out to be spiritual healing: 'Spiritual healing is more or less the ability to summon energy'. The energy summoned by the healer is then transmitted through the rituals to the sufferer in order to fight the evil eye. There was debate as to whether these rituals were most powerful in face-to-face situations or at a distance. However, the healers explained that the divine energy summoned does not work according to physical laws and can be effective even if the sufferer is far away. The healers also suggested that the ecclesiastical prayers and the folk-healing processes with regard to the evil eye share the same symbolic language, symbols and sacred elements. They stated that there is no distinction between the folk healers' rituals and the ecclesiastical rituals. Such commonality stems from the fact that according to Corfiot healers, the evil eye has nothing to do with the Devil's manifestations on earth, or in fact with any evil; it is instead negative energy which stems from internal psychical processes, and these in turn come from an individual's past; hence, no exorcism is needed.

Old and new join forces to fight the evil eye, and the materiality of the phenomenon takes interesting forms through amulets originating from East and West and from different traditions. However, as far as the material culture of the phenomenon is concerned, one of the most crucial revelations I experienced during fieldwork was the realisation that no adopted tradition is combined with the Christian tradition. To be more precise, folk healers used different amulets, such as horseshoes, phallic symbols, crystals, blue beads and blue eyes, or suggested their use to sufferers for protection. However, none of these were combined with sacred icons, crosses, *komposhoini* (rosaries) or other Christian artefacts, and there was a clear distinction between these two different forms of protection. This discovery contrasts with different regions, where a combination of protections is used (Roussou 2011a).

Having explored the importance of the healing process as understood by folk healers, and having considered laypeople and clergymen's views, there is another group of individuals that requires close scrutiny at this stage of the analysis in order to properly examine attitudes towards the evil eye. This group is none other than the mental health professionals of Corfu.

MENTAL HEALTH PROFESSIONALS

Among mental health professionals in Corfu, there appeared to be a common belief that talking about religious issues in the consulting room, and more specifically about '*matiasma*', was not something that fell within such professionals' 'repertoire', Dr Spiros stated:

> The evil eye is for charlatans, not professionals like us. Mr Souvlakis, sometimes I do not understand why professionals are interested in that phenomenon, if we can consider it a phenomenon. I get angry when I come across some people and priests trying to treat symptoms assigned to the evil eye with all sorts of rituals; such an attitude is dangerous. Imagine that there is an individual who is in pain, and these charlatans do nothing to treat them; in fact they try to gain respect through these rituals in order to feel important.

Dr Spiros told me that the phenomenon was not worth exploring and that it contributes negatively to a patient's treatment. Dr Markos, meanwhile, concluded that the majority of mental health professionals do not pay much attention to a patient's religiosity, as it has nothing to do with their treatment:

> After all, we are in Corfu and we are all Christians. There is no need to pay attention to these religious phenomena. These phenomena belong to the religious realm; not in the consulting room. What would be the point of paying attention to them? If we focus on specific religious phenomena we will stray from our profession and our actual role, which is to help people. I never ask my patients their religious beliefs and practices, and when they might bring up the evil eye in the consultation, I usually smile.

Such a view was further supported by other mental health professionals, who suggested that religion is 'nothing but trouble', and can sometimes be detrimental to a person's mental health. I was met with scepticism when I introduced the notion of the evil eye as something that might affect a patient's mental health. 'Nonsense', was the reaction of a mental health nurse, while Dr Spiros opined that 'our job is to deal with serious matters'. Many people told me that the evil eye is nothing more than the priests' manipulative attempts to gain money from patients, without thinking that such an attitude could cause serious issues to individuals.

It appears that many mental health professionals do not believe they have any pastoral responsibilities and do not have the time to assess the spiritual needs of their patients. It was the younger generation that raised the concern that the evil eye might contribute to patients' mental health. However, they mentioned that talking about a person's religion or religious concerns in the consulting room can only bring 'troubles'. Trainee mental health professionals who were almost qualified believed that they were not appropriately trained to deal with spiritual matters. There was a certain fear attached to talking about the evil eye. A psychiatric nurse revealed that she would be very interested to receive training in dealing with and supporting patients who brought spiritual matters to her consultation, saying: 'I do not think I am properly trained to do that, and there is no supervision that would allow me to practise to the best of my abilities; in fact, there is no supervision at all'. This nurse also mentioned that she was a religious person and attended church, but that that was for her own peace of mind. There was a clear distinction in her mind, as there was for most healthcare professionals, as to what was deemed to be her responsibilities.

A question that took me by surprise came from an established psychiatrist with many years of experience in Corfu, who said: 'Mr Souvlakis, I cannot understand all that fuss about the evil eye; if it was an important matter, don't you think that it would be part of the psychiatric curriculum? And I can assure you that it is not'. I found myself wondering about this question, and what he was trying to tell me. One thing that became apparent was that spirituality, or psychotropic manifestations with religious connotations, is not part of the Greek psychiatric curriculum – or if it is, it has not been given much attention. It is not considered the responsibility of mental health professionals, but instead that of priests. Almost all the psychiatrists told me the same thing. There was a certain hostility around the subject of the evil eye, and in my quest to discover the cause of that hostility, it seems like a Pandora's box was opened. The dismissive attitude towards the phenomenon on the part of psychiatrists revealed that there were certain biases against it which were informed by their social and cultural upbringing. It seems that they viewed the evil eye as a controlling attitude towards certain behaviours, and therefore did not feel it had any place in the consulting room. As one stated:

> I do believe in the evil eye, but I do not think that it has anything to do with mental health. As you can see, I do have amulets in my office; somehow I believe that it can bring misfortune. My mother has strong beliefs on the effect of amulets and I think she has transferred her beliefs to me. However, I do not believe that the evil eye has anything to do with mental illness manifestations, and how can it? It is just something that religions invented to keep believers in a state of fear so that they can be easily controlled. I have seen patients that brought their symptoms to the room and assigned them to the evil eye, but I have to admit that mental illness has nothing to do with the evil eye, and is far more complicated. Most of the time I become dismissive of them, as we need to treat the illness rather than negotiating the evil eye.

Many mental health professionals made the point that when a person's mood changes because of positive or negative attitudes towards them, this is not a mental health issue. However, some mental health professionals have come across cases of the evil eye and have found it difficult to admit that their initial reaction was of shock, due to its multifaceted nature. They approached the phenomenon with scepticism because it can take all sorts of forms; this creates confusion, as it cannot be placed in a category and therefore cannot be treated appropriately. A nurse in a forensic department with over ten years of experience said that men adhere to their role and find it difficult to admit to their problems; this could account for the idea that the evil eye might cause some mental health issues to patients, but the mental health professionals' medical arsenal does not equip them to understand these issues. However, the fieldwork revealed that mental health professionals do in fact believe in some kind of connection between the evil eye and an individual's soul and mind. The next section therefore engages with the contradiction between mental health professionals' attitudes to the evil eye and their actual beliefs.

THE EVIL EYE AND MENTAL HEALTH PROFESSIONALS' CONTRADICTION

Nearly all the mental health professionals I spoke to said they found it difficult to respond empathically to patients when they talked about the evil eye in the consulting room. When the issue arises in discussion, the mental health professionals consciously or subconsciously try to navigate the conversation towards what they deem to be more appropriate. These responses correlate strongly with their agenda as mental health professionals, while at the same time allowing less time for patients to discuss issues that might matter to them. Following on from this attitude, slightly more than half of the mental health professionals interviewed revealed that they do not encourage patients to practice their religious beliefs. Dr George told me:

> There is no benefit in telling someone to pray or practise their religious belief ... what good would that do for them? These people really suffer; they do not need prayers to make them feel better. I have a duty of care and I cannot give them false beliefs and hope by directing them to the church. We need to face the problem and talking about the evil eye and their religious practices will bring nothing more than destruction to the treatment.

Thus, none of the professionals deemed it appropriate to refer patients to a priest for spiritual support or guidance; most of them were inclined to pathologise the phenomenon in an attempt to understand it in medical terms. The fact that there was a certain agenda surrounding the phenomenon affected the working relationship with the patients, who were experiencing spiritual suffering. Many clinicians noticed a change in their relationship with patients who talked about the evil eye; they showed less attentiveness to the professionals. The medicalisation of the phenomenon appeared to be the main attitude of clinicians, and this was where they felt comfortable. Under no circumstances did psychiatric staff feel the need to refer patients to clergy. A psychiatrist stated:

> How can a priest help someone with mental health issues? I do not think that I would ever consider referring someone to a priest. A priest can be anyone, and in Corfu by anyone I mean anyone without any qualifications. They have no supervisors or regulatory body, they do whatever they want. How can I trust them to treat a patient, it does not make sense, and there is no way that I will

refer any patient to find comfort through religious practices. It might alleviate their symptoms momentarily, but in the long run it is very dangerous to treat mental health symptoms simply with religious rituals.

Most of the psychologists also revealed that they do not deal with spiritual matters, but rather try to understand the psychopathology that lies behind belief in the evil eye. Almost none of the psychologists would consult a priest to inform their practice with their patients. The psychologists were significantly less prone to belief in the evil eye, considering it a defence or distraction from the real issue. This means that they do not pay attention to their patients' narratives about the evil eye or assess how it might be affecting their everyday life. There was a strong correlation in the psychologists' minds between the evil eye and an early paranoid-schizoid position, in which a person desires to possess their carer in order to gratify their primary omnipotent needs. Some psychologists believe that the evil eye is a socially constructed belief that feeds patients' fear of being different. The evil eye is thus a maladaptive thought which keeps them 'caged by what it means to be socially accepted'. All the psychologists stated that they were Christians but that they did not practice their religion, placing themselves on the spectrum of agnosticism. They did not believe that the evil eye could cause any particular damage to individuals and thought it was more likely a self-fulfilling theory that created the symptoms of their belief. Nevertheless, I noted that all the psychologists had protective amulets in their consulting rooms, and upon exploration, it appeared that they all believed in the negative energy of the evil eye and the misfortune that it can bring to someone. However, there was no place for it in the consulting room, as the rational mind fails to understand it. Their attempts to understand the phenomenon had led them to develop certain agendas around the necessary treatment, which affected their relationship with their patients. It was a shared attitude among clinicians that belief in evil could only worsen a person's mental health symptomatology. A certain contradiction began to become clear regarding the evil eye. All the clinicians stated that they did not believe in the phenomenon, and that it should not be treated as a condition, but rather ignored because it is a self-fulfilling prophecy. At the same time, they did believe that it could affect a patient's mental health. Finally, even though all the clinicians declared themselves to be Christians, most of them did not regard religious matters as significant or as something to be assessed in the consulting room.

There was a certain split that became apparent when clinicians started talking about their patients and their experience of spiritual matters. Dr Marios told me:

We need to be very careful here when talking about the evil eye, and not approach the subject with naivety, thinking that it is a phenomenon that contributes to someone's mental health ... In my experience, when someone is talking about spiritual matters, and in your case about the evil eye, there are alarm bells ringing in my ears that we might have a delusional episode with religious characteristics.

During one of my late-night discussions with professionals, I sat around a dinner table with theologians and clinicians who had come together to discuss the evil eye. What was interesting was that each person was trying to convince the others about the truth of their own view, and at times, it seemed that it was difficult for them to listen to each other. The theologians were trying to convince the mental health professionals that the evil eye is a soul suffering which can affect the afterlife until the second Apocalypse, after which nothing will matter. They portrayed the evil eye as a condition in which the soul suffers due to possession, and which, if not treated appropriately, will affect the soul even after death. On the other hand, the clinicians were adamant that after death there is no soul, and that we only live on in the memories of our loved ones. It appeared that many clinicians shared this view; they had no room for any spiritual 'gibberish'.

'The evil eye has nothing to do with the soul; it is a social construction which allows people to behave in certain ways and constrains their cognitive space to "breathe"', a psychiatric nurse told me. A social construction is a construction that has been manufactured in the intersocial context to control, or rather eliminate, the 'other'. The idea of being different can inflict certain anxieties onto individuals such that they do not feel comfortable in their own skin. Thus, it is not that the soul suffers, but that the belief system is maladapted to a social norm of indifference. 'The psychiatric field has nothing to do with the philosophical idea of soul; we have patients to deal with who need support and not a philosophical discussion; they do not need a philosophical discussion about the soul'. The soul, therefore, has become a philosophical notion that has no place in the psychiatric field. On that basis, the evil eye is not the cause of suffering, but an excuse not to focus on the real issue. In the era of noesis parapsychology, it does not add anything to our understanding of human functioning.

A junior psychiatrist stated his fear of not seeing the whole picture. He said:

Within the omnipotent stance of being superior, we have forgotten the fundamental fact of being human ... I do believe in the evil eye, and it does not matter if it exists or not, but the fact that I created this belief means it can affect my emotional state.

What does it mean to be human, I asked myself. Indeed, the evil eye is a belief that, for some reason, is sustained by humans. The reason must serve a purpose, but many psychiatric professionals do not want to address it, either because it does not fit with their training, or because their social status does not allow them to admit that they cannot understand it; this creates a schism between mind and soul. This schism has caused the dismissal of anything outside the cognitive realm; the evil eye has become a 'philosophical matter'. The junior psychiatrist further stated that the evil eye exists and is closely related to guilt and shame. According his own personal account, he experiences the evil eye as a punishment for being pompous and preoccupied with his own achievements. Therefore, the evil eye has become a constant reminder of redemption; it is a 'slap in the face' to remind him of the importance of the soul's needs. He saw this as a reminder of human flaws, and it was his attempt to understand complex existential situations, often in an imperfect and materialistic way. Even though the effect of the evil eye was negative, its purpose was positive: to bring humans into touch with the long-forgotten soul.

MENTAL HEALTH PROFESSIONALS' ATTITUDES TOWARDS THE EVIL EYE

After a while, it became apparent through the fieldwork that time has had a significant effect on the attitudes of professionals towards the evil eye. I was confronted with ambivalent views about the phenomenon, which made it even more complicated. It was a shared attitude among psychiatric staff that belief in evil can only be detrimental to patients' mental health symptomatology. However, contradictions began to arise. The majority of psychiatric staff stated that they did not believe in the phenomenon, and that it should not be treated as mental illness but rather as a self-fulfilling prophecy that could be ignored. Nonetheless, they also acknowledged that the phenomenon could damage a patient's mental health. I began to wonder whether this ambivalence reflected what laypeople described as the intercultural element of the evil eye. What appeared to be an internal conflict within psychiatric attitudes might be the fundamental need to believe in the evil eye. I was curious as to whether this need was innate or learned. Almost 90 per cent of the data relating to mental health professionals revealed that as young people, they had believed in the evil eye, but later social constraints had led them to follow the views of other medical students, and subsequently, the attitudes of the professionals had 'forced' them to abandon their earlier belief. The evil eye was thus a belief that had never been forgotten, but was no longer accepted.

'When my daughter was seriously ill, I knew that it had to do with the evil eye, as there was nothing physical affecting her', a psychiatric nurse revealed. However, the evil eye had no place in her psychiatric work. The nurse was in her late forties, and even though she believed in the evil eye, she did not acknowledge it in her work, because if she did, she would be putting her patients at risk: 'there is no standardised measurement for the evil eye, so to hypothesise that someone suffers from it can put the patient at risk'. Katia stated that she believed in the evil eye and that her life showed that it exists, but she also mentioned that such a belief appeared to be outdated. In the past, when psychiatrists could not understand certain behaviours, they attributed them to the evil eye. Any 'weird' phenomenon that affected people and could not be explained was thought to be the evil eye. Scientific progress and a better understanding of human behaviour allow less space for the unknown.

George, a junior psychiatrist, argued that the evil eye is 'hocus-pocus' and that it does not belong to the psychiatric world. He could not understand his mother and the fact that she believed in the power of the evil eye. George was in his early thirties, and had never been actively religious, believing that religion has nothing to offer to a patient's well-being. However, he grew up in a Christian family, with both his parents practising their religion. He remembers his mother always being afraid of the evil eye and acting accordingly to protect herself from it. As a child and teenager, George was angry at his mother's attitude, and with the priest who reinforced such fear. Interestingly enough, George had some amulets for protection in his consulting room, and was wearing an amulet from the Venetian era. On reflection, he indirectly stated that he still believes in bad luck, but not in the evil eye. He believes in the power of mind, where energies can be emitted and cause damage to people. However, he does not believe that such energies have power over a person's mental state. It was commonly agreed among psychiatric staff that the evil eye is a phenomenon that allows parents to control their children, but that its power fades once the children become adults.

This realisation puzzled me during the fieldwork, as the contradiction between what was said and what was actually observed was rather significant. The majority of the psychiatric professionals disclosed that they had a strong belief in the evil eye as children and young adults, but that the more they engaged with their field, and the more they read, the more they came to understand that the evil eye was nothing but a social construction to control people. As children, however, they remembered being scared of the evil eye and its effect on their life. They all shared similar experiences of feeling sick, of losing their motivation and feeling disorientated. Some admitted that they saw shadows that did not exist. However, once they started reading and had qualified from medical school, they realised that all these experiences had been a placebo effect: 'I used to experience what I was expecting to experience. I started to have these symptoms because that was normal when mum said I had the evil eye'. As time passed, and as they gained a different social status, such beliefs did not fit with their new outlook. Dr Christos told me:

> I am a psychiatrist and I am trying to make people well and understand their conditions, not create a fear of their condition. What is the evil eye, after all, if not a fear that comes from the past, as people could not understand certain phenomena, but we do now?

The divide between the old times and the new era was supported by the psychiatric staff. What had been considered religious belief had now become noetic science; the power of God and evil, as described by older generations, had become energy of the mind.

Young mental health professionals, however, disclosed that they were open to spiritual matters. Maria, a mental health professional in her early thirties, stated:

> I really don't mind if my patients talk about God with me. Most of the time, though, I do not know what to do with this information, as I have not been trained to deal with such matters; but it seems that the patients want to talk about them and when they do they feel better.

Maria's view is supported by many young professionals, who said that even though they do not know how to deal with spiritual matters, especially the evil eye, they do find it interesting when patients bring such issues into the consulting room. It was commonly accepted that professionals do not believe in possession by the evil eye; however, they do accept that the phenomenon creates an illusory belief of possession, which is manifested through varying symptomatology. However, they maintained that since the evil eye is a construct of the human mind based on religious beliefs, the more patients talk about it, the more it loses its effect on them.

There was a counterargument from some mental health professionals in the same age group who do practise their religion. These professionals stated that the evil eye is not an illusory construct of the human mind, but something real. However, they argued that it would be inappropriate for them to suggest this or to perform the rituals to exorcise the evil eye. Even though they believed in the existence of the phenomenon and its various manifestations, they also believed that it would not be professional to engage in discussion about it. They would only acknowledge it if the patient were to bring it up; then they would talk about it. There is positive neutrality, as one of the mental health professionals put it; they do not initiate discussion, but they allow patients to talk about it should they wish. There is therefore resistance to addressing the evil eye in psychiatric or mental health settings; these professionals provide a platform for patients to talk about the evil eye, but believe that there should not be any regulations about the different ways to approach the phenomenon in the consulting room, as it is something personal and stems from a person's beliefs. George stated:

> You cannot teach someone attitudes, and how to approach spirituality ... it is impossible, and if the evil eye were to be included in the curriculum, then it would become something to be diagnosed, and we would lose the immediacy to listen to the patients and their spiritual needs.

Specific scepticism was found in the field of psychotherapy. There is a certain resistance from psychotherapists to talk about or even acknowledge the evil eye, or in fact any religious issues. A psychotherapist in his early forties stated that the evil eye is just a systemic construction stemming from the internal conflict of good and bad. He went further, stating that it is a psychical conflict originating in the carer's preoccupation during the children's developmental period (early years of their lives) and the failure of the carer to meet the children's needs. Such failure creates a split, and individuals feel a need to project the evil out, due to a fear that it might absorb and kill any internal goodness. However, there was a belief among some psychotherapists that religious issues, and especially the evil eye, do have a place in the consulting room, especially if they are important for the patient. The demographics were inconsistent, however, and no particular conclusion could be drawn with regard to whether younger or older therapists believed in the power of the evil eye. However, it was commonly accepted that the evil eye can have a negative effect on an individual's mental health. The therapists also maintained that they have no relationship with religious leaders, as the latter are not trained and can cause damage if patients are referred to them.

The majority of psychiatric nurses argued that it is important for their relationships with patients, and for recovery and treatment, to discuss religious matters if patients wish to. However, they said that religious matters, and especially views on the evil eye, vary from individual to individual. Tonia suggested that according to her experience, spiritual needs may differ from person to person, and having concrete guidelines on how to approach spiritual matters might help; however, in reality, this would only partially meet the individual's needs. Her colleagues also pointed out that mental health professionals should approach the phenomenon of the evil eye with an open mind, and should allow patients to tell their stories and be heard. They also argued that dialogue between themselves and religious leaders, which at the moment does not happen, should be developed and encouraged. Kostas, a young psychiatric nurse, stated that the evil eye not only causes mental health issues, but is also an esoteric spiritual phenomenon that needs to be treated with care. He went on to say that his training did not cover anything on the matter, and that he finds it difficult to deal with the phenomenon and support his patients; however, the local folk healers have helped him to learn a lot about the phenomenon and patients' needs. Kostas' account of the evil eye highlights the importance of integrating mental health and religious and spiritual knowledge in an attempt to treat people holistically as human beings. Meanwhile, Tonia stated that people 'are not just wired with neurons, and we are not just neurobiological beings; we are spiritual beings as well, and if we fail to understand that, then we fail as professionals'.

For these reasons, I concluded that mental health training should address spiritual and religious matters, and a dialogue with spiritual leaders should be established. I would also argue that mental health professionals should receive training about religious issues with specific content, instead of a generalised training. Furthermore, the different attitudes towards the evil eye among mental health professionals indicate that they would benefit from becoming more aware of the role of religious leaders, and indeed of the role of spirituality and religiosity in the consulting room. This would also benefit their treatment of those who believe in the evil eye, as they would develop better awareness of the different spiritual needs that patients might have when it comes to this phenomenon. Being aware of one another's views would facilitate innovative interdisciplinary treatment which would be more attentive to the patient's needs and would approach them as a biological and spiritual being.

CONCLUSION

In this chapter I examined the role of the Orthodox Church in Greek society as a fundamental part of the Greek Orthodox life and identity. The chapter also explored the attitudes of different social groups towards the evil eye, as identified from the data. Laypeople approached the phenomenon as a demonic energy which interferes with their spirituality. The evil eye therefore becomes a means by which the Devil weakens believers, allowing demons to easily access and possess their bodies through the evil eye. The data also revealed the diversity of attitudes towards the evil eye based on age differences. Younger generations agree that the evil eye is the Devil's means to weaken someone's spirit, but believe that if they keep their spirit and body fit, the evil eye has no power over them. There was certainly an ambiguous attitude towards the evil eye among the laypeople. It was concluded, therefore, that the evil eye is indeed possession, but a possession originating from humans rather than demons. The evil eye's maleficent energy towards another person appears to be interpreted by some as fear of closeness, or in fact a fear of being witnessed or seen; seeing or witnessing could take an actual form, or could be the capacity of one to keep another in mind so as so to be seen metaphorically.

The data prompted discussion of whether the evil eye is a natural or supernatural phenomenon, but was not conclusive. It reflected the informants' understanding of the phenomenon as both natural and supernatural. In a way, the informants saw the phenomenon in a more holistic manner and as an integrated part of their physical and spiritual being. Interestingly, the data revealed that the evil eye is not about suffering, or making someone suffer because they possess something that we want for ourselves, as the current literature would argue. Rather, the evil eye is a scream for help, as some of the informants revealed. It is a primal phenomenon that does not belong in the linguistic realm; therefore, the only way that its exigencies can be communicated is through experience. The data thus indicated that the evil eye is the caster's scream for help, achieved through making others experience their spiritual suffering. In this way, this chapter engaged with the idea that the evil eye is profoundly relational and stems from early attachment with the primary carer.

Despite the various beliefs and approaches to the evil eye in Corfu, the majority of the Greek Orthodox priests interviewed believed that the phenomenon is not a type of witchcraft, but rather something manifested in the human psyche that needs to be treated seriously. They argued that the evil eye is one of the living proofs that God exists, as it exposes our human deficit. Interestingly, though, the priests argued that evil is not inaugurated through the evil eye. The evil eye is part of original sin; the priests suggested that we, humans, felt impotent against God's power, and that therefore the evil eye is a reminder – through mental anguish – of God's power. There were some insinuations from some older priests that the evil eye is sin, stemming from our disobedience to the Greater Power.

For many priests, the evil eye appears to be a passive process by which demons find a way, through the eye, to possess and control us. The data from the clergymen also confirmed that despite the nature of the evil eye and its demonic associations, a relational structure is necessary in order for the phenomenon to be nurtured. The evil eye is thus a relational phenomenon. It was concluded that the evil eye is indeed a negative energy, but that in order to survive, it needs an agent: a human being. Interestingly, the fieldwork revealed that the evil eye is not about inflicting misfortune on another, but in fact causes damage – spiritual damage – to its caster. The rationale for this new idea about the evil eye comes from the fact that demons are attracted to hate and therefore possess those who are prone to hate: the casters of evil eye and not the sufferers. In clergy circles, it was believed by many that the evil eye can sometimes be seen as God's wrath, or punishment for our disobedience. It was thus easier for the clergymen to accept the evil eye as God's action, rather than the Devil's hate.

Finally, the chapter engaged with the importance of the phenomenon as related to the fear of absence. Priests argued that the evil eye is strongly associated with the fear of loss, or an existential anxiety of not existing as human beings. The data brings to the forefront, and adds to the current analysis, the fact that envy is not the primary feeling that fuels the evil eye, but is instead a shadow feeling that overlays the fundamental fear of the existential absence.

On the other hand, folk healers in Corfu expressed their discomfort with clergymen, due to the fact that their practice of casting out the evil eye has not been accepted by the clergy, even though it is strongly influenced by the Greek Christian tradition and faith. In addition, it was agreed among folk healers that the manifestations of the evil eye are nothing more than an expression of existential anxiety. At the same time, the folk healers differentiated themselves from practitioners of the psychiatric treatment of the evil eye, which equates the phenomenon with spiritual disturbances that can only be addressed through one's faith. Following this distinction within the psychiatric understanding of the evil eye, the mental health professionals interviewed – and especially the older generation – could not see the phenomenon as anything other than a construct used by 'charlatans' to manipulate individuals and make them dependent on their 'treatment' practices. However, it is important to note that the younger generation of mental health professionals do believe in the evil eye, and they feel comfortable enough to incorporate faith and rituals in their practice.

The following chapter engages with the phenomenon of the evil eye as it is expressed in the sociocultural reality of Corfu, but also as it is observed among the whole population. What follows, therefore, is a description of the common characteristics of the evil eye and its functionality among all the informants, regardless of their sociocultural groups.

Chapter 3

Fieldwork Observations
Symptomatology of the Evil Eye and Sociocultural Views

INTRODUCTION

Considering the archetypal dimension of evil eye possession, one might argue that fear and shame fuel and intensify the power of this phenomenon. The evil eye appears to be by far one of the most universal signs of fear, and it reflects the relationship between eye, mind and self. One might maintain that behind the evil eye hides an evil person; but is this always the case? In the minds of many, the evil eye has become a symbolic configuration that has the power to reflect the caster's malignity and project it, inflicting pain on the unfortunate recipient of its gaze. Gifford (1960), in a pioneering study, argues that the evil eye and maleficent gaze has been imprinted in humanity's collective unconscious for the last five hundred years.

Following Gifford's (1960) understanding of gaze, it can be assumed that the evil eye entails enormous maleficent energy, which human beings can emit to cause agony and suffering to others. Considering the spiritual and physical suffering that the phenomenon can cause, it is therefore closely related to mental health and mental illness; merely as a result of thinking of or looking at someone, excessive emotional states have been observed that can and do influence an individual's spiritual and mental state. Cultural influence in everyday idiom has reinforced a primitive notion defined succinctly as 'a look can kill'. According to informants, this phrase carries the primal idea of being watched, and some informants linked it to original sin. The idea of the evil eye has thus continued to have a metaphorical presence in society as the infinite anxiety and fear to which individuals are exposed; they are visible to the eyes of others and are consequently vulnerable to rejection or even abandonment. Some might argue that the perpetual belief in the evil eye is a feeling as deep as shame or guilt.

In this chapter, I look particularly at the sociocultural and linguistic aspects of the evil eye as derived from the fieldwork, in an attempt to deepen the understanding of the phenomenon within the context of mental illness. This includes exploring fear, anxiety, vulnerability and hostile powers in a person's internal and external environments, and therefore unravels the forms of distress caused by the fear of being tangled in another's mental content and gaze. The chapter also attempts to connect these insights with the construction of the self through the phenomenon of gaze. Interaction with the sociocultural and linguistic understandings of the phenomenon instigates the philosophical question of the construction of a self-agency, which is something that the chapter will also address. However, the importance of understanding how the evil eye is perceived within cultural and mental illness frameworks has emerged; this is the focus of the following section.

MENTAL ILLNESS AND THE CULTURAL FRAMEWORK IN CORFU AS RELATED TO THE EVIL EYE

Social distress and psychological discomfort among sufferers of the evil eye in Christian Orthodox regions, and most particularly in Corfu, appears in various cognitive, physical, psychosocial and existential ways. Sufferers of the evil eye have exhibited emotions related to grief, fear, despair, anxiety and depression; on a more cognitive level they have exhibited hopelessness, worry and loss of control among other symptoms. It was widely reported in the fieldwork that emotional and cognitive symptoms of the evil eye are always accompanied by somatic symptoms, such as fatigue, loss of drive and insomnia – all of which are medically unexplained. Furthermore, social withdrawal and interrelational difficulties have also been reported. Most of these symptoms have been strongly linked to a sudden violation of the psychical borders that the evil eye displaces.

Many symptoms may occur when a person suffers from the evil eye, as will be explained in more detail later. These symptoms occur to people who do not necessarily suffer from mental illness, but who feel distressed when the evil eye has been cast on them and feel possessed by it. Informants argued that when these individuals are in distress, their everyday lives are significantly affected. These different levels of distress are strongly related to the evil eye. It is also important to mention that spiritual or psychical conflicts can affect Christians' experiences of mental illness. Maria stated:

I feel like I am crazy when I am possessed with the evil eye. I feel as if I lose control of my own mind; my body does not answer to medication and I am losing it. During that time, only St Spyridon can save me. It feels like a reminder to be in touch with my faith and practice as I often get possessed when I do not practice.

The majority of Corfu's population believe that mental illness has its origin in discrepancies attached to supernatural or religious beliefs. It is pertinent to mention that during fieldwork, individuals expressed numerous different practices of their religious experiences, through prayers, rituals and church attendance, in order to heal mental issues. As the phenomenon of the evil eye is strongly linked to an individual's faith, it can be concluded that the evil eye and its perception and power are strongly related to people's life experiences and religious practices. It was noted in the field that cultural idioms of distress are associated with commonly accepted means of expressing distress within the community, and that they may be adopted to express various conditions. The evil eye has a specific place in the community's cultural idioms for expressing distress. Explanatory models can attempt to understand the evil eye, as it seems to be an idiom that Corfiots use to express and make sense of non-medically explained illnesses. It is also used to determine potential treatment (Fiske 2004). A greater understanding of the evil eye will provide a more comprehensive appreciation of the models and idioms that individuals use to communicate distress. As well as being in the interests of the study, this understanding can help individuals to develop resilience to the effects of this distressing phenomenon.

The majority of the Greek Orthodox residents of Corfu looked for supernatural causes of misfortune and mental illness in their attempts to explain the distress that they experienced through evil eye possession. It appears that such an attitude has been rooted in the priests' preaching about evil and hell, but it is also a trans-generational understanding of the phenomenon. Despite the sociocultural and educational background of Christians in Corfu, they referred to the existence of the evil eye in order to contextualise it within the realms of what they called 'madness'. Belief in various manifestations of the evil eye is common across the world, but from the fieldwork observations, it can be seen as an attribute of faith. However, a lack of understanding of the idiosyncratic cultural attitudes (the unique cultural characteristics as they stem from the informants) towards the evil eye might put mental health professionals in danger of falling into the trap of discrimination against patients who believe in it and feel that they have been possessed by it. According to the informants, mental health professionals therefore need to be culturally competent and able to explore spiritual elements in their interaction with clients. In other words, when the sufferer adopts or seeks understanding of their symptoms in supernatural terms, without having any particular mental health condition, and in cases where a supernatural explanation coexists with mental health symptoms, such as hallucinations or delusions, certain consideration is required on the part of the mental health professional to discern the sufferer's symptoms. An understanding of the local idioms assists mental health professionals in making these distinctions clearly and more accurately.

Within the specific region of Corfu, terms such as 'mental illness' or 'psychological well-being' are not fully understood by individuals. People are more likely to understand mental illness as 'madness' or 'craziness'. Mental illness thus has strong negative connotations. 'This person is crazy; depression and so on does not exist; he is just crazy', one 42-year-old informant stated. However, according to the Christian Orthodox tradition, suffering does not always imply medical intervention, as it is embedded in the Christian life. It was believed by the informants that spiritual suffering is a prerequisite for the afterlife. Emotional distress (spiritual suffering) therefore takes a rather more controversial linguistic form than the evil eye does among Christians in Corfu. Sufferers tended to use general words to express their psychological well-being, and avoid any direct mention of words such as 'mental', 'well-being', 'mental illness' or even 'psychologist' and 'psychiatrist'. It was also noted that sufferers of the evil eye firstly presented general practitioners with their physical symptoms and not with their psychological or spiritual suffering. A societal split was observed regarding the treatment of the evil eye: while visiting their general practitioners for their physical symptoms, the informants also visited folk or spiritual healers for their spiritual suffering. This societal split reflects what was later observed as a split between body and soul. This was opposed to the interconnection of body and soul as promoted by the explanatory models of illness. The understanding of the idioms attached to the evil eye facilitates a better understanding of Christian Orthodox attitudes towards mental illness; local expressions have been developed to express distress, and these are explored in the following pages.

EVIL EYE IDIOMS AND TYPES OF ILLNESS

Eastern Orthodox Christians in the Ionian Islands approach the phenomenon of illness from various angles, providing a range of accounts for illness or mental illness, and these accounts incorporate sociocultural, transhistorical, political and religious beliefs. Engaging with the idiomatic understanding of the evil eye gives a deeper understanding of mental health as a phenomenon attached to the culture in which the symptoms develop. The evil eye thus cannot be seen apart from the culture in which it develops, and it cannot be generalised as a universal phenomenon. The fieldwork accordingly revealed that the attitudes and behaviours of sufferers of the evil eye towards mental illness are strongly correlated with the geographical area in which they live; surprisingly, though, their attitudes towards the phenomenon were not influenced by their social status and education. Interestingly, however, the same sufferers appeared to hold a hybrid understanding of mental illness which enabled them to seek support from different sources at the same time.

Mental illness, however, is more likely to be attributed to divine or supernatural forces. Thus, underperformance (physical or mental) is interpreted as an after-effect of the evil eye, and more specifically of its envy aspect. In these cases, there was an intrinsic motivation to externalise the suffering in an attempt to find meaning for it. In other words, the sufferers tended to look for external causes for their suffering, rather than looking introspectively to identify their internal reactions and attitudes to it. Externalising suffering and trying to find other causes for specific symptoms can help aid recovery according to Desrosiers and Fleurose (2002). However, on occasions when mental illness is seen as the evil eye from God – incurred due to not being a good Christian – blaming other sources for the suffering does not help with recovery. This was the view of Katerina, a mental health nurse in her thirties. In these circumstances, sufferers pay more attention to their own spiritual engagement with the Christian faith in order to find strength to deal with the suffering. It is also believed that the evil eye is the cause of severe mental illness because it brings powerful negative forces upon a person, and these forces are beyond human control. Georgia, in her late thirties, works for one of the private surgeries in Corfu. She is the mother of two boys and has always been a Christian; she goes to church as often as she can, and she described her faith as 'a significant element in [my] life and important to the development of [my] ethics and morals'. I met Georgia in church while I was working in the field. Initially, she approached me because she wanted some clarification about mental health with regard to one of her best friends, and she was seeking understanding of some symptoms that the doctor could not explain. It was after a couple of meetings in the church that Georgia opened up and told me that she was suffering from 'something that I cannot explain'. She also told me that she was scared, because she felt that if she were to tell anyone she thought she was possessed, the doctor would lock her in an asylum. She was also scared because her doctor could not do anything about her symptoms, and she did not know how to support herself. Georgia stated that her grandmother had taught her that there were negative powers in this world that she needed to be wary of. These powers can affect her if she is not close to God, because demons would try to possess her soul. Georgia told me:

> My grandmother told me that I should always be close to God because negative forces will be cast upon me through demons while they manipulate their servants to gain more souls. I think that I am experiencing these negative forces; I cannot control myself; I feel as if my soul has been raped and it is painful, but I do not know what to do; I feel exposed and I cannot hide from these negative forces; no one can help me, and I was praying to God for a sign, a hope that I have not lost it.

She continued to describe how she felt embarrassed to share all these experiences with others, as they would not understand her. She felt ashamed and scared that she might be rejected: 'I do not want my kids to have a crazy mother; everyone will mock them because of that. I am also scared that I will lose my husband, who might not want to be married to a crazy woman'. In this case, shame appears to be present and experienced by the family of the sufferer as well as the sufferer themselves. Shame is attached to the evil eye, or 'madness', as Georgia described it. Certain idioms, then, have been attached to the evil eye in Corfu, and these idioms also exhibit certain symptoms when it comes to the phenomenon. The evil eye appears to be embedded in the Corfiots' idiomatic reality, from which they create meaning, but which also affects behaviours. There is a fear associated with the evil eye, linked with demonic manifestation through individuals' bodies, and this affects their understanding of mental health and mental illnesses.

THE EVIL EYE AND MENTAL ILLNESS SYMPTOMATOLOGY

In the Ionian Islands, and specifically in Corfu, mental health professionals identify particular mental illness symptomatology linked to the evil eye. According to their estimates, about 56 per cent of the population develop depressive and anxiety symptoms; 32 per cent develop symptomatology related to loss and trauma; a small percentage express psychotic symptomatology; and the rest receive some sort of folk diagnosis.

DEPRESSIVE SYMPTOMS AND EVIL EYE

A dichotomy was observed with regard to depressive symptoms. Westernised mental health professionals suggested depression and anxiety in cases where professionals with a Greek Orthodox background would assign the same symptoms to the evil eye. Westernised psychiatry understands depressive symptomatology through its nonspecific bodily manifestations (Ryder and Chentsova-Dutton 2012). However, Greek Orthodox mental health professionals add to depressive symptomatology the somatic elements as seen through the evil eye. Those who exhibit depressive symptoms as a result of the evil eye experience internal emptiness, distractibility, insomnia, erectile difficulties, loss of appetite and loss of energy. Among the Greek Orthodox Christians living in Corfu, it was believed that depression is not a mental illness but rather a consequence of the evil eye. On that level, the evil eye tends to trigger excessive worry in sufferers, who become obsessively preoccupied with traumatic events and the negative aspects of their everyday lives. However, most mental health professionals paid no attention to an individual's belief in the evil eye, and treated everyone with medication. In response, people turned to folk healers, from whom they received understanding and support. It seems that depression stemming from the evil eye is related to more existential anxieties, such as internal void, emptiness and meaninglessness. However, before I engage with these existential anxieties, it is important to understand the link between loss and trauma as related to the evil eye.

LOSS AND TRAUMA AS RELATED TO CORFIOTS

The implications of the current financial crisis in Greece and the perpetuation of this state of affairs have exposed Corfiots to enormous trauma. Many people have faced significant cuts to their salaries and pensions; they have lost their jobs, their houses and their dignity. Others have witnessed their families falling apart. This has been compounded by the moral and spiritual violation following the financial crisis, which has led them to find shelter in what has been a traditional refuge throughout the years: their faith and their religion. This in turn led to more attention being paid to the phenomenon of the evil eye, as the more society fell apart and social classes became more distinct, the more people started believing in the evil eye again. These traumatic experiences have had a detrimental effect on the Christian Orthodox understanding of mental illness. George stated:

> it is important to understand that the financial crisis might be an indication that we as human beings stray from our Christian paths. We were so much preoccupied with who we are in society that envy and jealousy overpowered us. We lost connection with God and therefore lost our meaning. The financial

crisis created a lot of unknowns in our everyday life, we do not know what will happen to our jobs, salaries ... the evil eye has become more powerful now that there are distinct social classes, which affects how we create meanings, how we engage with each other, and I really believe that Christianity can give us a new agency from which we can draw meaning. The evil eye is a calling to look again on who we are and how we relate.

It was also noticed that those who had previously been exposed to trauma were more affected than others.

Individuals from low socio-economic backgrounds are more likely to experience symptomatology related to loss and trauma. It appears that those who lost their possessions due to the financial restructuring process started to focus more on negative aspects of life, fearing the future and wanting to destroy those who had more. Their interaction with these negative aspects opened them up to spiritual violation and traumatisation of their internal psyche, and the shame attached to their loss of identity, in combination with the financial constraints of the last ten years, 'allowed demons to use us to play their games', George also mentioned.

In these instances, the evil eye has become an idiom of emotional conflicts and distress, and can be seen through the effects of trauma. The evil eye therefore represents through its symptomatology the shame and humiliation that individuals have had to experience due to the depletion of the conditions and circumstances of their lives. 'I do not care anymore; I want to see pain and I want to see others suffer because they possess more than me', a 43-year-old man stated. The evil eye has become a containment of their pain and an idiom of rage. Through the evil eye, they expressed their anger at losing their social status and identity. Through that experience, some informants started expressing a different element related to the evil eye that they called 'psychotic symptoms'.

THE EVIL EYE AND 'PSYCHOTIC SYMPTOMS'

'Being affected by the evil eye is like being crazy', an informant stated after visiting his mental health professional. Mental health professionals treat patients who know that the evil eye has affected them, and they revealed that the majority of these patients lack the ability to function in everyday life. The evil eye is similar to 'craziness, is like losing their selves, losing their ability to relate with nature and others'. In social contexts, others started to lose their trust in the sufferers, and their judgements and decision-making were no longer considered reliable. The analysis of the fieldwork data indicates that if mental health professionals were to see their patients' understandings of the reality of the evil eye and detach the phenomenon from their own religious beliefs, it would be more likely that psychotic symptomatology would appear. What the sufferers and mental health professionals classed as psychotic symptomatology refers to the idea that if the evil eye remains in the sufferer for a long period of time, then spirits or demons possess them and try to punish them. Maria argues that:

> What I have witnessed and know from personal experience is that when someone suffers from evil eye the capacity to think clearly is lost. It is like someone takes over your ability to think and act, like a third entity operates from within and you are just a spectator to your own life. I had that experience when I was suffering from evil eye and I could not recognise anyone around, I lost all my energy. I was sure that something demonic was acting from within my body. No medical treatment could cure me and the more I was left with the evil eye, the more intense the experience become.

Surprisingly, though, while the results suggested that the evil eye and psychotic symptomatology are strongly related to demonic possession, this is not always perceived in negative terms. Orthodox clergy and sufferers suggested that at times, individuals suffer from the evil eye for the 'greater good', and so have started seeing the phenomenon in a positive light. The sufferers interviewed stated that spiritual healers were more appropriate to address the issue than mental health professionals. The positive aspects of the evil eye can be manifested in specific circumstances, for example when sufferers absorb negative energy in the place of someone else. In these cases, they consciously attract the evil eye in order to protect someone else. On the other hand, negative aspects of the evil eye maintain the sense of a punishment. In both cases, if the religious element is ignored, the evil eye grows stronger and the sufferer starts to have 'visions', either of God telling them to do good deeds or of the Devil punishing them. Symptoms also include social isolation, disorientation and poor social skills. Sufferers experience a condition that makes them unable to recognise themselves, and also develop the belief that someone else is thinking for them. Thus, the self's internal agency is attached to the demon that possesses them through the evil eye. Under these circumstances, the term 'evil eye' encompasses the meaning of all of the above, and therefore the sufferers do not need to explain their symptomatology. Those interviewed felt that when they had tried to describe their symptomatology to mental health professionals, they were dismissed. It appears that informants found it beneficial for the alleviation of the evil eye symptoms to talk about the phenomenon. They also stated that it is important for healers or mental health professionals to respect the context in which the evil eye is manifested. The folk diagnosis is the focus of the following section.

FOLK DIAGNOSIS AND THE EVIL EYE

The evil eye can produce a trance state with different dissociative forms. Faith and belief is the counterbalance to the evil eye, and it is faith that empowers people – mostly women – to become folk healers and treat the affliction. The majority of the men who can heal the evil eye are priests of the Greek Orthodox Church who use a specific ritual. The evil eye takes the form of subordination, in which sufferers lose their own ego and surrender to the evil eye, acting out forbidden desires and feelings. Based on the content assigned to the evil eye, Corfiots have developed certain diagnoses to describe its specific effects on a person's mental health.

One symptom that was described by many informants is the frozen state: when the evil eye penetrates someone's body, they experience momentary paralysis. Further analysis sheds light on this: the paralysis shows that the evil eye causes narcissistic injuries and blurs the person's ego state; the paralysis is the result of the ego's defence, which the evil eye breaks. In this moment, certain psychosomatic symptoms have been witnessed, including high blood pressure at the edges of the motor and sensory cortices (measured during the possession via blood pressure machines), as well as momentary blindness and an increase in pain. If these symptoms are not acknowledged, the evil eye begins to become established in the person's body (σώμα), and it becomes harder for the healer to cast it out, as Maria described previously. In folk diagnosis, emotional distress is expressed through the evil eye. However, the level of emotional distress attached to the evil eye is of an excessive level and is characterised by a sudden loss of consciousness. This loss of consciousness is similar to the frozen state; it is a reaction to the extreme pain suffered when the evil eye penetrates someone's defences. It appears to be a negative societal norm to want to hide the suffering and to not acknowledge mental illness, in order to protect individuals from stigma. Individuals keep secret or deny the existence of a mental illness, due to the shame invoked by the possibility that divine intervention has caused the suffering (Gopaul-McNicol et al. 1998). At this point, a rather controversial understanding of the evil eye starts to emerge from the field. It was clear that envy and jealousy are indeed parts of the evil eye in certain cases, but what links all cases together is something rather different. The picture that I was confronted with led to an understanding of the evil eye through shame. This understanding is discussed in what follows.

SHAME AND THE EVIL EYE

'Shame is a feeling that haunts my soul'; these were the words of Maria, an informant in her mid-forties. She continued that human beings cannot escape from this feeling; we are defined through others' eyes, and we crave to be seen, but when we are, it feels like 'a cold death breeze covering my body, scared of the outcome of that look and ashamed of my inadequacy'. Maria here was describing one of the fundamental elements of the evil eye: shame. This is the concept of being seen through the eyes of another, which brings human beings to face relationality with themselves and others. A fear of being seen emerges from our fear of being abandoned because of our inadequacies. As such, the evil eye becomes a psychical mirror through which another can 'penetrate our defences and see us for exactly what we are', as another informant, in his late twenties, stated. Genesis (2:25) gives an account of the lack of shame between Adam and Eve. Before their eyes were 'opened', 'they were both naked, the man and his wife, and were not ashamed'. Humanity caused its own descent in the world through original sin; original sin brought humanity into its own existence and subjectivity and embodied its own relationality; even though people are in relationships (as with Adam and Eve) they now begin to realise, through the presence of another, their individuality, which at times they are scared of. In the context of this descent, the data from the field suggests that shame has changed its own constitution and become a moral matter. It has become a duty, a social construction that as human beings we need to obey; society has its morality of good and bad. Therefore, through shame, social norms dictate how a person should behave within the civil state (Klonick 2016). George maintains that:

> Sometimes I do believe that the evil eye is like an indicator that we need to follow the rules. What I have observed is the fact that when people do not behave as their social environment might have wanted them to behave, they get sick, sick as if they get the evil eye. I cannot stop making the link that the evil eye has something to do with the morality that we held in the Corfiot community. It is like we feel ashamed, and therefore you get the evil eye from things that we are doing that do not belong to the Corfiot norm.

Based on George's and others' accounts, it can be argued that such a belief is indeed a traditional representation of shame and the way in which shame has commonly been experienced throughout human history, as moral conduct shaping behaviour and ways of thinking. However, this chapter presents a different rendering of shame that has emerged from the fieldwork. In this study, shame was firmly within the scope of the evil eye, as it was suggested that it is not a moral construction, but rather the opposite; it is free from moralistic good-or-bad interpretations. Shame is not associated with civil conduct, and it is certainly not interested in passing criticism, or even focusing on the accepted ideas of the 'ideal'. Instead, shame is strongly associated with the notion of exposure. It has started to be transformed into something far more important than moralistic societal conduct; it has become a living experience of 'being-with', the objectification of the human experience before another human being. My research is starting to build the rather controversial theory that shame is an essential component of the human soul, and hence that it has become an ontological matter regarding the phenomenon of the evil eye.

Shame epitomises the human right to exist in the world: the fieldwork also suggests that this feeling is associated with the notion of self-awareness and awareness of others, in other words, the sense of the 'other' as self and self as 'other'. Genesis (2:25) reads 'when their eyes were opened'. The idea here is that when one is confronted with the reflection of oneself in another's eyes, shame declares its presence, and it is through this that the process of knowing oneself can begin. Shame, then, becomes coexistent with the presence of self and of the other. The revelation of the first moment of being seen through another's eye is like the shame felt by Adam and Eve when they were watched by God's eye. At this point, shame is linked to one's basic existence, rather than to moralistic applications. So far, my research has also advanced the idea that shame becomes the vessel in which self and others can forge a reality. It is essential here to distinguish between shame and guilt. The epistemological existence of guilt gives a true representation of self by aligning all the accessible aspects of the self. Guilt therefore becomes a raft of knowledge that has been transgressed, and is the juridical verdict against the pathway from society's moral milieu. One might argue that guilt is the knowledge of self-transgression. In contradistinction, shame is the experience of being, not just the knowing of being. Thus, shame becomes an ontological rather than an epistemological phenomenon. Even though these concepts were clearly distinguished in the field, there was confusion at times, and some interplay between the two, since both phenomena have been seen as constitutive of one's own responsibility and accountability (Levine and Levine 2011; Broucek 1991; Kurtz 1981).

As older informants described, the evil eye has historically been related to shame, which in turn has been a controversial phenomenon, invoking contradictions and ambivalence. Within the psychoanalytic tradition, shame has been perceived as a repressive phenomenon that affects the efficacy of the instincts and drives. It also negatively affects the process of individuation that is attendant upon the fundamental human need of autonomy (Erikson 1987; Stipik 1983). On the other hand, recent queer theories suggest that shame is a fundamental part of human development, especially for the development of personhood, and highlight the importance of relational aspects of personhood (Sedgwick 2009). Both psychoanalytic and queer perspectives address significant aspects of shame and its hermeneutics, and indeed play significant roles in shaping the landscape of shame. However, they do not address the ontological manifestation of shame, as they fail to examine its experience. Given this limitation, one might wonder how shame can relate to the evil eye. Katia, who comes from a working-class family and is in her early twenties, attempted to give an answer to this. She grew up in a village in Corfu where she spent most of her childhood and teenage years, and where the Church and the Christian faith were part of her weekly routine. Her mother was a 'housewife', in Katia's words, and her father was a very hard-working man. She hardly ever saw him during the week, but she remembers going to bed and staying awake until she could hear his bike, at which point she would fall asleep. I met Katia in a social environment through another informant. She was initially reluctant to talk to me, and did not trust me sufficiently to discuss matters surrounding her faith, as if I were a threat. She had a good relationship with her grandmother, from whom she had learned to respect folk rituals and healing processes. Katia admired her grandmother because she was a 'strong woman who offers support to others'. Her grandmother was also a healer of the evil eye. Once Katia had learned to speak, she used to ask her grandmother frequently about the ritual, and the latter's response was: 'You are not ready to be seen yet'. From that moment on, Katia began to think that there was something wrong with her that had led her grandmother to say this. Katia took part in many discussions about the evil eye during the weeks following our meeting. In our one-to-one discussion, she disclosed how difficult her childhood had been, because she was often 'getting the evil eye', and her grandmother was doing 'her thing'. Later on, her 'thing' became to say prayers and perform oil rituals. Our discussions continued and became deeper, and at some point, Katia linked the evil eye with an existential sense of shame. She said:

> I do not remember my mother being there for me at all. Well, do not get me wrong, she was there, and she was doing her best, but there was something empty in her eyes. Every time she looked at me I felt nothing. I could not identify with my mother when she was looking at me, especially as a child. I remember I wanted to make her disappear because I felt scared next to her, as I could not see myself, or define myself. I felt as if I had no existence through her gaze.

Katia was interested in understanding this, and wanted to explain to me the fear she had experienced through her mother's gaze, so she continued:

> I think that my mother was giving me the evil eye, not because she was envious of me but because her gaze was giving me nothing; it was as if I was looking into empty eyes, and I do remember that when I was looking into her empty eyes I started having pain in my body. I could not really locate it anywhere in my body, but there was a strong sense of body paralysis or something like that. If I think of it now, I cannot stop thinking that I was scared because I could see that my mother was disappointed in me, and she was giving me the empty gaze. I was ashamed of not being able to meet her expectations of being a good girl, and that allowed her evil eye to possess me. The evil eye, for me, goes hand-in-hand with my own shame. I was ashamed and scared to be seen because I felt that I was lacking something, as if a piece of me was not fitting well within me; or there was a gap; my mother's eye reflected that and I was sure that she could see that. I felt that there was a vortex in me, that if someone could see it, then I would be abandoned. My mother could see it and she could not relate to me; she was upset and therefore the evil eye that she was giving me, for not being her 'dream girl', was fuelled by her anger; she was unavailable for me to be able to see myself through her eyes. Therefore, the evil eye for me is a tool that the Devil can use to reach my existential emptiness and shame of not being in God's image; and therefore, when I sense that someone can truly see me, I am paralysed.

What Katia indicates here is that shame is another important source of the evil eye. Shame is not constructed, but emerges internally from the fear of not being good enough. Katia associated her mother's inability to reflect her existence as a child through her eyes with the internal vortex that brought shame to her. The eye becomes the vehicle through which, according to Katia, the devil can penetrate her bodily boundaries and paralyse her from within. There is a strong correlation, she believed, between the evil eye and the embodied self. The evil eye can be fuelled by an existential shame of being empty, and its manifestation cannot be separated from the individual's bodily identity. Katia's story finds support in those of other informants, where victims' reflection on the internal vortex reminds them that they might not act in accordance with God's image, and therefore that they are 'less'. Shame, in that sense, becomes a source through which individuals start to develop an agency in which to place themselves in the world. However, the agency that develops reflects their existential entity, and is closely related to the mirror reflection through the eyes of others.

In her narrative, Katia gives an answer regarding the relation between shame and the evil eye, in which 'seen' becomes a primordial state from which shame arises. In addition, being seen within a moralistic social construct, which is regulated by a given transcultural milieu, becomes a secondary phenomenon where shame operates. To this extent, the theory has been confronted with the fundamental query of how shame has been mobilised as a secondary phenomenon within the evil eye; thus, the evil eye is 'the big eye that can see you for who you are', according to informants. This generates shame, which is a systemic effect of policing individuals' behaviour within the regulatory civil state. It has been argued that even though the evil eye emerges primarily in relationships, it can, at the same time, be internalised for the 'lesser self' to be able to generate shame without a significant life event (Kaufman 1985). What is now encountered is the displacement of the primordial shame to the ascendant of the internalised morals of the civil state in which the informants live. The data reveals that such a displacement creates an existential mask, a false sense of modesty, which the evil eye can penetrate and see through. Therefore, from a very young age, the informants had learned to wear these masks in order to be socially accepted (Seidler 2000). In Katia's case, she was trying too hard to become the acceptable girl for her mother, and so she locked herself into her internal prison, fearing to be herself. Later on, such imprisonment finds refuge in the fear of being seen through another's 'evil' eye. For Nietzsche (2003), shame is 'bad conscience'; however, reflecting on his theory, similarities could be drawn between shame and the external moralistic influences that informants have internalised. Therefore, individuals start regulating themselves in front of others, and start exploiting their desire for concealment. Parallels can thus be drawn between a bad conscience and shame; the provenance of Nietzsche's bad conscience is compatible with the mobilisation of the self, which is exposed before the eyes of others and becomes known as the evil eye.

Analysing the phenomenon of the evil eye (and more specifically, its primary action, the gaze) along with the data, especially Katia's story, reveals that gaze includes elements of shame. This is a fundamental shame that stems from the notion of the embodied self as a separate entity from the individual's psyche, but one which is also in communication with it. Psychical conflicts can thus affect, communicate with and disturb bodily functions. On a constitutional level, the gaze involved in the evil eye shares the existential understanding of someone's being and reveals its interconnection and coexistence with the being of the other. I can therefore conclude that the evil eye is a relational phenomenon. However, as Seidler (2000) elucidates, shame can easily be confused with the moral implications of the action of gaze, which carries societal judgements and certain consequences. George, a 31-year-old Christian living in Corfu, said that at times, what he sees in other people are elements and capabilities that he lacks, and as a result, he feels shame, as the reflection he is getting back reminds him of his deficits.

When he has these feelings, George wants to run away from the reminder of his deficits and make it disappear. George's statement was supported by many other informants, who argued that it is easier to try to eliminate the reminders of their deficits than to accept them. Such a statement brings the evil eye to the fore and supports Levinas' (1998) argument that individuals appear to be passive in respect of their responsibility to expose themselves before they face the 'other', because of their fear and shame of being 'seen' and being 'less'. Derrida (2008), however, aligns himself with the Corfiots' view of shame and gaze, suggesting that individuals' responsibility to expose their personhood comes from the fear of the gaze of others, and not through fear of the gaze of self.

'Sometimes, when I [intentionally] give the evil eye to someone, it feels as if I am not sure of what is going on ... it feels as if I am losing control'. Maria is a devoted Christian, and this statement of hers found support among other young informants. In these instances, gaze has become something outside the individual understanding of self. The question that now arises is: what happens when an individual develops awareness of the existence of the gaze outside of their own being? Before we develop the capacity to bestow any systemic gaze on others, we have been born under the oversight of others. What makes the evil eye uncanny is the element of gaze; we learn throughout our lives that when we look into a mirror, the reflection looks back. Thus, individuals become subjected to gaze; but gaze becomes something more than the individual, which is the source of the internal pain, triggering fundamental anxieties of what it is that has been reflected back (Žižek 2006).

Gaze therefore becomes a central element in everyday interactions. In his attempt to understand the power of gaze, Lacan (1949) engages with the theory of the 'imagination and mirror' stage, which focuses on fantasy images and the illusions of gaze. He suggests that gaze can lead a person to certain interpretations and lure them into false beliefs about the meaning of their reality and personhood. In short, Lacan says that human beings have an innate need to be seen, and the 'imagination and mirror stage' enables them to recognise themselves in a reflection from the external environment. Most importantly from the perspective of this chapter, the mirror provides a way for a person to recognise themselves in a symbolic image, and from this to start appreciating themselves. In other words, Lacan suggests that people turn unconsciously to objects visible to the external world in order to be able to identify themselves as human beings; and by grasping the eye of the other, they are seeking a symbolic reflection. The contribution made by the present chapter to Lacan's theory is that the reflection that reminds people of their deficits is understood as the evil eye, due to the fact that it produces existential pain, which is manifested through their bodily functions.

The informants explained that they sometimes experienced fear when engaging in social interactions, because their whole 'appearance' and later 'existence' was susceptible to 'the gaze of others'. Sandra stated that she likes to look beautiful and that this makes her feel good. She likes to put her make-up on and wear nice clothes; she likes to look after her body, as she then likes what she sees in the mirror. However, she also expressed her anxiety about being seen from outside. Sandra went on to say that she used to get the evil eye when her 'mask was not strong, and people could see how insecure I was feeling'. What did she mean by this statement? One answer might be found in the social and cultural context in which the interaction took place; others might turn to the subjective understanding of her statement. However, engaging with these statements has led to an appreciation of the connection between the evil eye and the fundamental phenomenon of shame. Shame stems from an intrinsic existential anxiety triggered by a person's need to catch another's 'gaze' in order to start developing a sense of personhood. Yet at the same time, there is the fear that 'being seen' can expose one's vulnerabilities. The use of shame in the sociocultural contexts with which individuals interact can lead to an experiential fear, through the gaze of others, which threatens the fundamental feeling of 'being'.

The attribution of shame to the socially constructed moralistic code of disobedience is a constitutional attempt to create a system in which a person may use the power of gaze to delimit others. The shame of casters can therefore generate the evil eye, which in this case is meant to punish the disobedient person for moral transgression, rather than to shame the exposure of another. 'I knew that I had done something wrong, but I could not help it. I felt shame for being happy with their misery'. Nikos, and most of the informants, shared this same view regarding the evil eye. As Orthodox Christians, we have been conditioned to believe that shame brings pain, and therefore we have developed an intrinsic mechanism to try to hide ourselves from it and keep it out of view; 'it is an attempt to protect ourselves from a gaze, through a gaze', in the words of one mental health nurse. This intrinsic attitude is a means to escape from the realisation of falling short of the false self. By emitting negative power through the gaze, we are trying to escape from the profound bond between our being and the world, and also between our being and others. The struggle with which I am engaging is the phenomenon of the evil eye, which can now be seen as an experiential phenomenon with physical and psychical manifestations. However, the fieldwork indicates that there should be a systematic way to interpret the evil eye in its primary stages. How, therefore, can we summarise the spectral nature of the evil eye, which can at times escape symbolisation? The findings from the fieldwork provide an answer to that question, through the emergence of seven crucial interpretations of the maleficent gaze from the point of view of the sufferer.

The first interpretation of the maleficent gaze is estrangement. Sufferers revealed that when they feel that someone is looking at them, they start to feel as though they are losing their existential subjectivity: 'At that moment I do not exist; I become part of the environment like I am a piece of furniture or an object with no will', Giannis stated. The lack of clarity of expression when talking about the gaze allows the sufferer to interpret reality differently; this corresponds to Lacan's (1949) theory of the 'gaze of illusion'. This study supports Lacan's theory, with informants demonstrating the conflicting nature of the evil eye through their engagement with the phenomenon. Their experiences highlight a dual relationship, which not only indicates the coexistence of someone's self and body, but is also described by the illusion of the need to be similar to others. The gaze of illusion also depicts relationality between the imaginary and the real. The data reveals that the informants develop an imaginary wholeness based on the visual reflection that they have received from the 'mirrors' which inform their fragmented reality. Žižek (2007), on the other hand, argues that such a gaze is the landscape in which the subject becomes meaningless. The bond between the caster and the potential sufferer does not exist, and therefore the sufferer starts to experience the horror of the void that is created by both sufferer and caster in the fragmented reality. The void, in its turn, leads the sufferer to interpret the evil eye based on the fundamental experience of shame, and this leads to the anxiety of being absorbed by the void, because of the shame of failure of being: as Nikos stated, 'I failed as a person; I am not sure what makes me want to keep going; anyone can see that I am a fraud and have nothing to offer; when people can see that I feel empty and paralysed, I lose not only the sense of who I am but also the meaning of living'.

The second interpretation stems from the crucial phenomenon of human subjectivity that relies on the reflection of one's self from others. Xenia, a young informant, stated that she knows when she is suffering from the evil eye because she feels as if she has invited it. How is it possible for a human being to invite such suffering? Further analysis of her narrative revealed a profound need, stemming from early childhood, to be noticed. This is an objectification of being, in order to be 'used, seen and appreciated', as Xenia put it. When Xenia was a child, she remembered wanting her parents' attention, and trying so hard to make them see her that she started to lose herself; she was trying to please them and trying to fit into their boxes. As a result, she said that she always remembers looking at others' needs first, and at her own last. Sometimes, when she is unable to foresee others' needs, she is petrified that they will see her as a fraud because they can see her real self behind her masks; this brings her to face 'the monster in her'. The evil eye, for Xenia, is the ability of others to see the monster inside her. She also said that at times, she does not want to be in touch with that monster, and is doing her best to build her masks by screaming non-verbally at others to look at her and notice how good she is, which, in a way, attracts their evil eye. Many informants related similar accounts to Xenia's, wherein they described simultaneously trying to deny their internal 'monster' while also feeling the need for external reassurance, resulting in the evil eye. During these moments there is an internal voice screaming: 'Notice me!', 'Look at me!' or 'I feel as if I do not exist'.

Upon reflection, the informants stated that during these times, they were often going through some internal existential crisis of not feeling important or 'not existing', and wanted acknowledgement and reassurance from others of their existence. One could therefore conclude that the evil eye is a conditioning phenomenon manifested through painful embodied experiences; at times of crisis and fear, however, it can also indicate the presence of someone who doubts their existence. The sufferer thus regains their personhood through attracting the evil eye. After all, we all exist in an amalgamating intersubjectivity within the whole.

The next interpretation derives from the field observations and from the fundamental need to be recognised. It became apparent that in Corfu, unless individuals are socially recognised, they can develop the fear of not existing. They therefore do everything in their ability to attract others' gaze, in the hope that they will be recognised and therefore will exist. The powerful element of the caster has been identified as the action of gaze without engaging. What makes the gaze, or the evil eye, painful for the sufferer can be traced to a failure to have their desires met. In other words, the sufferer starts to believe that the caster sees in them a misinterpretation of who they are, a factor which is responsible for the misfortune befalling them. Green (1983) attempts to describe this phenomenon by introducing the theory of the 'dead mother complex'. The dead mother complex is what Katia described as empty eyes. It is the ability to see others without reflecting back their image. What is enacted through this gaze is fear, which sufferers feel when there is no one there to see them and acknowledge their existence. Because of the unresponsive gaze of the caster, existential anxiety is triggered and manifested through physical and psychical pain. This leads to the fourth interpretation, which I call provocation. Following the existential fear of not existing unless we are looked at, Christian Orthodox Corfiots operate from a polarised view. To be more precise, on the one hand they fear attracting the evil eye, and on the other they long to be seen in their social environment; in a way, they try to seduce their environment in order to be noticed. However, the difficulty for the sufferer is to understand the admirer's gaze. Here, we are aiming to understand the individuals' attitudes, and to answer the question of whether the sufferers examined were imagining that the casters desired what they wanted, or whether the sufferers' existential need to 'be seen', in order to fulfil their intrinsic need to know that they exist, was at play.

Laplanche (1999) tried to answer this question by introducing the concept of the enigmatic signifier. In this way, he provided a partial answer, stating that adults cause disturbance to children and other individuals by emitting unspoken messages to them that cannot be disguised. Even though this concept has made a significant contribution to the understanding of the question, it nonetheless fails to address the internal need of the sufferer to be understood as a human being through the gaze of others. The concept does highlight the fundamental fear of extinction, but does not provide an in-depth account of this fear. On the other hand, my research suggests that it is the sufferer's seduction – the fifth interpretation – that can attract the evil eye, based on the existential need to be understood through the eye of the signifier. This provocation from the sufferer appears to unconsciously excite the caster, while at the same time bolstering the sufferer's internal construct for trying to understand the signifier or caster's gaze and creating meaning from it. Engagement in such a process exhausts the sufferer's internal resources, leaving them 'internally dry', as Stamos stated, through 'experiencing body pain and headaches'.

The provocation then gives rise to persecution, which is the sixth interpretation that came out of the fieldwork. Persecution can be observed in the informants' need to attract the evil eye, which, as mentioned, originates from the internal fear of not existing unless seen. This internal fear is strongly associated with the lack of a sense of one's efficacy, which prevents the sufferer from having a strong internal voice with which to declare their existential presence. One might argue, therefore, that the sufferer is stuck in a vicious circle which feeds the existential fear. To be more precise, the results from the fieldwork reveal that people are looking for the gaze of others, while at the same time perceiving it as an intrusive, judgemental and penetrative action that violates their own internal frame of self. The gaze of others, which is manifested as the evil eye, thus penetrates a person's defences, takes residence in their cognition and exploits their need to be seen. It is little wonder, then, that this becomes a judgemental exploration of one's internal faults, and that the 'gaze' becomes a threat, exposing the individual's existential meaninglessness. It is also something that can take place at a distance. Subsequently, the gaze grows into an atrocious quest to destroy any good that is left inside an individual. 'I feel like it is eating me from within; it leaves me with an empty void', a sufferer in his forties stated.

The seduction and persecution lead to the final interpretation of the phenomenon, which is pity. Behavioural conditioning, through society and education, has focused attention on compassion and pity, and this has been imprinted in people's internal processes from a very young age. The internal need to be pitied not only attracts the evil eye (or gaze), but also the caster's attention; people therefore learn to enjoy suffering through being seen and develop a certain attachment to it, because this gives them the joy of existing, not only through being seen but also through being treated well by healers. It also attracts compassion and sympathy, as for example when Xenia and George asked their mothers to cast out the evil eye; their mothers felt sorry for them and spent time telling them how bad their cases of the evil eye were, which made them feel better. In addition, Xenia stated that she was pleased and felt great when people told her how much she had suffered from the evil eye, and how no one else could have suffered so much. The internal ungratified narcissistic need appears to cause individuals to feel the need to be subject to the evil eye. It is much better to receive an aggressive, envious gaze than nothing at all, Stella stated; at least individuals can then believe that they possess something worthy of envy.

The findings from the fieldwork also revealed that the complexity of the evil eye's symptomatology comes from a lack of understanding of the phenomenon. Up to now, the majority of the available literature on the subject has focused on the phenomenological understanding of the evil eye, and has failed to investigate or explore its deeper meaning. In other words, researchers have focused on the symptomatology without paying attention to the true underlying meaning. Although they have tried to understand the effects of the evil eye, the existential meaning has been missed. The plethora of symptomatology associated with the evil eye thus appears to be people's need to be seen through it, and individuals have developed different symptomatology according to their ecological environment. Symptoms continue to appear as a means to communicate the 'lostness' of the individual, and until we understand the deeper meaning of these symptoms, the evil eye will continue to exist, as Father Andreas stated.

The symptoms of the evil eye also disappear when sufferers are taken back to the fundamental anxiety of being looked at. However, if attention is not given to this anxiety, the symptoms recur in a different form each time. When informants became more aware of their own shame around being watched, the symptoms disappeared: 'I felt that when I asked my grandmother to cast out the evil eye, I was more in touch with myself;

something has been alleviated and somehow, I felt alive, free. It feels as if I am not scared of being seen, it feels like I am weirdly proud', Sandra stated. Her statements found support in the narratives of other informants. The realisation of the discomfort of being watched alleviates the pain from the symptoms. Merleau-Ponty (1973) suggests that people's need to develop a sense of self through the reflection in others' eyes originates from a lack of self-consciousness and consciousness of the embodied self; this is the subject under discussion in the following pages.

EMBODIED EVIL EYE

The analysis of the collected data suggests that the evil eye cannot be distinguished from its key element, the gaze. Therefore, in this section, the terms 'evil eye' and 'gaze' are used and considered interchangeably. The gaze was experienced by the informants as a force, or an energy, which alienated them from their bodies. This energy radiates from the eyes and can penetrate the mental and physical boundaries of another human being, creating a sense of disembodiment in the sufferer. As stated by many informants, 'the body is the vehicle that carries one's soul'; the body as a shelter performs in subtle ways, and it is only when its basic functioning is affected that the idea of the body comes to the forefront and we become aware of it. The primary feeling that epitomises this bodily failure is shame: 'It is painful to think that people are looking at me; I think that my body is exposed to the criticism of the other's eye', Kerkira stated. If the body is not sufficiently robust to sustain the penetration from the other's gaze, this is reflected in the body, and in the embodied agency, the self through somatic manifestations. Corfiots referred to such processes as the failure of the body to sustain the evil eye's attacks. Many informants aged 55 and above proposed that the best protection against evil eye attacks on the body is the sign of 'an erect phallus'. 'The construction of the gaze is the primary facilitator of one's personhood', Katerina stated. In support of Katerina's statement, Father Andreas reminded me that Narcissus represents a significant moment in the dialectical development of personhood through looking at his own mirror image. Narcissus, and whatever he later represents in the psychopathological field, is related to the attempt to connect with the fluidity of the gaze by trying to give a body to it, and to correct it through someone's reflection.

A new development in the analysis of the evil eye, emerging from the findings of the fieldwork, is the absence of boundaries. 'When I attract the evil eye, it is usually when I do not feel certain about who I am', Katerina suggested, while Stamos argued, 'I know that I have the evil eye not only because of the symptoms, but mostly because there is a strong sense of not belonging anywhere, a sense that my body is not part of me and I am just like a ghost, not grounded anywhere'. The informants, and especially the younger generation, therefore attempted to understand their subjective experiences of the evil eye through an intellectual presupposition, blocking at the same time the embodied understanding of the phenomenon. This was the typical defence adopted in the face of failure to understand any phenomenon that did not make sense to them. There was a tendency to rationalise their experiences by trying to fit them into their cognitive reality, which in turn led to intellectual prejudice (Merleau-Ponty 1962). The informants' unconscious need to rationalise the phenomenon by blocking its relationality and its need to communicate the internal psychical conflicts through the body left them with a sense of not belonging to their bodies. However, the research reveals that despite the informants' need to separate the phenomenon from its embodied functioning, they engaged in behaviours that contradicted that need, suggesting that within its functionality of disembodiment, gaze does not serve intellectual prejudices.

> It is hard to believe that a look can affect my emotional well-being and in fact make me feel that my body does not belong to me. I think that all these are stories from the past, because we had a lot of uneducated people. Nowadays, I do not believe that many think that the evil eye exists. It is irrational to think, and I am sure that when I experience symptoms that cannot be explained it is not because of the evil eye, but because I might not have knowledge to explain it. My grandmother believed in the evil eye and misfortune, but all these are superstitions; it cannot be explained, and it does not exist.

This was said by a young informant in his early twenties, who wore several protective amulets against the evil eye. He was also spitting in front of people whom he thought were negative. Another informant, Alexis, stated:

> I believe that my understanding of my body and how I feel about it plays a significant role in how I feel but also my well-being ... the evil eye plays a role in that, as it affects my physical being; when I have the evil eye, I feel more emotional than ever and I feel that my body does not represent me. I have the tendency to try to explain it so that I can understand what is going on.

There is an assumption here, and through the narratives of many other informants it was revealed that the frame of the body, and the body's functions, are an integral part of the emotional understanding of one's self. The conclusion from Alexis' statement above highlights the division between the internal and external personification of one's self, which is affected by the others' gaze. Sofia added that 'being looked at reminds me that I exist ... it is something that comes from others and it goes straight to my core, and then I feel that I exist'. Indeed, the findings from the fieldwork have shown that prior to the cognitive understanding that we are actually visible as entities, there is a primary feeling of being invisible. In Sofia's narrative, it is obvious that she becomes herself as the object of the gaze through the evil eye, which is detected outside her body. Then, without considering the actuality of the fact that another person is really looking at her, she feels her existence as if the gaze is an extension of herself. Sofia was primarily preoccupied with the existential understanding of being looked at, rather than the actual gaze from the other person. Here, then, gaze is more metaphorical than cognitive. The gaze becomes an experience in adulthood that enhances vulnerability due to the fact that it is experienced as disembodiment, which is in constant need of others' gaze in order to become embodied reality. This is due to the disconnection with 'the vessel of the soul'. As Marios said:

> most of the time I feel that I have been overlooked, but I do not know who gave me the eye. No matter how much I want to know who gave me the eye, it is impossible for me to identify it; however, there is always a gravitas around me, but I feel empty.

Meanwhile, a 50-year-old informant stated that 'I am scared of the others' gaze, but sometimes I catch myself thinking that I want to be looked at ... such need feels so real; my body becomes intense at the look of others'. Marios' statement above was supported by other informants, one of whom said: 'I need to be seen; I feel real when I feel that I am overlooked, but then my body reacts'. On further reflection and analysis of the findings, it appears that attracting the evil eye enhances the sense of being visible, and to an extent heightens the sense of personhood. It would seem that the need to attract the evil eye stems from the feeling of losing one's embodied personhood in the physical world. Most informants experienced a fear of fading away. By attracting the evil eye, they were able to enhance their understanding of self and their position in relation to the physical world. The need to exhibit oneself in order to be overlooked can be traced to the mother's eyes (Kohut 1971). According to Kohut, the mother's eyes become a mirror, a reflection of the physical body. 'I feel that I exist when I cross eyes with someone, despite the feeling of shame', Andreas said. His fear of being dissolved in his environment and not existing physically drew him to want to be 'loud', and attract others' attention; this caused him pain on a surface level through the evil eye, but at a deeper level it gave him a sense of existing through being visible to others. As all the informants suggested, the evil eye is nothing more than the discomfort, anxiety, pain and shame of being visible to others because of the lack of internal reflection of the self, and the fear of being judged and abandoned if we are seen.

Contemporary scholars would agree with the above theory, stating that the power of the gaze or evil eye is associated with the existential manifestation of the body, and the need, which sufferers from the evil eye have, to be visible and observed as a pathway to the development of personhood. However, such needs are not only accompanied by positive effects; they also contain the threat that the body might be objectified in the other's gaze. Thus, the shame of the evil eye becomes a sudden denigration of the self (Sartre 1992; Lewis 1995). 'It is always that fight; I want to be seen when I feel invisible, but then I am scared, thinking of the after-effects of my visibility to others, and I prefer to be hidden, which then causes me other problems ... it is like a vicious circle', a 36-year-old teacher stated. What is the nature of this fear? From the data collected, we might say that the evil eye or gaze is initially understood as a form of energy affecting the body, and one which can penetrate bodily boundaries. From this, it becomes clear why informants want to hide from such a gaze. As the informants mentioned, human beings feel protected by the body; there is a need to look after it, because it is the shield against external threats.

At this juncture, it is important to highlight one of the prominent elements of the evil eye, which is the gaze in its disembodied form. A universal understanding of the evil eye is that it emits energy that can cause suffering, disease or even death to others (Bohigian 1997b; Maloney 1976; Fenichel 1953; Reis 2005; Tourney and Plazak 1954; Roussou 2011b). However, universal understandings pay less attention to the phenomenon as communication from one person to another through the eye. At times, in their everyday communication, the informants would say, 'If only looks could kill', perpetuating the primal fear of the magical elements of the eye. This primal fear illuminates the phenomenon; within that belief, one can start to draw a picture of the need to be hidden while craving to be seen. The body becomes the frontier, protecting the soul from the energy that emanates from the eye. Shame, therefore, is not strange to the evil eye; the shame of being exposed to someone's gaze creates the desire to hide behind clothes or tattoos. As Costas stated, 'Sometimes I feel as if my tattoos allow me to hide from the other's gaze; ... it is scary to know that I am watched even though it gives me pleasure'. Costas continued to say that 'my body becomes my protective shelter where I retreat to find comfort when I loose my sense of self'. One might argue that Costas is completely wrong, as the nature of tattoos is to attract the gaze of others. However, this argument allowed me to delve deeper in terms of my understanding of the evil eye. As Costas stated, his body becomes the shelter where he can retreat when he feels threatened by the gaze. His tattoos, to that extent, destroy the gaze, because others are preoccupied with the tattoos rather than actually looking at him. I find similar perceptions when I examine the history of ornaments and other body beautifications; their initial role is to attract the gaze and create a false focus of attention. This mechanism appears to have a dual role. While these techniques of beautification attract the evil eye, they are used at the same time to create a diversion, producing a new kind of visibility that takes away the focus from the individual's personhood. In other words, when the evil eye is transmitted and captured by the other's bodily shelter, its energy and manifestations are directed to the surface of the shelter, and away from the individual's personhood.

The body therefore becomes the agency through which individuals comprehend their own existence. 'It is interesting', Maria stated, 'that when I observe others or even when I think of others, it feels as if I see myself, and then a weird feeling of existence goes through my body'. Maria's statement highlights the importance of seeing our reflection. Like a reflection in a mirror, the gaze becomes a single moment of the synthesis of personhood, in which a comparison between personhood and others is drawn to create a consciousness of one's self. When this consciousness is developed, individuals link gaze with shame and inhibition. The fear of being looked at then breaks the communion with the other, and initiates the process of feeling sick. When the communion between two individuals through the evil eye is broken, individuals feel 'separated and isolated, fearing that I am the object of others' observation', as a 25-year-old male explained it. The oneness is now disturbed and the individual experiences the gaze as a disembodied moment. Maria also stated: 'It feels like an attack when I sense that I get the evil eye; I feel alone, that there is a gap which separates me from everything'. Here, I am starting to engage with the existential puzzle of personhood, which requires the evil eye to be resolved, as the data reveals. The question of the evil eye in relation to the understanding of self will thus become the focus.

THE RIDDLE OF THE EVIL EYE AND THE SENSE OF SELF

Many informants, in their discussions with me about the evil eye, mentioned the memory of their mothers' eyes. There was an uncanny fear of being 'overlooked' by their mothers, or in more general terms, by their carers, as infants. Such memories led them to understand that the evil eye and its antiquity seem to haunt individuals uncannily, producing terror that can affect their mental health. The evil eye often prevails in the lives of people who have suffered from emotional conflicts and disturbances. It was here that I often witnessed the evil eye being attached to shame and guilt. Further exploration of this relationship led to the realisation that the evil eye has become a survival mechanism for coping with extreme shame. In other words, in cases of extreme shame, a person can express internal masochistic attitudes of dread of being bad and the need to be punished through other's witnessing. We read in Matthew (5:29) that 'if thy right eye offend thee, pluck it out and cast it from thee; for it is profitable for thee that one of thy members should perish, and not that thy whole body should be cast into hell'.

Delving into antiquity, one can see the association between the evil eye and shame. The findings of the fieldwork, however, highlighted another aspect of this connection: the petrifying terror of shame in younger people, which indicates the prominent link between the development of certain aspects of personhood, the mother (carer) and the evil eye. Children have not yet developed an internal sense of personhood that enables them to sustain frustration, and they therefore suffer a situation that makes them susceptible to the evil eye. In addition, many informants pointed out the importance of communication through eye contact between them and their children. Others also argued that the evil eye might have affected their later social skills, 'sight' and attachment. It is argued that eye contact can stimulate psychotic anxieties; visual contact is an intense interaction, as it creates a potent emotional space where individuals are confronted with 'raw' material from their relational narratives. Winnicott (1965) argues that eyes become the focal point of an emotional connection between two individuals in which they can reflect their ways of being, and in which instincts and intense emotions can be triggered. As eyes become the mirror of one's self and needs, those with a weaker sense of being appear to dread being seen, out of fear that others might see their 'lacking', or that they might be seen as empty. A high percentage of these individuals become casters of the evil eye.

The fieldwork also revealed that the evil eye has a strong connection with the sense of self. There was a certain dependency of the Orthodox Christians' spiritual needs on the cultural and interpersonal context where evil is most commonly witnessed. The sense of self created through interpersonal interaction can easily be distorted by changes in the cultural and social environment, and the evil eye is part of that distortion. People also communicate this social and cultural distortion through the use of the evil eye, which affects their stable sense of who they are. Therefore, people have started to recognise, through the pain caused by the evil eye, that they do not have power; this in turn destroys the reality that they are agentic beings who can govern their own lives. Before any further analysis, it will be helpful to explore further the term 'self' and to spend some time defining it.

Stamos, one of the informants, stated, 'Self is not that complex; it must be a simple term'. Every individual has a sense of self. It is the self that generates desires, thoughts, behaviours and fantasies; these products of the self build the sense of self-agency, as reflected in culture and society (Fiske 2004; Leary and Tangney 2012; Sedikides and Spencer 2007). Through this understanding, researchers such as Reis (2005, 2009) have developed the notion of the self as a stable part of being, with a certain self-awareness and rationale. However, it was not long before this idea was challenged, on two grounds. First, Freud (1978) postulated that there is no unified self-agency, and that even the ego is not master within its own space; then James (1983) went further, defining two aspects of self: the subjective and the objective self, 'I' and 'Me' respectively. He also stated that there is no metaphysical 'I', and that the 'I' is responsible for cognitive functioning. However, an understanding of a self-agency emerged from the findings of the fieldwork, and it is a reformulation of the Jamesian notion of 'I'. It is, therefore, the integration of the physicality of one's being – the body – and the psychical experience of the same.

The way that the body interprets and interacts with experience informs the core construction of the emotional experience of one's self. In other words, the Orthodox Christian understanding of the self agrees with Johnson's (1987) statement that an individual's bodily experience constructs a symbolic language to understand and interpret reality and to conceptualise experiences. However, what Corfiots actually consider the self is just a part of the whole self. In fact, the sense of self-ownership is a complex phenomenon indeed, and one mostly defined by efferent and afferent signs. The evil eye thus becomes an afferent sign in the attempt by individuals to better comprehend the sense of self, and to exert ownership over somatic activities. However, no matter what the afferent and efferent signs are, the question that puzzles social scientists is how the self develops. The phenomenon of the evil eye partly answers the question through its somatic manifestations. In 2010, Gallese and Sinigaglia examined mirror neurons; in their research, they found that prior to understanding a sense of self, the sense of the body develops. Hence, the development of the body schema is the source of action upon which a sense of self can develop. According to the Corfiots' narratives and experiences, the evil eye plays a significant role in the development of the body schemata, as it is projected to others in an attempt by the caster to develop a sense of self through the reflection that comes from the sufferer. Therefore, one can conclude that the development of the self is not a static stage, but rather an interactive development throughout life; it is significant that it is influenced not only by the sociocultural environment in which individuals live, but also by transhistorical elements of the culture they inhabit.

The development of the self has been the main focus of attention for many decades and in many disciplines. Similarly, the informants addressed the importance of the development of the self through different behavioural and psychical attitudes. The evil eye is a phenomenon which stems from the failure of maternal preoccupation to allow the infant to develop a secure self; this was revealed in the data analysis. This constructionist and relational approach to the evil eye and the self has been at the heart of this research. Schore (2009) argues that the development of a self is an amalgamation of many different perspectives: social, intersubjective, constructionist and constructivist. However, the findings of the data analysis suggest that new interrelational experiences, commencing with early attachment to the carer's gaze, significantly contribute to the development of the self. The sense of an individual's self is thus embedded in the interaction with the narrative that they uphold, but the sense of self also widens and is transformed via the understanding of the self-with-other(s). Therefore, self is interpreted as an agency that can influence and affect the physical and relational entities of 'others'. The evil eye therefore becomes a phenomenon through which casters attempt to develop a self-agency based on their first early interactions with their carers. Palmer (2007) supports the above statement, suggesting at the same time that a self-agency has the capacity and power to intentionally affect results and cause somatic reactions in other members of the social group. In addition, Bandura (2001) agrees that a self-agency has the capacity to control one's physical life. He goes further, stating that the self-agency affects and is affected by the broader sociocultural network and the subjects that build it. However, Gallagher (2000) is interested in the inter-structures of these networks, suggesting that the self-agency builds upon intention prior to action. A self-agency is thus built upon the sense that an individual gets from initiating a course of action. In other words, the evil eye has been seen by most of the informants as the initiator of action. This attitude allows the building of a sense of self-agency that was otherwise lacking from the informants' internal psychical structure. Self-agency, however, appears to be dominated by the adjacency sense as revealed by the fieldwork; this is discussed in the pages that follow.

CHARACTERISTICS OF THE EVIL EYE: ADJACENCY SENSE

The analysis of the fieldwork data revealed another important characteristic of the evil eye; even though informants talked about their fear and the need to be looked at, they also disclosed their understanding of the evil eye in terms of 'another sense'. It is the sense that allows them to absorb and understand their environment at a distance. Taste, smell and touch all require proximity to another object or person, while the gaze allows the processing of information at a distance. However, the gaze can easily cause mischief; the blurred gaze originates from an individual who finds it difficult to be confronted with something they are not ready to see. The fieldwork therefore revealed that the evil eye is at times used as an alert of something threatening. Such use of the evil eye does not need proximity, and it was described in the field as adjacency sense when associated with the phenomenon. 'When I saw M. being so bright and so lucky, I was so angry because I was not so privileged, and I know that I am better than her', Sotiria said. At that point, Sotiria felt ashamed of herself, and said she was not ready to reflect upon it. Her shameful feeling had become so painful and unbearable that her gaze became powerful and able to penetrate those who reminded her of this pain; she therefore projected onto these others the pain that she was not willing to deal with. Steiner (2006) would argue in support of Sotiria's narrative that her eyes had now become the mediator of her introjections and projections.

As manifested through the gaze, distance can represent loss, through which both individuals (caster and sufferer) are connected via the eye. The internal pain that the individual is not ready to confront tries to escape through the eye. In an attempt to escape the realisation of loss and shame, the pain thus becomes poisonous; neither the sufferer nor the caster can resist it, and therefore both suffer. The gaze takes the form of a channel that transfers the inhibited shame and guilt, as well as unbearable existential anxieties, from one mind to another (Freud 1978). The findings from the fieldwork also revealed that when something is outside the norm of Corfiot society, or even outside the individual's tolerance level, there is a scopophilic attitude towards it; this is an impulsive desire to look upon things that are different, while at the same time looking to develop destructive behaviour through the evil eye that aims to destroy that which is different. The word 'different' is used in broad terms by the informants. Fenichel (1953) discussed the equation of sight. Even though his theory is old, his ideas are relevant to the present times, as he talks about the look with the intention to devour that which reminds us (human beings) of our 'falls'. He further states that this devouring gaze contains something sadistic and masochistic, and this statement can be supported by the data: individuals (casters) find unconscious pleasure in the destruction inflicted on others, but also onto themselves, which is also painful. However, what the findings of the present research add to the scopophilic attitude is the risk that gaze includes: the risk that something might be stolen from the person to whom the gaze is directed. Further analysis of this risk revealed that the caster's scopopholic attitude incorporates two polarised and at times antagonistic intentions. The first is to destroy and impose pain on what reminds the caster of internal imperfections, and the other is to communicate pain to the other through the empathic look.

We are confronted with the eye's appetite for destruction and the meaning of this. Undoubtedly, the evil eye contains an element of envy and admiration; however, this appetite for destruction has been added, exemplifying the hypnotic elements of the gaze that serves the needs of both caster and sufferer. The gaze's appetite, therefore, depletes the other, who reminds the caster of their 'falls'. This builds a picture of the voracity of the eye, which from a Christian perspective could be considered to be 'sin'. In connection with the voracity of the eye, a statement given by a mental health professional, in which she made a link to the legend of Lady Godiva, was recorded in the fieldwork. In her attempt to describe the evil eye's voracity, she said that in the story of Lady Godiva, all the window shutters were closed so that the lady would be able to ride naked in the bright light of day. Her seductive body and the voracity of one man's eyes meant that he could not resist looking to see her beauty, with the dreadful result that he was turned into stone (blinded). Father Athanasios also mentioned, in his description of the evil eye, the gluttony of the eye in Gomorrah, and how everyone was turned into stone (specifically a pillar of salt) when they opened their eyes. This is how the image of voracious eyes is sometimes represented in the evil eye.

The statement above by the mental health professional and the comments by Father Athanasios highlight the conjuring notion of the evil eye and its need to turn what is most treasured into dust. Envy, therefore, becomes one of the things that fuel the phenomenon. However, while envy appears to be the most universal explanation of the evil eye, analysis of the fieldwork data challenged this explanation. It is important here to mention that envy is the fundamental desire to have what is not possessed, and therefore operates through the evil eye to express an interest in the object of desire. However, the evil eye is not only about envy. According to the fieldwork, envy is a product of the phenomenon, and not the cause of it. When the phenomenon is examined more deeply, it is discovered to be about destroying what is most treasured. Its aim is not therefore to gain, but to ravage what is not possessed. There is a fundamental instinct here that drives both caster and sufferer, which is the desire to destroy and gain pleasure from the experience of witnessing the pain that others feel and experience.

It is helpful to look at the terms 'caster' and 'sufferer'. Death, destruction and voracity are concepts connected to the evil eye, and analysis of the collected data reveals, through the attitudes of casters and sufferers, another element of the phenomenon: that caster and sufferer are one. The sufferer is in fact the caster, and vice versa; they both share the same existential anxieties, expressed in opposite but also complementary powers (that is, their roles as caster and sufferer). There is a fundamental anxiety and fear of death and of losing something we have that is precious to us. The fear of separation from the attachment developed with the subject or object leads to the projection of 'fear of death', and this attitude is shared by both caster and sufferer. Therefore, others become a source of torture, holding the threat that what is valued can be destroyed either by envy or admiration. Since it is unbearable to envy ourselves for the good fortune we have, and as we cannot sustain such pain, we are led to project it out in an attempt to protect ourselves from our own envy and fear of exposure. Although this sounds paradoxical, it has elements of truth; destruction and suffering through the evil eye now appear to be self-inflicted out of fear of love. What is meant by fear of love is the focus of the following section.

FEAR OF LOVE, INHIBITED SENSE OF SELF AND THE EVIL EYE

During the fieldwork and field observations, there was a similar narrative that Orthodox Christians often brought to their everyday interactions with others. This narrative attracted my attention not only because of its frequency in conversations but also because of the importance it conveyed about the fear of love through the emission of the evil eye. In these interactions, there was a strong impression of an inhibited sense of self from those casting the evil eye on others. Even though the phenomenon was clear, its true meaning was hidden behind linguistic metaphors and social interactions. The way that casters related to those who were envied was thus achieved through passive compliance.

Further exploration of these attitudes, and interaction with the informants, led to a deeper understanding of the nature of the evil eye, revealing that it contains a psychical element stemming from early experiences recounted by individuals. The evil eye projected a certain amount of anger towards those who appeared to have good intimate relationships with others in their adult lives. Furthermore, the findings of the fieldwork revealed that all those who had the ability to cast the evil eye had shared similar experiences during their early years. Most of them described their childhood as 'suffocating', or discussed having an 'overprotective mother' or even an 'absent father'. It was also apparent that they had been undermined to the extent that their own understanding of autonomy had been disturbed, and they found loving and being loved equally dangerous. Therefore, there was anger towards their parents, and this anger had not been allowed to be expressed; it therefore took the form of the evil eye through envy towards those who had healthy relationships. The informants disclosed that they had somehow lost their own self-identity by thinking that others' needs should take priority, and they were aiming to meet the needs of others instead of their own. One might wonder what this has to do with the evil eye. Again, the fieldwork observations and the narratives of informants can provide some answers. It emerged from the data that the evil eye is an attack on individuals who reinforce and cherish the idea of a self-agency to another. These attacks, on secondary analysis, contain elements of self-destructiveness; the evil eye plays the role of a masochistic sacrifice of the caster's need to create relationships, projecting their pain out through the evil eye and the unconscious devious force of destroying anything that reminds them of love that is outside their understanding (Miller 1988).

For the informants, the evil eye included an element of the fear of being loved. A commonality between the casters was that they believed that being loved meant ceasing to exist; that it was necessary to destroy their own creativity, aliveness and sense of self in order to meet the needs of others and therefore to be loved. The evil eye is therefore the agency by which casters are protected from the overwhelming experience of true love; they then perpetuate what seems familiar to them, pleasing others through the absence of their sense of self. This element of the evil eye does not arise from acute trauma, but rather from everyday activities and, indeed, from the less obvious experiences of self-deprecation and self-devaluation. Therefore, by maintaining this position and using the evil eye as psychical defence, casters create the illusion of protection from potential individuation and separation. This protection takes the form of Christian Orthodox rituals and language, a topic that is explored in the following pages.

ORTHODOX CHRISTIAN LINGUISTICS OF THE EVIL EYE

The circle of life is considered by Christians to be an alchemical outcome of feelings, thoughts and emotions; these three elements, along with other sensations, play an integral role in Christians' everyday lives. However, the way they are experienced not only communicates the fullness of their internal state, but can also indicate social status and relationship styles. The abstractions that Christians use are interesting, and examination of the collected fieldwork data reveals that these linguistic abstractions are an attempt not only to cognitively define an idiosyncratic experience, but also to contextualise the experience within the specific social environment. The purpose of this section is to look at the use of language with regard to the evil eye and to consider how individuals express their discomfort.

The way that individuals interacted with one another regarding the evil eye during the fieldwork differed according to their cultural and social upbringing. Based on that differentiation, it became obvious that cultural constructs influence an individual's cognitive processes in their effort to understand their emotional experience, but also that they construct a discourse in order to communicate their suffering to others. It is important, therefore, to examine the somatic and verbal idioms that individuals use to express their distress. The aetiological concepts that they share in their attempts to communicate their suffering allow them to identify the need for help, and also enable the healer to understand exactly the suffering process and the healing that is required. For the Orthodox Christians who were observed and participated in this research, the evil eye constitutes suffering and appears as one of the idiosyncratic attempts to communicate this suffering. It is an idiom which specifically allows someone to be in touch with their spiritual pain, and to be in a position to express it and finally seek support. Therefore, a closer examination is required of the interrelation between the evil eye and suffering as a linguistic idiom that incorporates fear and bad luck.

When engaging with the evil eye, I found myself puzzled by the question of what it is about this phenomenon that is so hard to understand. Why are people afraid even to mention the word, let alone engage with the subject? At that point, the play *The License* by Luigi Pirandello came to mind, and more specifically, the section in which Pirandello quotes the exact root of fear which is attached to the evil eye. He states that 'in these eyes of mine, I have the power to reduce an entire city to rubble! Look out for me!' (1964: 136). This phrase reminded me of the power that is inherent in the evil eye – to destroy an entire city, to create ruins – and the threat that it can hit at any time: 'Look out for me!' In a sense, the evil eye can be seen as a persecutory phenomenon that can hit anyone in any moment.

The notion that a mere look or thought can impose suffering or destroy objects can be observed in different cultures around the world. However, the way in which individuals gestate the evil eye varies not only from one culture and tradition to another, but most importantly, from one individual to another within the same cultural context. Following that logic, I am proposing the idea that there are as many definitions of the evil eye as there are individuals describing it, based on their own experiences and understandings. What I intend to discuss below is therefore my personal understanding and interpretation of the phenomenon, as it has been presented to me during my observations and through analysis of the data I collected during the fieldwork. This has created a tapestry for me, with which I engage in the next section, and from which I may fully comprehend how Eastern Orthodox Christians interact with the evil eye – more specifically, through an emotional construction as seen in the field.

THE EMOTIONAL CONSTRUCTION OF THE EVIL EYE AS SEEN BY GREEK ORTHODOX CHRISTIANS

Greek Orthodox Christians in the Ionian Islands believe in what Moss and Cappannari (1976) describe as the Mediterranean view of good and evil. Corfiots therefore exhibit in the rituals of their everyday lives a clear understanding of this dichotomy. Their religious beliefs and interaction with their religion and rituals seem to reinforce the dichotomy, which governs their actions and attitudes. The dichotomy was clear in the informants' linguistic interaction with others; they often talked about heaven and hell, and about who sins and who does not. Such a dichotomy takes the form of socially accepted attitudes and behaviours in interpersonal exchanges that accentuate views of what is right and what is wrong. Further investigation led to the understanding that what is right within interpersonal relationships is seen as respect for one another, while wrong is linked with disrespect. It is this disrespect – to which envy is attached – that attracted my interest; envy has been interpreted by Orthodox Christians as disrespectful behaviour towards others or the Divine. It is important to mention that envy in this context was described as the evil eye.

An interesting point that came out of the fieldwork was that the evil eye is not only a person's need to gain what someone else has, and which they do not possess; rather, it is the wish for the person who possesses that thing to lose it. The envy that is attached to the evil eye is therefore about the other person experiencing the loss of the object, and not necessarily about the caster acquiring it. Thus, it was out of fear of losing something that people appeared to want to always be in control, or attempt to be in control, of their impulsive envy. On the other hand, they believed that by attempting to control their envious impulses, they were showing respect to the interpersonal social norms and were therefore safe from the evil eye.

The evil eye has had a strong influence on Greek Orthodox interpretation, and on the way in which Orthodox Christians interact with one another and with the Divine. The duality of right and wrong influences their perception of reality. It also creates fear of the future, as the evil eye can be projected into the future to inflict spiritual suffering. This is where the logic of bad luck or misfortune is born for individuals; the evil eye brings bad luck to others, and bad luck is the source of illness according to the informants. Further exploration of this logic is presented in the following section.

CONTEXT OF LOGIC AND THE EVIL EYE

The question that arises, therefore, is about the linguistic aim of using the idiom 'evil eye' in the context of everyday life. What was the real purpose of such an idiom? The data revealed its aetiological construction as the means through which individuals communicate their psychical suffering. This aetiological construction appears to be vital for the later healing process, as understanding the foundation of the suffering allows the spiritual healer to construct an action plan for healing.

It was noticed that informants were particularly disappointed with mental health professionals who had been influenced by what is known as the Westernised medical model, and with their attempts to treat conditions stemming from the evil eye and spiritual trauma. Due to their disappointment with this model, people had begun to seek support from folk treatments. The majority of those interviewed were unsatisfied with their failure to alleviate their suffering through medication, and gave this as the reason they were turning to spiritual healers. They were re-evaluating their understanding of, and trust in, the medical model by which they felt 'let down'. They were developing an idiomatic understanding of the phenomenon of the evil eye and considering where to go for support. The spiritual healers, therefore, were able to cast out the suffering from the victims' systems, and this validated their suspicions about the evil eye.

One can conclude that in these particular cases, where people had felt let down, the idiom of the evil eye played a fundamental role in exemplifying pain, and also became a compass by which the sufferer and spiritual healer could come up with a treatment plan. In addition, it helped the sufferers to ease their anxiety about the symptomatology, whereas their symptoms had persisted during treatment through the medical model. Waldram (1993) would argue that the positive outcome of a spiritual healer's course of action depends primarily on the sufferer's willingness to comprehend and accept the explanation of the suffering that is given.

It will enhance our understanding of what follows to introduce Ms Maria, who is in her mid-fifties and has partial paralysis, although she stated that she has had no formal diagnosis. She introduced herself to me after a long process of messaging, through which she was trying to understand who I was and what my role was as a researcher. Ms Maria is a devoted Christian with a strong Orthodox Christian background; she is from a wealthy family and is an only child. She described herself as an exceptional child who forfeited many opportunities in her life due to her gender. She was beautiful and intelligent in her youth, she said. At the age of 21, and after a major fight with her best friend, she had an accident which resulted in muscle apraxia, which has affected her ever since. Through numerous attempts to cure her condition, or at least to make it less painful, Ms Maria started to realise that medical treatment was not effective. The doctors could not identify the cause of her muscle dyspraxia and her condition was worsening as the years passed. It was later in her life that she engaged with spiritual healing, even though she was an active Christian. When she visited a spiritual healer, she was surprised to have a spiritual experience; the healer entered a trance state in which she realised that Ms Maria had been cast with the evil eye, and in fact exposed to it repeatedly. The spiritual healer could not help her, however, because of the timeframe in which Ms Maria had been subjected to evil; the muscle dyspraxia had become permanent.

The importance of Ms Maria's case is the fact that she was disappointed with medical treatment, which had 'killed the hope', and even though the spiritual healer could not help her, she had given her a narrative which provided her with a logical rationale for her condition. It was easier, therefore, for Ms Maria to accept the healer's rationale and reduce the negative effect that her condition had on her mental health. From this, we can conclude that the evil eye provides a logical rationale to sufferers that helps them to understand their condition and build up a sense of hope, instead of trying to identify and blame external causes. The significance of Ms Maria's narrative is that it exemplifies the inability of the medical model not just to treat but also to diagnose the condition, while at the same time showing how the evil eye contextualised her suffering.

Among the Greek Orthodox population of Corfu, the evil eye is not just a phenomenon, but a specific idiom of distress with religious connotations. Therefore, Corfiots do not perceive the phenomenon simply as an idiom that can exemplify how they feel; they believe it contains a duality. It is a description of their suffering, but it also transfers the meaning of the suffering to others and enables them to comprehend the experience. Considering the accounts that were given about the evil eye, it became apparent that it is used as an activating force. It holds the power to start a process that reflects the anxiety experienced within social interactions. People thus talk about the evil eye as bringing a rapid somatisation of this anxiety. This might lead to the question of whether the evil eye is a discursive device, but the answer to that is not simple. The analysis of the collected data showed that the evil eye encompasses cultural symbols which carry the causes of suffering to one's psyche. It therefore becomes almost impossible to understand the evil eye outside of the interpersonal context in which social and moral transgression takes place. The evil eye reflects the penetration of the interpersonal context through violation and conflict, as it was represented through individuals' narratives.

The phenomenon of the evil eye is not used diagnostically, however; it incorporates time as a factor and represents chronic difficulties. In an interpersonal context, the evil eye becomes the mirror of constant failure to meet expectations, and generates feelings of 'not being good enough'. The sense of being 'not good enough' is embodied in the sufferer, and it is in those moments that the symptoms appear and become noticeable. Ruptures in relationships can thus become an issue that reinforces the symptomatology. At that point, people start to seek support from medical professionals, who usually prescribe specific medication. However, the lack of effective Westernised treatment, and the increase in seeking alternative folk healing, is all represented in the words, 'I have the evil eye'. To conclude, the evil eye serves as an interpretative device, one that expresses pain and suffering. It is, therefore, the communication between the sufferer and others, and the call from a sufferer for healing. Finally, the evil eye is the channel through which the sufferer concretises an experience in order to start the transformative process of healing.

CONCLUSION

This chapter has explored the phenomenon of the evil eye through each common understanding held across cultural and social groups. Despite the common view that the evil eye can cause misfortune through envy and admiration, the data from the fieldwork revealed that it is part of humans' collective unconscious. However, the informants exhibited a wide range of symptomatology, ranging from the physical to the spiritual and with a particular emphasis on existential anxieties. The fieldwork revealed that there was always a connection between cognitive, psychological and existential symptomatology with somatic manifestations. It is also important to mention that the symptomatology associated with the evil eye was not correlated with mental health issues, or in fact with any mental illness symptomatology, despite the fact that individuals were using mental health language to express their understanding of the evil eye's symptomatology. However, there was a strong correlation between the evil eye and religious beliefs and rituals.

One of the significant findings from the field regards the casters' attempts to externalise their internal suffering through the evil eye so as to derive meaning from their 'pain'. Concurrently, there was reluctance from the casters to work through their internal pain and try to understand it. On examination, this reluctance was shown to be an expression of existential turmoil that was expressed through the evil eye. Such turmoil has been interpreted as the need to be seen by others in an attempt to define personhood, alongside a fear of being seen due to a fear of inadequacy – of not being good enough, and therefore of being abandoned or rejected by the community. Due to this fear of being seen, the evil eye was strongly related to shame. To this extent, gaze, which is the evil eye's primary function, appears to include shame projected outwards in an attempt to make sense of the turmoil experienced internally. It is important to state here that according to the fieldwork, shame is in constant dialogue with the caster or sufferer's embodied self, while the individual's psyche is diseased. This chapter has opposed the current trend in the literature by suggesting that the evil eye upholds an existential understanding of the individuals' being, but also honours its fundamental need to be in connection with others, as well as its otherness. Therefore, the chapter concluded that the evil eye is a relational phenomenon. It criticises the current literature for its limited focus regarding the evil eye, and argues that in order to understand the phenomenon in depth, researchers need to go deeper than its symptomatology and triggers, as this chapter has attempted to do. When the evil eye is examined with regard to its archetypal characteristics, its symptomatology fades away.

This chapter also engages with the understanding of the evil eye as an embodied phenomenon, arguing that it is fuelled by early ungratified narcissistic needs in adulthood. The evil eye therefore becomes the vehicle for the caster, or indeed the sufferer, to gratify these needs. Such needs, however, can generate a sense of disembodiment in the sufferers, as they perceive an energy from the casters which seems to be alien to their own physical and psychical energy. Another important finding that was revealed by the fieldwork was that concerning the adjacency sense. It is through the evil eye that individuals in contemporary Corfu understand, but also absorb, energies from their surroundings at a distance. Distance can however be perceived within the relationality of the phenomenon as loss and shame. The gaze in the evil eye thus becomes the channel through which inhibited shame and guilt are transmitted to the other.

The fieldwork made a clear distinction between what is known to be the evil eye and what is actually experienced by the informants. According to the data, the evil eye is not the individuals' internal need to possess what they lack but others have, but rather the need to make others lose these coveted things. This subtle difference allows an analysis of the evil eye that shows it to be not the envy of an object, but the desire to make the others who have it experience its loss. It is the fear of losing and the need to always be in control of things that generate the evil eye.

The data also revealed an uncanny memory concerning the evil eye: namely, the similar experience regarding the mother's (or carer's) eye, which mirrored or created a misinterpretation of the individual's own being. The following chapter therefore explores the association between the evil eye and personhood.

Chapter 4

Personhood and the Evil Eye

INTRODUCTION

In the previous chapters, different understandings of the evil eye among different social groups have been examined and analysed. The analysis has suggested that despite the effects of the evil eye on mental health and well-being, the phenomenon provides a deeper understanding of mental health as something that is attached to the culture in which its symptoms develop. The current chapter deepens our understanding of the evil eye through an analysis of its interaction with personhood ('I'), based on the empirical data collected from the fieldwork. More precisely, this interaction is investigated in relation to the different philosophical and ethnographic understandings of personhood. It is expected that this approach and analysis will facilitate a better understanding of the evil eye through the accounts of individuals' journeys in the process of their development of personhood. The intention of this chapter is to bear witness to the importance of the evil eye in the understanding of personhood, which is created from a relationship between the sufferer and the caster of the evil eye (the subject and the other); it also promotes the individual's personhood in their relationship with others. Finally, the chapter aims to offer a detailed analysis of the particular element of eye ('I'), and more specifically, of 'the others', as they relate to the phenomenon of the evil eye.

ETHNOGRAPHIC UNDERSTANDINGS OF PERSONHOOD

'Self' has become one of the areas that attract great interest in the field of ethnography. However, ethnographers approach personhood in different ways; some understand it as the common element that characterises all humans, while others are fascinated by the variations it can take. Many scholars retreat to what is known as 'society' in order to understand 'personhood'. Yet, as Kuper (1999) suggests, 'culture' is the primary source from which to start unravelling the mysteries of developing personhood. Therefore, on the basis of cultural elements, the findings of the present study similarly reveal that the development of personhood in Corfu appears to be modified by its particular culture. This chapter thus aims to uncover how the phenomenon of the evil eye is seen within a specific cultural environment in order to examine whether culture plays an important role in the development of personhood. It is important to mention that every single biological organism – including humans – is embedded in the cultural setting in which it lives, as the field shows. This study adopts the belief that every human being is deeply rooted within a particular cultural environment, and that each individual is identified by a unique cultural focus when it comes to understanding the relationship between the evil eye and personhood.

The various views promoted by ethnographic studies regarding personhood as culturally oriented are rather simplistic (Triandis 1995). The supposition that personhood is developed despite the cultural environment in which an individual grows up has been extensively attacked by Spiro (1993), who argues that the concept of personhood is not developed individually but is in fact a combination of the self and cultural ideologies.

Ever since Mauss (1983), anthropologists have been confronted with the difficult task of identifying the ways through which a person develops a self. Within that spectrum, I lean mostly towards Bloch's (2011) argument, in which he talks about the notion of a 'blob' in his attempt to define the self. The blob, according to Bloch, refers to the narrative self and how it is linked with autobiographical memories and the meta-representations of self in others. The idea of the blob therefore supports the theory that there is an interconnected network in which we all deposit our collective memories and relationalities. Like other scholars before him, Bloch is interested in understanding the development of self through the tendency that some individuals have to project themselves to others. Bloch is greatly influenced by the philosopher Strawson (1999), who argues that people talk about their psychical and physical states based on their relational style and their understanding of 'blobs' ('selves', 'I', 'person'), which have been influenced by their culture and history. Bloch (2011) based his theory on his fieldwork in Malagasy villages, and suggests that individuals are in touch with their psychical states through their understanding of both their culture and other people. This argument is in accord with my contention about the evil eye, and supports the idea of understanding the evil eye and its manifestations through the attempt to understand the development of personhood. Therefore, similarly to Bloch, I seek to interpret the collected data regarding the evil eye and personhood through the relational notion of personhood.

The contribution of cultural anthropologists to the understanding of personhood among Orthodox Christian traditions and cultures remains limited even today. Stewart's (1998) theories, however, represent a landmark in relational aspects between cultural ethnography and personhood, based on his fieldwork on Naxos Island on the Aegean coast. He highlights the important role that tradition plays in the process of developing personhood, while examining the effects of this process on an individual's relationship with the other. Following Stewart, this chapter examines the Greek Orthodox tradition in the region of Corfu in an attempt to understand whether the evil eye appears to affect the development of personhood.

On the other hand, other ethnographers and anthropologists, such as Whitehouse (2004), apply cognitive theories in their attempts to understand personhood among Orthodox Christian societies. This approach actually ends in a dichotomy between the beliefs and the imaginary states of a person's being; therefore, I do not support these cognitive theories as a process for understanding the link between the evil eye. Whitehouse also describes personhood according to her findings from fieldwork in Romania, a country with an important Orthodox Christian element; she maintains that it is more likely that personhood is developed through the influences received from others.

An interesting account that contradicts what I have explored so far in terms of personhood comes from Mauss (1983). Mauss uses the term 'persona' to describe personhood and maintains that the route to person-hood is through the different personas that an individual adopts during their lifespan. These personas are inherited from one generation to the next and are probably reincarnated and expressed through folk beliefs. Mauss was interested in antiquity and personhood, stating that during the classical period, and more specifically in the Roman Empire, personhood had become a set of social roles. Mauss's views on personhood have some bearing on the Christian understanding the concept, which stipulates that it needs to be seen through its indivisibility and that this stems from the nature of the Trinity; it is in this context that Corfiots place the evil eye. Tonia suggests that *matiasma* (the evil eye) is possession through the eye. For Tonia, possession is undivided from its culture: 'I do not think that I would experience the same symptoms if I was not Corfiot. The symptoms that I experience are closely related not only to my spirit but also in relation to my body and my whole existence'. Tonia continues:

The evil eye is like a clear glass through which I can see myself as a whole – spirit, body and agency. However, the glass is in between me and myself and only through some self-exploration would that glass break. Besides, glass is a liquid with very slow movement, and therefore if we think symbolically, water represents emotions, and through that glass emotions are regulated with great difficulty. The evil eye, therefore, becomes a greater reminder that I need to give further consideration to my trinity (body, soul and agency). Every single time, the symptoms reflect where I lack self-awareness of body, soul or agency, and hence I experience different symptoms at different times of my life. Nikos, the evil eye is not a singular phenomenon, but in fact has three major components that you need to look at and explore. That is who we are since the beginning; we learn to be like that from generation to generation.

Tonia highlights here the importance of the indivisibility of the different facets of the phenomenon, and the fact that only through its tripartite nature can it be understood. She also makes a connection between personhood and the transhistorical heritage that human beings share, but highlights the importance of the other in developing a sense of personhood.

In contrast, Hallowell (1955) argues that for many years, he has seen personhood as separate from its culture, but as having generic attributes. In fact, he proposes that personhood is universal to humans and is an important element for social functioning. However, he develops his thinking further, suggesting that personhood cannot exist outside a cultural environment and that personhood and culture are interconnected. In other words, he points out that personhood is constituted in a community, and a community consists of group(s) of individual personhoods.

During the years since Hallowell's work, a significant amount of research has been conducted regarding the different understandings and perceptions of personhood. Markus and Kitayama (1991) promoted two models to explain personhood from an ethnographic point of view. The first is the independent model, in which personhood is developed through the experiences of the uniqueness and individuality of each human being having their own internal attributes. Conversely, the interdependent self model highlights the importance of the relational aspect of developing personhood and the importance that the society plays in witnessing the development of personhood. They conclude by stating that personhood depends on the interplay between independent and interdependent models. They therefore emphasise the importance of the effect that culture has in the process of developing personhood, but also the significant role that self-awareness plays in that journey. Despite their thorough research, their models have attracted a lot of criticism due to their lack of theoretical clarity, which leads to an understanding of personhood that remains inadequate. Spiro (1993) – an

American cultural ethnographer and anthropologist – extensively criticises Markus and Kitayama's models of personhood, and proposes that culture and society are not necessarily manifested in someone's journey towards developing personhood.

One of the most important findings about personhood comes from Morris (1994) and his extensive research in Malawi. He reveals that personhood can be classified in three elements. Firstly, personhood can be seen as the manifestation of human being. Morris goes further, explaining that human beings are the embodied manifestation of their consciousness, while at the same time they are social beings with agency composed of morals, ethics and linguistic abilities. The second element of personhood that he proposes is the idea of personhood as culture; this element appears to be more inclusive that the first one. It describes personhood in an ecclesia; personhood is thus affected by its ecology. Finally, Morris suggests that the third element of personhood is that it is different to others; he thus supports the idea that personhood is developed through the differentiation of one's self from otherness.

I am in agreement with Rasmussen's (2008) suggestion that personhood is influenced by the cultural and social settings in which an individual lives and with which they interact. Rasmussen also argues that without examining the influence and the effects of culture and society upon individuals, it would be challenging to talk about personhood, as although personhood is an individual construction, it is based on relationships with others. She argues that personhood expands beyond local relationships, and that it is necessary to consider existential matters in order to better understand it. Moore (1996), however, suggests that a culturally bound investigation of personhood can only bring confusion, and that therefore a multidisciplinary approach needs to be adopted. It can be concluded that there is a vast amount of research on the concept of personhood from an ethnographic perspective, especially through data stemming from Asia, Africa and Oceania. However, the literature reveals that there has been limited research on the relationship between the evil eye and personhood within Greek Orthodox regions. This study suggests that there are two major aspects that need to be addressed when discussing cultural anthropology. First of all, until recently, ethnographers and anthropologists grouped Eastern cultures together, viewing them all as 'non-Western' and thereby failing to identify the variety and particular characteristics of different regions. Secondly, as Said (1978) maintains, cultural ethnographers tend to see non-Western cultures as 'the rest' and assign to them static qualities. The division that therefore appears between the West and 'the rest' – wherein the West is mostly monolithic in its understanding of personhood as a process of individuation – is that 'the rest' focuses mostly on society and culture. Because of these complexities, the present study not only approaches the relationship between the evil eye and personhood from an ethnographic point of view, it also investigates the marriage of such disciplines through the lens of a philosophical understanding of personhood.

PHILOSOPHICAL UNDERSTANDINGS OF PERSONHOOD

While cultural anthropology and ethnography focus on the importance of culture in the development of self, philosophy pays particular attention to the elements, experiences, feelings and thoughts that separate one person from another (Thiel 2011). Contemporary debate engages with the notion of personhood as a philosophical matter, without however indulging in its relational aspects. Therefore, from a philosophical point of view, personhood is often interpreted either as different levels of consciousness based on an individual's ecology, or as an agency which informs someone's decisions and choices (Sorabji 2006; Thiel 2011). Within the realms of philosophical metaphysics, personhood is identified as immaterial substance (Cory 2013). In addition to an ethnographic view, this study also aims to take a philosophical and metaphysical approach to the phenomenon of the evil eye and the development of personhood, in order to examine the relationship that the evil eye might have with the development of the immaterial substance of the self.

In line with the existing literature on the subject, it is important to mention the statements, from philosophers ranging from Descartes to William James, that personhood can only be described using the first person. However, when examining the metaphysics of personhood we see that the use of the third person signifies only the researcher's tendency to objectify their understanding of 'personhood' (Gaynesford 2006; Brower-Toland 2012). Therefore, the present study opposes Gaynesford's (2006) understanding and objectification of personhood and follows the traditional philosophical view of the phenomenon through the characteristic of the identity of the self (Dennett 2016). In other words, this study adopts the view that personhood might be formed through the exhibition of the self to another, while the quality of the discourse and conduct of the self belongs to the individual who exhibits these elements of the self. Therefore, adopting this definition of self and placing it within a cultural setting, this study aims to explore the interaction between the evil eye and the development of self through the gaze of the other. I engage with the relationality of personhood through others' eyes (mirrors), which can cause the evil eye.

Morris (1994) approaches the philosophical quest for personhood in a holistic manner. He differs from the above scholars, stating that approaching personhood with a singular view of the phenomenon does not add to our understanding of it, but rather confuses the issue. For this reason, he proposes that personhood is a combination of culture, embodiment and otherness. To be more precise, he suggests that personhood has an embodied consciousness, which allows the individual to fit in with social norms but also enables the experience of one's self through the body. In addition, he states that personhood is born from a unity, and therefore that it is formed in relation to the cultural elements in which it is manifested. Lastly, personhood is the ability to individuate through interaction with others and allow space for the 'I' to form through others' reflection, without being absorbed by others. Father Ionas, a priest in his early sixties, spoke about this:

> Many of the believers who approach me in regard to the evil eye suffer from different symptoms. Sometimes I do not think that my studies prepared me to deal with something so complicated as the evil eye. When people are possessed with it I see a battle, a battle that can destroy people because it is challenging the fundamental elements of their existence. Most of the time, what I experience through my discussion with the possessed believers is a battle between the need to be a person, a person close to God, and the fear of being dissolved into society. The symptoms, according to my experience, start when they are afraid to allow themselves to be independent, to find their own truth, and to connect with God, even though that is what they need, they become however part of the mass identity. In a way, possession with the evil eye creates some kind of an oasis in their internal torture to stop and see themselves, understand themselves, and decide what they want to do in regard to who they are as Christians. During these times, the evil eye is a product of a relationship with the society, but also the other(s) that allows them to see themselves.

Within such an understanding of personhood, the question that emerges is what roles the 'I' and others play in the formation of personhood.

This chapter analyses further the findings of the fieldwork, through the philosophical understanding of personhood as portrayed by Frankfurt (1971), who argues that personhood is defined as the individual's need to be in touch with their existential desires. In this chapter I therefore discuss the idea of personhood in an attempt to pinpoint the effects of the evil eye in developing an individual's ability to identify with their desires as expressed through the reflection of the self via the gaze of others. However, despite Frankfurt's attempt to define personhood, it seems that he pays less attention to its relationship with reason. To bridge this gap, it is helpful to refer to Raz (2011), who maintains that in order for individuals to develop personhood, there must be a reason for this development, and that individuals reach personhood when they are acknowledged by others. Raz emphasises the importance of recognition and acknowledgement in the development of individual personhood, and this study supports this idea of recognition in regard to the formation of personhood through the evil eye. However, Raz's conception of personhood incorporates two fundamental ideas that oppose the view of its relational aspects: the first is his suggestion that the development of personhood is linked to the necessary separation between an individual and their environment; and the second is his suggestion that personhood promotes an internal dialogue stemming from the external and internal experiences that are experienced differently for each individual. However, the philosophical understanding of personhood pays little attention to the individual's relational consciousness, as described in the Gospel of St John: 'Whoever does not love does not know God, because God is love' (I John 4:8). This suggests that human beings are relational souls, and that it is through relationships that we derive meaning from our existence; personhood develops as we live in a community (Plass and Cofield 2014). I adopt St John's view in the interpretation of the evil eye and personhood, while maintaining a critical philosophical and ethnographic view.

Considering the various interpretations of personhood from both philosophical and ethnographic perspectives, this study aims to provide a different account to the Western theories of individual personhood; that is to say, that personhood is dependent on culture and on the individual's ecology. The approach taken here sees personhood as not only promoting individuation, but also as the development of an individual self within its own boundaries and frame, yet within a system and in relation to that system (Said 1978). However, the discussion in the present chapter does not engage in the debate on different views of self between the West and other regions, but rather promotes the concept that personhood is in constant interaction with the culture and ecology in which the individual lives.

The challenge is not to oversimplify the influences from the culture with regard to personhood and the evil eye. Corfu does not appear to promote an individualistic culture governed by individuals apart from the society in which they operate, whose goal is to become independent of any social norms and systems. If that were the case, the relational phenomenon of the evil eye would not have any significance. However, after the financial crisis in 2008, there was a societal shift which affected individuals' sense of self. This shift included the development of different values, affecting the concepts of self-agency and personhood. Therefore, keeping in mind the concept of self, the following discussion examines what might be known so far in terms of the current understanding of personhood, as observed in the field.

Father Alexios pointed to the importance of the Trinity in understanding the evil eye and personhood. He suggested that the evil eye is a sign which testifies that individuals are distancing themselves from the Holy Ghost: 'Those who are acting through the Holy Spirit have nothing to fear, as Satan would not be able to find a vessel to act upon the earth through his manipulations to cause harm through the evil eye'. He went further and maintained that the evil eye can be understood through its ultimate damage, which is death, 'the absolute telos'. Faithful Christians approach Father Alexios, asking him to cast the evil eye from them and feeling:

> a sense of pointless existence; they come to me and say that they have the evil eye; they feel as though nothing has meaning anymore, and they are scared of the absolute internal void. Some from my congregation say that they have the evil eye when they socialise with those who are not as faithful as them; then they feel that what they see in these others is something dark, something that can absorb their own existence. They say that when they start feeling bad from having the evil eye, it is as though someone has planted something bad in them, something that they cannot recognise, and which brings them chaos, darkness.

Father Alexios is suggesting here that the evil eye stems from the individual's death drive, the drive that Yannaras (2006, 2012a) would describe as Thanatos or telos. This drive is deeply implanted in the human psychical existence and causes dysfunction or self-destructiveness. On the other hand, Father Alexios argued that the Holy Spirit does not make human beings all the same; in fact, Trinitarian theology, as described by Yannaras (2006), promotes person-centred ethnographic theology. Yannaras (2004) proposes two models within Trinitarian ontology. The first is uniformity, which derives from what he suggests as a form of nature, and the second is individuation as a form of freedom. Therefore, as the current study argues, the self within its freedom form is in constant relationship with the Son and the Spirit and highlights the divine relationship with the Father. Yannaras' Trinitarian ontology promotes the development of self through the consciousness of otherness and others.

Father Alexios expanded his thinking, stating that the evil eye is part of person-centred ethnography and can be seen in a theological context because Christian ethnography is relational, as Yannaras (2012) would argue. The evil eye, therefore, is an ontological construction of human existence, as the eye ('I') is a fundamental element of the *prosopo* (πρόσωπο, or face). Therefore, 'the evil eye is the absolute mirror of the sufferer's soul';

> The symptoms are not all the same because the evil eye reflects back the uniqueness of the sufferer, whether good or bad, and hence it expresses an onto-

logical and existential understanding of the individual, as dissimilar from any other; each one is an unrepeatable subject in relation to others and to God.

According to Father Alexios, this is what personhood actually is, and this is closely related to the mirror element of the evil eye; and as Frankfurt (1971) suggests, personhood is a unique construct of the individual's understanding of their existential anxieties and desires. Here, Father Alexios indicates the importance of the individual being in touch with their own existential image as transmitted by the evil eye. The evil eye therefore forces the sufferer to face the existential anxieties of goodness and badness, which can create an internal void. The witnessing of that existential void can lead to petrification, and then the evil eye becomes a threatening phenomenon. Maria, a mental health professional and a devoted Christian who often suffers from the evil eye, confesses that:

> The evil eye is the royal pathway to my absolute self through the witnessing from others; despite the fact that I am in pain and I experience very painful symptoms, I cannot deny the fact that it is through the evil eye that I emerge. I feel alive; I exist and flourish through connection with the otherness. If it was not for the evil eye, I would not be able to confront and be in touch with my dark side. This is the side that I have hidden so deep and blinded myself to for many years, because it was not 'socially acceptable' as my mother would say. Through the symptoms that I experience, the evil eye takes me deep to where I have hidden all the bad me. It does that as this bad me comes through the other's eye through the witnessing of me; then I can see this part of me that I am scared of and own it. I know it sounds simple, and I am sure that you do not believe what I am saying, or think that I am naive, but I can assure you that the realisation that I have when I am possessed with the evil eye brings me in front of a self that was not known to me. Through the rituals and the afterwork that I am doing with that new self, I can say now that I have a sense of who I am; I exist.

Maria is suggesting here that the evil eye is a tool through which we can start to know ourselves through others. Her testimony is significant, in that personhood cannot exist by itself, but only in communion with the community to which we belong and to which we witness. There is no coherent self without reference to the other, a fact which actually supports the views of Strawson (2005) and Kuper (1999) that self cannot be seen in separation from its social setting and culture. However, Maria's narrative links ethnographic understandings of self with what Bloch (2011) describes as the meta-representation of self in others, which is then reflected back through witnessing and the evil eye. This chapter therefore promotes an ontological relationality which appears to be fuelled through the phenomenon of the evil eye, bringing to the surface one's personhood in relation to others and to the universe.

'My parents used to tell me that it is rude to stare at someone because it might make the other person feel bad and give them the evil eye', a 23-year-old informant stated. What we have here is clear avoidance of developing a direct contact with the real other. Further exploration of this statement led to the understanding that the avoidance of the gaze of the real other was propelled by internal anxiety and the fear that the self might be mirrored back by the other; 'the other person that you look at might feel bad about themselves because of your look; you don't know what they might think about your look'. In this circumstance, the evil eye functions as an agency of opposition, which maintains that if human beings do not know anything about the fear of being witnessed, they have a faint idea of their personhood. The evil eye then becomes a scapegoat for our own fear of personhood through acceptance of our relational need to be witnessed by the other(s). In the depiction of the evil eye as a quest for personhood, the 'I' of others becomes the mirror through which the individual's personhood becomes not impossible, but traumatic and sinister, as it sheds light on the hidden parts of our self. The fieldwork data indicates that encountering the sense of self through the 'other' challenges us with the primitive and raw feeling of vulnerability and anxiety about human existence, because we are being watched. Thus, anything that threatens human nature is often avoided in favour of a more idealistic abstraction of humanity. However, to understand personhood, its real dimensions need to be debated. 'The evil eye comes from outside to show us a damaged picture of ourselves. We need to be brave and get the courage to face that image in order to start developing the essence of our personhood'. The 35-year-old informant quoted here had thought through his personal experience of the evil eye in a way that re-evaluates what Buber (2002, 2004) and Ricoeur (2005) refer to as the conflictual nature of personhood. Kristeva (1991) supports the informants' narratives about personhood and the evil eye, emphasising the human tendency to demonise the other's gaze, which reflects the internal process whereby we avoid direct contact with any internal foreigner. The evil eye, therefore, becomes the agency through which we transcend the projection of the evil foreigner.

In order to develop personhood, the informants suggested that human beings need to be in relationship. There is no possibility of establishing a genuine and true personhood unless 'we are in communion with others and experience our own existence and form through the others' eyes', Father Andreas stated. He was also opposed to Nussbaum (1994), who suggests that personhood is formed purely by developing a relationship with one's self, independently of culture or community. However, Father Andreas and other informants argued that there is always a temptation to see the self as a separate entity from the community. These conversations introduced the idea that it is impossible to develop a relationship with one's self in which a good understanding of self is acquired without first interacting with others; the true self is reflected through these others. 'We cannot talk about personhood without considering the fact that we are born from a relation in order to be in a relationship', Father Andreas maintained. What Nussbaum (1994), Zimmerman (1981) and Hadot (1995) propose therefore pays no heed to the relationality of personhood; rather, they focus on the individuation of self through the separation from the 'other' and the self's ability to survive alone. This idea can only be sustained by ignoring the fundamental human need to be seen. In other words, what the above scholars suggest is the insignificance of intersubjective space where two or more individuals come together to create a new reality and a deeper understanding of self. One might query why there is a desire to take the individual out of their natural environment, the relationship, to develop personhood. Christopher Bollas (1987), in his book *The Shadow of the Object*, highlights the idea of the objectified self through identification with others. The need for such a philosophical statement to distinguish between individualisation and individuation might stem from the very simple, but extremely meaningful, statement of Kerkyra, a Christian informant in her early thirties:

> I am not sure what to say here; I think that the evil eye cannot be seen outside my family's tradition. It would not be me if I was seen outside my upbringing. I do not understand how anyone can start talking about the 'self' without talking about the past, the present, the family, the history and the culture. The evil eye is part of that ecosystem, which, as someone, I belong to. The evil eye is nothing other than a shared culture that reminds us of who we are; a culture or phenomenon, if you wish, that shows us who we really are. If you dig deeper to understand what the evil eye really is, you will see that it is our common culture, which we share by living in it. It also reflects who we are, and sometimes gives us a nasty image of who we are; at other times, it gives a more positive image. Those who believe the evil eye has nothing to do with the sense of who we are and who is separate from our culture, are just scared of their past; they are scared, because judging from me, they might be insecure in their own skin. They might have an insecure sense of their personhood.

Indeed, this statement might apply here, as fear of allowing the self to identify with the other, and with the ecology, is due to the fear that encompasses the eye ('I'). There is also the possibility that it might bring to the forefront the fundamental anxiety of surrendering to the other's objectification, imagination and identification; all of this can bring confusion to the sense of personhood. It is important therefore to explore the evil eye and its association with the agentic elements of self as related to the inner and outer.

SELF: INNER AND OUTER AGENCY

Corfu can be considered a unique location in Greece, where East meets West; and, of course, these influences can be observed in the understanding and construction of the self. There are two different constructions of the self that were observed in the field: the self-I and the self-Me. However, to avoid any confusion, it is necessary to explore these two different approaches to the self in order to understand them better. The first can be interpreted as the inner agency and the second as the outer agency. The inner is the agent of action and seeks to be acknowledged in order to declare its existence through the other's reflection, while the outer is the accusative 'me', which develops a sense of personhood through the other's mirrors. The self-concept is therefore bound to both selves, inner and outer. However, I do not wish to imply that these distinctions are universally adopted; rather, it suggests that the self can be developed through two different functions, the inner self and the outer self.

Maria, a young informant, shed some new light on this, stating: 'I do not want to be subjected to others' eyes and be constantly worrying about whether I will be cast with the evil eye or not. I think and try to remind myself that myself belongs to me'. The confusion comes when Johnson (1985) suggests that the outer self contains society within it. In other words, the self as an outer self is part of the projection of the social self onto others in the attempt to define itself; but it is also an introjection of the self in order to develop a sense of personhood. The evil eye has become a complex phenomenon because it combines both these self-attributions. In the process of developing personhood, the evil 'I' (eye) refers to one's action in developing a sense of self through self-perception, but also to the action upon which the perceived self is projected out to be witnessed. George, a Corfiot in his mid-thirties, pointed out that sometimes he is able to find out more about himself through the look of others and the way he is seen; through the evil eye he is able to understand what others reveal about him. In addition, in the actions of the evil eye, the process which one undergoes in order to be defined as a person with a social image is conventionalised, and this is collectively perceived through the gaze of others. However, sometimes the image that is perceived is not the one that the person wants to project, as one young priest argued. This discrepancy can lead to the phenomenon of the evil eye, and anxiety can find soil in which to grow.

However, even though the Corfiots engage with the phenomenon of the evil eye in order to develop a sense of personhood through its duality as outer and inner, they also ask questions that have so far remained unanswered about the self as the knower of itself. Katerina states that even though she knows herself through her reflection by others, when she is by herself she becomes anxious, because her own self is bound up with the others and their gaze leaves her with the feeling that 'I don't know who I really am without the others; when I am alone I feel empty, as if I do not know myself; it is an empty moment'. Katerina is proposing a fundamental idea of the self that either knows or does not know itself; this is similar to the dualism in Confucianism. A self should be able to be seen when alone; however, for this to happen, two functions are required, the self as an outer agent and the self as an inner agent. Graham (1989) – concurring with Hsu (1963) – points out that the two self-attributes should not be seen as two different selves, but rather as the self that is unified in its capacity as the knower. Therefore, engaging in a debate about the self as inner versus outer agents would lead nowhere. Father Andreas stated that the self is not made up of pieces that fight against each other, but rather pieces that complement each other in order to create an image. Yannaras (2006, 2012b) would argue here that according to the Trinitarian ontological understanding of the self, in order to reach spiritual healing and construction of self, all the elements or attributes of self should live in harmony, rather than being at war. Approaching the self as an outer or inner agent within a social construct thus detracts from the process of creating a self. The evil eye then becomes something negative, rather than a process which brings us into unity with ourselves. Kerkira, a devoted Christian who has spent most of her life serving the common good, stated in her attempt to explain personhood through the evil eye that 'Most of the time I believed that the evil eye was nothing more than the self using the eyes to look at the I'.

The Corfiots' understanding of personhood regards its attributions (inner and outer) as a hindrance that needs to be surmounted in order to lead individuals to a deeper consciousness where they can be closer to the transcendent. Rao (1988) argues that the transcendent is where self-inner and self-outer meet and cease to exist separately. In that space, where the self is neither inner nor outer agents, personhood is absent and the self as the knower starts to emerge (Crook and Rabgyas 1988). In a similar manner to Crook and Rabgyas and to the Corfiots' understanding of the effect of the evil eye on personhood, Paranjpe (1988) suggests that within that trans-cognitive space where two eyes meet and produce a no-thought zone in which individuals start to experience different symptoms, there is no dichotomy between the known and the knower. Within that no-thought zone, individuals are confronted with the fear of losing self-boundaries: Tonia, a folk healer in her mid-forties, said, 'When I have the evil eye it is like I am losing myself; I merge with the one who has cast the evil eye. I always know who cast the evil eye because of that feeling. It is not a pleasant one and feels like I need to fight for my existence'. Tonia's statement is another example of the complexity of the evil eye. Sampson (1988) maintains that when the eyes meet, the self and non-self come together and threaten an individual's personhood. This threat is culturally and individually subjective, so each culture and each individual needs to be examined separately in order to better understand the phenomenon (Sampson 1989). In this approach, further engagement with the agentic elements in relation to the evil eye is important.

FURTHER ANALYSIS ON INNER AND OUTER AGENTS AS SEEN THROUGH THE EVIL EYE

Tonia, a Christian in her late fifties, revealed in her narrative that:

> Sometimes, when I am possessed with the evil eye, I lose the sense of me; I don't know where I start and where I finish. I feel like a person with no personality and I think that others during these moments are not taking me seriously; it is like I am not being listened to; it is like I am part of the furniture in the room. The evil eye for me is an experience from which I lose what I know as self to find myself through the others.

In fact, we are talking here about the painful element of the outer agent of personhood through identification with the narrative of others, in an attempt to develop a sense of personhood. Here, I do not completely agree with the self-objectification theory, which proposes that objectification is the behaviour or attitude towards someone in which the individual is treated as an object which can be manipulated in order to develop certain sense of personhood (McKinley 2011; Bartky 1990). On the other hand, I agree with Nussbaum's (1995) second and third definitions of objectification of self, in which personhood lacks self-boundaries and a sense of agency. The fieldwork reveals that there is a constant need to look for transformative others with whom we can live in symbiotic harmony; it is this which allows personhood to develop and which can also allow it to metamorphose. However, negative past experience(s), especially those related to our own initial carers, might cause difficulty in working towards individuation in the relationship, and may create a desire to individuate in separation from the other, as a misconception of the self as an object which is at the disposal of other(s) might have developed. Sandra, a Christian in her mid-thirties and a mental health nurse, told me:

> The evil eye for me is a slap in the face. It reminds me of feelings and experiences that I would never be able to retrieve from my past. These are painful experiences and memories, or at least, that is how I recall them. The symptoms that I have when I have the evil eye remind me of something familiar, even though it is painful. When I get the evil eye, I lose my sense of subjectivity. I feel like I become someone else's object. The reflection that I get when I look at the symptoms of the evil eye are something like a distant memory; something that is weird, even though I can see that I am looked at, and even though I can feel that I exist. At the same time, I feel that I am not me, but I am part of someone else's subjective experience. The person who always came to mind when I had these symptoms was my mother, so I started asking to find out whether there was something I did not know, or did not remember, about my early upbringing. Finally, it was my grandmother who told me that when I was a baby, my mother engaged with me through her own understanding of how a mother should be. My grandmother also told me that my mother made me a perfect baby; I did not cry or demand anything. The sensations that I get through the evil eye seem familiar with what my grandmother described as a 'perfect baby'.

Winnicott (1965) argues that there is no such thing as a baby in separation from its mother; a baby exists in relationship with the mother. To some extent, that is what this chapter proposes; similarly to Winnicott's idea regarding the baby, there is no self-existence without the other.

Now that we have begun to examine the problem of personhood when it comes to the 'I' and the fear of being seen, the question remains as to the meaning of being seen that is attached to the evil eye, and of whether the phenomenon does indeed contain elements of 'I' or 'self'. Undoubtedly, the evil eye plays a fundamental role, but how is personhood manifested through it? And is it even possible to examine personhood through the evil eye without in fact altering its primitive givenness? So far, what the literature reveals – although it is not necessarily supported by the fieldwork in Orthodox Christian Corfu – is that personhood within an Orthodox Christian society can indeed be examined phenomenologically through the phenomenon of the evil eye, without any negativity towards the latter. It is important at this stage to expand upon some current theories of personhood in order to be able to further unravel this phenomenon, starting with the tripartite theory of personhood as revealed in the fieldwork.

THE EVIL EYE AND ITS TRIPARTITE STRUCTURE OF PERSONHOOD

Despite other approaches that could be taken to understand the phenomenon, what emerged from the fieldwork was the tripartite structure of personhood: world, self and others. These three elements are closely interrelated and are associated with the evil eye. Costas, an informant in his late forties, said:

> Sometimes when I get the evil eye I am not sure what to make of it. There is a strong sense of separateness from my own self. My self seems not to exist and in addition to that I feel like I have no connection with my surroundings. I feel as if I cannot be understood, and that no one can see me as I really am. During these moments I need to make a double effort to be able to feel present and another effort not to be misunderstood. The worst for me is when I experience all the symptoms of the evil eye as a disconnection with my own environment, as if I do not belong. I start experiencing the symptoms badly when I feel that I do not belong. There is a sense of me wanting to be present to belong, and when I am not properly seen, I feel like I do not exist.

Costas' narrative about the symptoms and feelings he experiences because of the evil eye is linked to a theory proposed by Metzinger (2003), who in his book *Being No One* discusses the idea of conscious personhood. Metzinger comes to the conclusion towards the end of the book that it is a mistake to talk about personhood alone, as being separate from the world; indeed, he maintains, there is no such thing as developing personhood. Personhood, he argues, is rather a social construct designed to make sense of the projected self in the external environment. He continues by stating that whenever personhood is referred to, it is more likely a reference to the projected self, rather than an existential entity that human beings cannot comprehend. Human beings, therefore, are nothing more than operational processing systems; personhood is thus mistakenly taken as an existential entity instead of a cognitive self-representation. Costas and other informants argued that every individual is indeed part of the self that is projected to the external environment, but with a unique internal substance. However, this study also proposes that the sense of belonging to the environment comes after the disconnection from the internal sense of self. Sandra, in her mid-twenties, said:

> A sense that feels like I am nothing; a sense that it feels as if I am not me; I have no substance as a human being. Most of the time when I have the evil eye it is like I cannot understand my body, or that it is dissolved in space. My physical space is disappearing, which then allows me to emerge in order not to stop existing.

In a way, Sandra is suggesting that even though personhood is part of the world, it is at the same time an existential element that starts from within, and it is highlighted when threatened by the evil eye. Costas and Sandra emphasise the importance of self as a singular element within the social ecology. Sandra's experience of the evil eye as a threat to her physical boundaries, as well as her engagement with the experience of the evil eye as promoting self-emergence, supports Ricoeur's (1992) view that personhood is not just about making sense of the experience, but stems from a rather primitive need for a deep existential engagement with the experience. In other words, Ricoeur indicates that personhood is not static, but something that constantly undergoes metamorphosis through interaction with the other – a suggestion that agrees with the overall argument of my research. Following this view, one can conclude that personhood is not as transparent as we may wish; rather, it is a complex phenomenon that requires careful consideration and understanding of the environment in which it develops.

Stamos, in one of our discussions about the evil eye, responded to my question of how he thought the evil eye contributes to the development of personhood through its possession by replying:

> My grandmother kept telling me that the evil eye is a nasty thing and I should be careful not to engage in activities that would make me stand out. As a child, I could not understand why. I still remember wanting to be different and to be seen; it was my attempt to make my parents acknowledge me. I wanted to be like them. Back then, it was like I was existing through their acknowledgement, but such acknowledgement did not come without cost. When I realised that I had substance in the world, I would fall ill. My grandmother kept telling me it was the eye ['I'] I could not believe that my own parents could give me the eye, but it was true. It was later, as an adult, that I realised that the evil eye is nothing bad, but rather my own anxiety of being existentially present and confronted with my absent false self. When someone noticed me I felt threatened, because I was not on good terms with myself. I felt uncomfortable when I was acknowledged, because I could sense that they could see my blind spots and were reflecting them to me through the eye. When I was working with myself through my therapy, I realised that it was indeed my attempt to define myself, but despite my attempts to do that internally, I could not fully embrace myself unless I was exposed to the external environment and could therefore see my reflection holistically.

He continued:

> What I have learned in my life is that I react to the story that I tell myself about myself. I therefore become the story; I learned how to be a child based on the story that my parents told me. Then, in school, I was the story that the teachers

wanted me to have, and later on, I became the ethics that Corfu wanted me to live. But what was common throughout was my outermost need to be seen. This worked as my link with who I was, or who I really am, seeing myself through others; no matter how scary it is for me, it reminds me of myself.

What Stamos describes here is his understanding of personhood through the narratives that he has adopted. It was common practice in Corfu for individuals to conceive personhood through certain narratives in their lives, and there was a deeper need to share these narratives with others in order to build a more coherent understanding of personhood. Therefore, personhood does not exist by itself, but together with the other; personhood is a product of a linguistic and existential union. What Stamos argues again supports Ricoeur's (1990) ideas about personhood, and its constant metamorphosis through engagement either with the narrative or with the experience of self through others' reflection through their mirror eye.

The current study furthermore suggests that personhood is not just the narratives born out of union with existential and linguistic communities, but that it is in fact a real givenness in a person's life through experiential expositions. Phenomenologists like Damasio (2010) focus on the experience that constitutes personhood. Damasio thus maintains that it is the experience that reveals personhood as one's property or being; personhood, therefore, is something that is not simply perceived, but requires a background where the individual can reflect and better comprehend the experience of personhood (Damasio 2010; Zahavi 2008; Shaun and Zahavi 2010). The findings of the current study suggest that the evil eye becomes the field on which individuals play out their own need for developing mine-ness, and to an extent understand the meaning of being. Father Andreas says that:

> in many cases of the evil eye, I was facing individuals who were lost; they could not find meaning in their own theology. 'I' was nothing more than an empty vessel which was looking for an eye to show them their shape. However, the evil eye was a cruel realisation that personhood cannot be reached independently but only in communion with others. In a sense, the evil eye possesses the individual in order to force them to look inwards and engage them in a quest to find themselves after the external triggers.

Father Andreas suggests here that the evil eye becomes an imperative element in someone's conscious life through interaction with the 'I' and the 'other' in the quest for personhood. Due to the subtle reflectivity of personhood in the arena of being seen through the eye, the eye becomes evil, because there is no explicit awareness of personhood; therefore, anything outside the individual understanding of the supposed personhood experience is threatening. Bermúdez (1998) suggests that there is no personhood without reflexivity; personhood emerges when we stop being preoccupied, and therefore absorbed, in the experience, and start reflecting on the consciousness of personhood. To this notion, the fieldwork data adds that the facilitation of the reflexivity, and the termination of being absorbed in the moment, comes at times with the abrupt experience of the 'I', which was revealed as the presence or possession of the evil eye and otherness. Personhood therefore has a connection with otherness as it is manifested through the evil eye; this is engaged with in the following section.

THE EVIL EYE AND ITS RELATIONSHIP WITH PERSONHOOD AND OTHERNESS

Who would create the space for the 'I' to be experienced if there were no 'others', one informant asked? This was a question that I pondered during my time in the field. The 'I' of the others, according to the informants, embraces existential and philosophical conceptions of personhood. Therefore, otherness constitutes the fundamental idea of personhood. But what does otherness imply? I maintain that the theory of otherness is something unique, and that it is in fact a complex term that is involved in the process of acquiring personhood. Such uniqueness is not to be understood simply as a singular phenomenon, but one that is deeply anchored in witnessing, as stemming from the evil eye.

> The evil eye, I think, represents something unique that originates in the relationship that we have with the other ... the relationship is weird, as it creates pain, but it is also something that I cannot describe; something that I cannot put into words. When I am possessed with the evil eye, it makes me see myself as something special and unique, but also as something in relationship with my body and my whole existence; and part of it is the result of the fact that I am observed by others. It is then, I think, that with the help of the caster I can claim back my own personhood and sustain, if not eliminate, the symptoms. It is with the help of the caster that I can sustain what the eye mirrors see and accept my reflection.

This was the statement of a 49-year-old informant. It is something that cannot be put into words; the evil eye therefore becomes the product of the 'other', which is created within the relationship and works for the relationship in developing personhood. The 'other' becomes the process through which the individual starts to hypostasise the exact notion of personhood and elevate it to an agency that can sustain the pain of abandonment; yet it is also able to hold this notion without losing the feeling of existence. Therefore, the evil eye becomes the agency through which otherness is seen not as άλλο (other referring to an object), but rather as άλλος (other referring to a subject), according to the majority of the priests in Corfu. Otherness, in this case, becomes a person instead of nature. It appears that the above narrative links with the philosopher Leo Stan's (2017) attempt to engage with the idea of 'other' in the journey of discovering personhood. Stan engages with four different interpretations of otherness in the process of acquiring personhood. The current study agrees with two of these: first, the self as it is abandoned and in fact forgotten in an individual self, to the point that it becomes the other, and is reminded of this through the reflection of the self from the evil eye; and second, the otherness of the other as experienced through the subjective self as reflected by the evil eye. The evil eye, therefore, becomes the agency through which otherness is now actualised through a person. A priest commented:

> I wonder whether the evil eye and its painful manifestations have anything to do with the martyrdom to which we ascribe the evil eye. It seems to me that the evil eye is nothing more than an agency from which we come in touch with what is long forgotten and alienated, because we do not like it. It seems to me that it is the other aspects of self that we do not want to be in touch with, and in fact they are coming to the forefront through the experience of others, through the reflection of us by the evil eye.

Otherness can be morally challenging and painful, due to the fact that it is created from a relationship and not from the self; yet it facilitates the development of personhood. Thus, another's eye represents the ontological sense of self to those whom the eye sees. However, due to the phenomenological difficulty in comprehending the other as a general category, we cannot assume that the other's eye always represents such homeostasis. The evil eye appears to reinforce the relationship with otherness and the person's freedom to be an individual self. The evil eye highlights, through pain, the right of each person to be different; but it shows that they are also in communion with the other, even as they are at the same time separated from the other. In other words, we are defined through the other's mirror; personhood therefore emerges through relationship with the other. However, we might make the mistake here of interpreting otherness as individualism, when in fact it is not. The evil eye does not promote individualism, but rather a deep relationship with the other from which personhood and freedom to be oneself emerges; we constantly develop the sense of self through the mirrors of others. It is important to state that this deep relationship with the other can take two forms in relation to the evil eye: it can be a negative relationship through oversight, or a loving one through admiration. Positive relationships through admiration can stem from a loving partner, a parental carer or even a supporting friend or peer. They are not limited to any relationship role; both positive and negative relationships with the other, however, can trigger the phenomenon of the evil eye in an attempt to understand one's own personhood.

PERSONHOOD AND THE ESSENCE OF HUMAN EXISTENCE

A monk from the northern regions of Corfu stated that:

> We need to understand the evil eye well. We are talking about the essence of human existence, and not necessarily about the physicality of the phenomenon. The evil eye hits the essence of human existence, and that is probably the reason why we are confused and scared of it.

In the case of personhood and the evil eye, there is a certain conflict between what is deemed to be natural and what is seen as essential or general. The conflict that the evil eye represents here, between the essential and the physical, is the beginning of the existential tension that gives birth to personhood. The evil 'I' conflict is created through relationship. It is the relationship that brings the self to the forefront, as it is nurtured and integrated into the physicality of human existence; yet it is also the essence of it. To achieve personhood, it is therefore necessary to go through painful conflict, and the evil eye is the pathway to this. A 65-year-old informant asked:

> Have you ever wondered why we cannot understand the evil eye except through its social and physical manifestations? It is not just a phenomenon; it is a process through which we need to go to understand, to experience what it means, or what it feels [like], to shed light on very deep parts of our consciousness in order for the self to derive and become an actual self. It is only through the evil eye that we are in touch with the self experientially, and that we are able to embody the true self.

A discussion emerges from this journey into personhood concerning the meaning of self-definition. The aim is thus not to attain a universal truth of personhood, but rather to uncover a subjective understanding of it from an Orthodox Christian perspective and in relationship to the evil eye.

Sartre (1992) would argue that before making any attempt to define our own existence it is necessary to engage with the world – in order to understand our position within it – and also to engage in encounters with others. The other's gaze thus becomes an imperative stage, where the mirror eyes play a significant part in the later understanding of self – as an informant named Spiros argued. The evil eye, therefore, is not just a multifaceted phenomenon, but an existential one which negotiates our own element of personhood through interaction with the others' eyes. Spiros also stated:

> If we are not in a relationship with the other, how are we supposed to understand who we are? It is how I experience myself through others that allows me to understand my own existence as a person; otherwise, I would be haunting my own shadows in a cave, thinking that my shadows are in fact others when they are mine.

It is important to acknowledge that the gaze contains a phenomenological element of the experience of being exposed and 'seen' by others; therefore, the evil eye might be related to the significant psychological and spiritual elements of one's existence where fear is present. As one informant stated:

> Fear becomes part of who I really am; fear of being watched feels as if there is an empty vortex in me and others will be able to see nothing. It is easier for me to be loud, and you know what I mean by loudness; it will obstruct people from seeing who I really am. I do not know what is going on, but every time I think about it, eyes are coming into my mind. I cannot escape from them; it is as if they follow me everywhere, reminding me of that empty space that I do not know how to fill. Throughout my life I have tried to achieve things, and I managed well; but I lost happiness as I was achieving, so others could define me through my achievements and not for me; and then I was thinking that I do the same. Most of the time, there is malice in my gaze when others remind me of my behaviour, hiding behind the brightness, the loudness ... ! Quite often, I wonder what these symptoms are that I face when I cast or receive the evil eye; and most of the time, if not all the time, I conclude that I fear the others' eyes, and their ability to see me, to see me for who I am. Then I start to defend my very existence, by hiding or running away, departing more and more from myself. I feel at the end that there is nothing there for me, as if I have no presence.

What is it about the other's gaze that reflects our own existential nothingness? The gaze of the other is the ultimate beast that threatens our own existence. It feels precisely like the invasion of something utterly alien that terrorises our personhood into the intersubjective space. This study therefore supports the philosophical idea of scopophobia: the fear of being watched, the absolute dread of the evil 'I' (eye). Within that fear there is the sense of losing one's self and of being with no purpose, due to the fact that through the process of the evil eye, the 'I' is altered and transformed to self (Henelly 1998; Goffman 2010). The same informant stated:

> Sometimes I go back to my own childhood, remembering the circus in town and the room of mirrors ... that is how I would describe the evil eye; as a room of mirrors so terrifying that you cannot define yourself through the reflections. It is not the others that cause you all these symptoms, but the internal fear; at least, that is what I think; that it is caused by the confusion of the self through these reflections. The others just remind me that I do exist and that I have developed a distorted sense of self.

These reflections are transformed into grotesque distortions that put at stake one's sense of personhood. It is through the other's gaze that we uncannily recognise something of ourselves, and this can seize hold of us. When Maria was 6 years old, she could not recognise what she was seeing in the mirror, though she had no diagnosis of prosopagnosia. She said that her mother was always preoccupied with other things and that she was left feeling that she was a waste of time (existentially). She remembers her mother's eyes only when her mother was criticising her or was angry with her. Later in her life, she started to become scared of the gaze of the other because, somehow, she could see the reflection of her own 'wastedness'. One might ask what connection the evil eye has with the above description: it is the fear of being existentially absent that allows the evil eye to become something negative when bringing us closer to personhood. This chapter aims to demonstrate the association between the evil eye and the development of personhood, and the fieldwork revealed that even though there is fear attached to the evil eye, which causes certain symptomatology, the evil eye itself is part of the process of developing personhood. It allows the person to be in touch with existential anxieties, to develop a dialogue with them and to start developing a sense of self.

The interaction with the other's gaze through the evil eye is often described as a painful experience: of being locked in someone's eyes. This feeling caused some of the informants to experience a type of catatonic response, with a strong element of paralysis, during which there is no sense of self. This catatonic paralysis appeared in the narratives of many of the informants when a gaze was present: 'I feel as if I am frozen'; 'I can understand when there is the evil eye because I cannot move my body. It is like a heavy weight that does not allow me to move'. This frozen state is accompanied by the internal threat to one's own existence. One informant related that 'During that moment I do not know what is going on; it is like I am seeing myself from outside, as if I cannot recognise myself'. It can be concluded that the presence of gaze triggers fear. This fear can also be observed in the animal kingdom; lepidoptera often display eye patterns which scare off other animals by making them fear for their lives. In the same way, the evil eye can act as protection, rather than as an aggressive act of envy. Gaze can be employed when a person feels existentially threatened. There is an uneasiness when being watched, and the more someone feels it, the more anxious the person becomes; this was expressed by a female informant. Prolonged gaze can result in anxiety and intense feelings. Gaze, therefore, fosters negative responses through the subjective fear of being watched (Ayers 2003).

Further exploration led to an association between the subjective experience of being looked at and the lack of internal reference. A male informant maintained that when he is being looked at, it feels as if his body is turned into stone. What is it that makes the gaze so powerful that it can absorb the vitality of a person to the extent that they feel threatened with petrification? The phenomenon of the evil eye not only reflects the experience of defending one's own existence and the need to be watched; it also involves surrender to the unknown fear of the other's eye. Most of the informants felt as though there was no freedom in their surrender to the other's gaze. It was as if they were trying to be in touch with their paralysed selves: 'I was losing meaning of everything when I was paralyzed, from thinking that others are staring at me. I felt that I did not exist'. People said that they felt completely objectified by the gaze of others. Surrender to the eye removes responsibility from the individual and takes away their choice in the matter of becoming a person. 'It feels like I am stripped of ... I am stripped of my own skin'. The informants' stories regarding the phenomenon of being overlooked are consistent with their sociocultural norms. The subject of the evil eye has now become an object without being; this is the attempt of the individual to avoid the journey of personhood.

At the outset of this chapter, I proposed that personhood requires acknowledgement of the cultural construction of a person, which could hold importance for both soma and soul. On this point, it is important to highlight that personhood derives from a strong transcultural construction. In a way, the evil eye has become a cultural element that keeps in its focus an individual's soma and soul and sets the foundation for a better understanding of personhood. In other words, personhood can be seen not only as soma and soul, but rather as soma, soul and transculture. Therefore, and as a result of the fieldwork, I take a specific interest in the significance of relatedness in the developing, functioning and meaning of personhood. I will therefore reconsider the description of primary shame as described in Chapter 3, and start to reshape it.

CONSTRUCTION OF PERSONHOOD THROUGH THE EVIL EYE

The analysis of all the narratives about the evil eye received from the informants led me to an understanding of how they constructed their sense of personhood. When I asked them to tell me how they saw themselves fitting as human beings within the experience of the evil eye, I noticed that their responses were structured differently from what I was expecting. Being influenced by Western traditions, I was expecting a coherent narrative about themselves and the evil eye, with a beginning, a middle and an end. However, what I received was scattered, incoherent fragments; stories without a coherent plot, as Bruner (1986, 2002) would say. The existence of a plot would have created a sense of wholeness for both the self and the stories. In contrast, the stories that the informants told me were fragmented incidents and had no traditional properties of storytelling. This experience presented me with a cultural challenge, which led me to the quest to find alternative ways of expressing the self through the informants' narratives of the evil eye.

I was also aware of a postmodern approach wherein everything can be considered a story; this therefore needed to be examined within their ecology. Culture – as already discussed in this chapter – has a strong influence on the way in which individuals construct their personhood; it influences their views about societal and cultural matters, and this includes the phenomenon of the evil eye (Rasmussen 2008). According to postmodern narratologists, it appears that personhood is developed through an individual's interaction with cultural themes, and is not inherited; this idea may conflict with Jung's collective unconscious (Currie 1998; Gibson 2004; Herman and Vervaeck 2005; Jung 2015). Therefore, adopting such a view in the quest to understand the development of personhood through belief in the evil eye and its mirror functioning undoubtedly reveals that the self is a difficult phenomenon to tame; it consists of monstrous elements about the self as it is perceived by the person through 'mirrors'. The stories that a person tells themselves are thus not synthesised with a coherent cohort, but are disjointed stories through which the person is struggling to understand personhood. For that disjointed sense of self, the evil eye appears to serve as the string joining everything.

> I am scared to look at myself because of the fear of what I might see through the others' eyes; and having all these symptoms, I start thinking about my fear of being nothing. At times, I question why others envy me or why I envy others; and I think it is because I fear to see myself ... the evil eye is bad; that is what my grandmother taught me, because it causes me pain. But is it really bad? The more I read, the more I come to the conclusion that I should challenge that traditional view.

This statement was made by Katerina, a woman in her late forties. The self, therefore, starts to be constructed through the narrative of the evil eye, and the informants' position is based on this construction. 'I do believe that the evil eye is something that I create when I feel that I am not seen. The evil eye gives me a sense of existence. When I talk about it with others to be healed, I feel alive', Michael stated. It can be concluded from Michael's story (and this is supported by other informants) that the stories we create for ourselves develop our sense of personhood. Thus, personhood is an organic construct that takes form through speaking; whenever we speak, the story that we tell develops a new sense of self. Therefore, evil 'I' is another story that is revealed to us through others and upholds a new meaning about ourselves; and, due to the fact that the phenomenon is deeply existential, it can affect our own understanding of personhood (Davies et al. 2004). An abbot stated that 'The evil eye is about connection, even if we are scared of it. No one can harm anyone unless there is somehow a connection. The evil eye is a form of connection through which we understand each other better'. The evil eye is about being seen; the eye becomes a constant reminder of our own pitfalls, our own self and our own existence.

Personhood, then, is constructed from multiple stories and reflections, rather than one unified story with a plot and a specific meaning. The evil eye becomes part of the multiplicity of the construction of self, where individuals are confronted with different aspects of themselves through the casters and the symptomatology. 'I do not always have the same symptoms. I suppose it depends on where I am with my life. Sometimes I have headaches, and at other times more severe body difficulties', Maria said. 'Where I am with my life' – what does that really mean? The evil eye has become a significant part of the multiplicity in which a person's story resides. Therefore, informants revealed through their interaction with the evil eye that personhood is constructed through different self-stories about the 'I' (eye), which have a certain continuity, but not in time and space. In this disjointed spatial continuity, the evil 'I' (eye) manifests a unity in personhood through its multi-voiced attributions. However, approaching personhood through the evil 'I' (eye) as a multi-voiced phenomenon does not imply embarking on an completely chaotic or fragmented journey to personhood. Andreas, an Orthodox Christian in his mid-twenties, said: 'Sometimes I do not know what is going on, or what I did; I attracted the evil eye, but when I experienced the symptoms and the healing rituals, something like cleaning happened, and meaning seemed to take the place of the symptoms'. The evil eye presents a structural framework in which individuals can retrieve, and find meaning for, their own existence, in a way that is painful at times; this gives a coherent meaning of their own sense of self. The 'I' is on a quest to pursue unity. The evil eye, therefore, becomes the context within which the 'I' seeks unity.

VISION OF SELF THROUGH EVIL 'I'

Katerina, an Orthodox Christian in her late thirties, told me:

> Most of the times when I have the evil eye, it feels as if I have a big eye above me, seeing every single movement or thought that I have. I am scared of it, because through it I can for some weird reason see myself ... and that makes me feel more stable, even though I have to go through the draining bit of having headaches, etc.

Maria said:

> I feel so restricted when I want to express myself, because society in Corfu will judge me and not accept me. At times, I tell myself not to do things that fulfil me, out of fear of the others' eyes, but then yet again I attract their gaze because I act like a weirdo.

For Katerina and other informants, the search for security and permanence often originated in their need to create an acceptable self. This is a self that despite its origin – whether collective or individual – necessitates constriction of its potential relationships with others according to social morals. Mauss (1983) and Kuper's (1999) theories would support the statement that Katerina made about the imprisonment that someone might feel when it comes to the true expression of self within a normative social environment. It is difficult and frightening for someone to allow the self to be fully displayed in a society with such specific morals and culture as Corfu. The individual thus develops a false self-departure from the true self, which is hidden deeply in consciousness and awakens through the experience of the evil eye. Maria, along with other informants, led me to explore further the question of social morals in the vision of the self and the development of personhood. The resulting attempt to understand Maria and Katerina led to the assumption that the experience of relating to another person is influenced, and in fact narrowed, based on the vision of the self. Self-sufficiency, as developed within Corfiot society, creates an illusion of self, which allows the 'self' to withdraw and hide behind these illusions of self-knowledge. Fallibility is therefore avoided, or even neglected, in favour of false security. However, this false security can only be maintained through the avoidance of the possibilities of self, which is approached with ambivalence. The evil eye, as a phenomenon, has become a constant reminder of the vulnerability of the self, and at the same time invites the individual to see themselves and reflect on themselves through the eyes of others, while being exposed to the reality of taking responsibility for their own inner and outer agentic self, rather than hiding behind the false security which has developed from their ecology. Ayers (2003), in a similar vein to Jung (2015), would argue that false security and the fallibility of one's self indeed support the idea of departing from the true self with the aspiration of pleasing others, so that the individual can acknowledge the other in their attempt to be in touch with the shadow self and integrate it into the true sense of personhood.

'Before I get the evil eye, I am confused, as though nothing in my life has any meaning; then after the rituals I feel more at peace', Stamos stated. The self as a story and the search for unity and meaning appear to be integral to the journey of developing personhood, in which the evil eye becomes the mediator between personhood and being. The evil eye becomes the mediator between the complexities that an individual has with personhood and the self; the relationship between these two is important for an individual to develop a meaning of personhood in the encounter with the external environment. One might conclude that the evil eye has become an integral ingredient in the development of the relationship between oneself and others, but also with the self itself. So far, the evil eye has become the agency through which an individual receives their reflection and self-affirmation through others. It could be argued here that this need might originate in early childhood. I do not want to indulge in the past to create associations with the need to self-affirm our existence through others, but I will try to examine the quest in its rather peculiar manifestation through the evil eye, which does, in fact, outline what has so far been explored in relation to the fragility of a person's identity. The fragile identity which constantly seeks affirmation creates attachments that are based on provision and linked to the eyes of others. Georgia, an informant in her mid-thirties, said:

> I am not sure sometimes what is going on, really; the evil eye is some kind of a paradox for me. I am so scared of it and it is painful to have it because it drains you, and with no particular reason. Many times, I have tried to understand what is going on and why I often have the evil eye; and most of the time I reach a dead end. One thing that I am sure about is that I am not sure about myself; and others have become an extension of me. It feels like I am seeing myself through them. I am not sure if they are jealous of me, because surely they have more and better things than me, but it is my fear of me, I suppose.

Georgia's statement was similar to those of three other informants of a similar age or younger, and highlights not only a definitional problem with regard to the evil eye, but also the fragility of our existential being. What Georgia described was not only her quest to find herself through the mirrors of others, but also her constant anxiety stemming from her reflection to others. Depending solely on the reflection and convictions of others means that our own existence is not only defined by them but also threatened by them. Therefore, the frailty of the self causes a fear of denigration to develop, and this is then concentrated in behaviours designed to protect against the evil eye, instead of engaging in open encounters with others and allowing relationships and love to develop.

I emphatically place personhood in close proximity to 'I' (eye). Recognition is influenced by the perception of others first, and then the self. The fieldwork reveals that personhood has no existence unless reflection is present; the eyes of others provide the reflection of the self that we constantly seek (Ricoeur 2005). Ricoeur maintains that personhood is an organic sense that constantly seeks to be experienced in order for one's personhood to declare its presence. The experience, though, is developed through the relationship with the other, and as this study suggests, the metamorphosis of personhood begins not just through relationships with others but through engagement with their 'I' (evil eye). What the informants implied, for instance in Georgia's statement – which is supported by Kearney (2001), who takes a more explicit view than Ricoeur – is that the self is never satisfied with itself, and is constantly searching for meaning and purpose through others. Within that constant battle for recognition, pain is inflicted. When the informants were at peace with their own internal need for recognition, the pain dissolved, as with the oil in the water. Harris (1983), in his work on Hegel, describes an intense master-and-slave relationship which creates pain to both parties, and can only be resolved, he says, when both parties recognise their need for recognition by the other; in their case, the other is itself. The misunderstanding associated with the evil eye arises because it has been seen and examined only through the master–slave relationship, which causes pain to both parties; there has been no attempt so far to dig deeper into its existential underpinnings. Therefore, all the informants suggested that the meaning of oneself can be lost if it does not answer the call of recognition by others. The reflection of self is therefore strengthened through the opinion of others, as this is projected out through their 'eye'. However, this creates tension between one's personhood and diversity. The interaction between self and others can be witnessed as the threat of unfamiliarity to the 'eye', and ominous protective energies can be emitted.

INTERSUBJECTIVE DIALOGUE WITH THE EVIL EYE

Katerina's statement about fascination as an element of the evil eye brought into the analysis another of the evil eye's fundamental elements, which is love. She said:

> What is interesting is when I cast the evil eye, there is a need for me to admire, to love; I do not even think of causing any harm, let alone damage. When I see something that I like, I admire it; I want to see it more and more; or, if it is a person, I want to do good to her, but I end up casting the evil eye. I never understood why, or what it says about me. Am I an evil person after all?

Here, Katerina indicates that there is an element of possessive love within the evil eye; but what does this really mean? She did not know initially that she was casting the evil eye, but she realised that she became a caster when she started having thoughts about what kind of person she is. In a further attempt to understand love in relation to the evil eye, informants stated that love can be a deep desire to be friends with someone, love for oneself or sexual love. At the same time, when someone truly loves another person, they do not want to be possessive or overpower the other person. However, as Katerina pointed out, the existential need for recognition – for acknowledgement of one's own existence – and the attempt to develop a sense of self drive individuals to get in touch with their own frailty, which diminishes any possible opportunity for love. Therefore, the journey of constructing personhood starts with conforming, and this is based on the expectations and needs of others. The fear of absence of personhood then propels a person on the journey towards the need for acceptance through the eyes of others, which develops the feeling of being possessed by others. Ricoeur (2005) argues that personhood cannot be determined or developed without the involvement of others at each stage of the quest for it. However, he goes further and states that the relationship with the others' eye does not rule out the recognition of the need for solitude. Katerina did not have a need to extinguish the presence of others, but rather a need to allow deeper connections with them through coexistence, which respects the intersubjective aloneness.

The dialectical dance between the need to develop a sense of personhood and the need to relate to others means that the two cannot help being intrinsically interconnected. In many cases, the informants implied that one's own personhood is personhood for the other, which is accessible through the eyes. In other words, as Stamos stated, 'it is funny, but I think that others are the self, as the self reaches its own meaning only in another'.

However, because of our own existential anxiety of meaninglessness, and non-existence, there is a primary tendency to understand the self in a one-sided way, which, as Katerina explained, is confusing and is a non-genuine attempt to understand personhood. Thus, in the attempt to develop personhood, human beings operate in an egocentric manner; self-definition and concern for the common good are necessary. However, it was observed in the fieldwork that the opposition to this egocentric attitude was not altruism, but something fundamentally different, which defines the evil eye – namely, envy. Envy creates resentment and leads people to act against their own needs. Žižek (2007) agrees that envy is in opposition to the egocentric need for personhood, which blurs the pathways to our interests. Egocentric aloneness brings to the fore the anxiety and fear of denigration which drive a person to want to fuse with the other to create an illusion of 'partnership'. The fear of being alone boosts the illusion that the person is actually the other; however, through the eyes of others, the person can be in touch with the deception they created. 'What scared me most is that through the eyes of those who cast the evil eye I can see myself; but I do not know if it is truly me or something else', Maria stated. Kearney (2001) argues that the illusion of fusion with the other can only be seen as a deception of personhood, because we can never be the other, and neither can the other be us. However, the fact that the union between myself and the other is not possible and cannot be seen should not be taken as a failure. In fact, understanding and respect of self-solitude in communion with the other can promote a dialectical personhood within which the uniqueness of the self can be recognised. It is the recognition of our existential solidarity through the eyes of others that creates anxiety, but which also allows intersubjective dialogue with the other.

The question that now arises is: if we are bound to the eyes of others, where is our freedom to exercise our own autonomy? It appears that freedom of personhood is strictly bound up with the recognition of the other, as this is the pathway to personhood and individual responsibility. One priest stated:

> The evil eye seems to govern my life, and wherever I go I have in mind the evil eye. What shall I do to protect myself from it? In a way, I am always conscious that it can happen to me at any time; but then I do not know why I worry so much, or why I allow others to control my life in such a way. The only conclusion is that I must be crazy, because for some reason I feel good within it.

Listening to him, I found myself wondering about this 'feel-good' aspect of his narration, and what it really meant. It appeared to me that he was talking about the importance of otherness, where the deception of one's individualistic personhood is passed over and one reaches the true meaning of one's existence: the recognition of personhood that celebrates the union and the need for the other. Personhood is not an individualistic phenomenon, but rather a phenomenon in union with the other. The evil eye therefore becomes a constant reminder that we cannot exist in separation, but only in union with the other, under conditions that respect a person's individuality. The informants disclosed that there is a knowledge that cannot be articulated; they feel that their self is not enough, and it is only through the reflection from others who manifest the evil eye that they can be in touch with the whole. The evil eye, therefore, illustrates the importance of union with the other, without, at the same time, obliterating the other's personhood, but rather highlighting it. In other words, personhood requires mutuality where other and self come to a communion and create warmth, in which the individual is in touch with the self in its frailty, strength and vulnerability. There is thus a certain paradox of personhood as it is developed through the evil eye.

PERSONHOOD AND ITS PARADOX

The evil eye, existential anxiety and the self become central to ethnographic study, within which a fundamental question of personhood inevitably arises. Personhood becomes a paradoxical construct of one's own experience, but is also appraised objectively. The subjective experience that is important for the development of the self now becomes subject to the objectified public arena through the others' 'I' (evil eye). Personhood and its fragility thus trespass into the need to be loved. Such need intrinsically motivates individuals to seek the gaze of others in an attempt to be loved and recognised. However, the process of recognition in this quest threatens the person, through exposure of one's frailty to the public gaze. Kerkira said: 'I am scared of the others' eyes; I get the evil eye easily and then I suffer. When I get the evil eye, it is like I am seen, and I am not sure if I am scared of the evil eye or of what I realise about myself through the evil eye'. Nikos followed with: 'there is an internal need to alleviate the sense of aloneness that I feel when I consciously seek for external attention, which then makes me feel sick because I get the evil eye'. The true self disjointed from the morally constructed self is expressed through projection to the eyes of others. It is the attempt not only to find the bond between the selves, but also to understand one's own personhood: 'the reflection makes it clear to me', one informant stated. Myers (2003) agrees with Žižek (2006) that it is the big Other that acknowledges one's personhood over the many other selves that the contemporary being can take.

We are confronted here with the presuppositions of personhood, illustrated by the cultural field in which the fieldwork took place and in which the evil eye becomes a radical agency from which to re-evaluate personhood and the meaning of being. In this context, the evil eye becomes a threatening, but also liberating, agency with no binary antithesis of good and bad, right or wrong. However, when it comes to personhood and the evil eye, a question remains: why, despite the other's gaze and the reflection that such a gaze brings to the subject, is the subject still bound in the tyranny of the socially constructed self and its morals? A young informant mentioned: 'I would not know what to do with the images about me that come from others; the way I experience the evil eye is scary'. Fear of freedom, therefore, not only enslaves the subject to their own fear of self, but also reinforces the sense of shame of being.

> I do not need anyone else to tell me who I am; the evil eye is a bond to the other because we are insecure ... the evil eye is just a weak phenomenon which does not allow progression ... and I am still confused about why I get the evil eye when I do not believe in it.

The denial of the need for the other brings the individual to confront the absence of a reflection, leaving the self with no meaning. Therefore, the repeated phrase, 'I do not need anyone', which many (especially younger) informants used, causes an oppressive enslavement rather than freedom. The absence of meaning through the other's gaze generates confusion in those who feel lost; and there is confusion within the phenomenon of the evil eye, which has given rise to prohibitions and difficulties in people allowing themselves to be seen and to be loved.

CONCLUSION

In the contemporary Orthodox Christian society of Corfu, the 'I' has become the evil 'I' through the fear of exploring one's self through the eyes of others; it is a fear of discovering the self through others that has transformed the gaze from love to evil. Such a transformation is an attempt to overturn the constraints of a society that has been influenced by its history. The integration of East and West has overshadowed the invisible codes necessary to allow personhood to develop and to lead to a sense of belonging in society. The merging of East and West drew attention away from these secret codes, which had promoted individual growth through the warmth of the gaze and without separation from society. The eye therefore reminds individuals that personhood comes in union with society, but also in respecting one's own boundaries. Within that context, 'I' and 'being seen' have become a pervasive demand that stems from an egocentric position with no respect for the other. An informant in his mid-forties said:

> I feel like the evil eye is about narcissists who cannot accept that others can have more than them; they cannot accept that others are more important than them. The need to show off attracts the evil eye and showing off is against Christian beliefs; there is no humility in it.

The internal need for early narcissistic gratification has been deemed egocentric in the Orthodox Christian society of Corfu; the individual's need to be seen as a journey to their own personhood is therefore suppressed. Thus, any attempt which allows the possibility of being seen creates guilt: 'Sometimes I feel the need to be admired, and then I feel bad because that is not how I grew up. I need to be humble, otherwise I will get the evil eye', Sandra explained. Guilt, therefore, accompanies the fundamental attempt to be seen, which is the pathway to personhood.

In the quest to understand personhood, the fieldwork has revealed that love and gaze are significant elements in its development. However, the guilt of wanting to define the self accompanies the individual in their quest, as this is opposed to the Christian doctrines of humility and love for others: 'Love thy neighbour as oneself – the evil eye and the want to be seen has nothing to do with that. It is bad to want things. There is nothing Christian either way: to want to be seen or to want to destroy'. The demands of these doctrines disavow the fundamental ingredient of love, which is the autonomy of the individual to make the decision to love and to be loved, and to choose to love whoever they want. In the commandment 'love thy neighbour', one of the questions that arises is who or even what a neighbour is, and what it implies to love them. The field showed that it is not reality, as Lacan might have argued in his correspondence with Žižek and Daly (2004). The neighbour represents the other's gaze, through which we can see our reflection, the informants argued. Thus, the neighbour becomes an extension of the self, in an attempt to engage with that aspect of the self with which, as human beings, we cannot or are afraid to have direct communication from within. Therefore, in the admonition 'love thy neighbour', the neighbour is the self as represented through the other's gaze. Fear of the gaze now becomes fear of the aspects of self that we see through it, and therefore 'love thy neighbour' brings us closer to personhood. However, in the frailty of human nature, loving one's neighbour grows into a traumatic reality that takes the illusory form of the evil eye. According to some informants, 'love thy neighbour' means the universal idealistic love, which the evil eye threatens.

At this point, it is important to engage with the philosophical question of the totality of personhood and the pain that a person experiences through the evil eye. The conclusion might lead to advocating a misanthropic cycle, given the likelihood that pain through the evil eye initiates personhood. Maria, in her late twenties, stated: 'I am not sure what is going on; the evil eye can kill me; it exhausts me and makes me unable to concentrate. I lose energy, but through the rituals there is a strong sense of warmth through which I feel full'. It was also suggested by other informants that the suffering of the evil eye might be a mask behind which we are afraid to see. If we were to start exploring the face of the evil eye behind that mask, we might encounter the primordial sense of omniscience; the uncertainty connected with this 'encounter' creates fear which, in a sense, is projected to 'I'. Therefore, the fear of incompleteness that this uncertainty causes to some individuals forces them to want to obliterate the fear, and then the 'I' becomes evil. The individual becomes aware, through the eyes of others, of a certain lack of being, and is then also aware that the others are in possession of something that the individual most needs. The evil eye also becomes the agency through which a person attempts to answer the question: who am I for the other? In other words, the evil eye becomes the phenomenon through which the other's eye reflects the missing parts of one's personhood; this means that the other's eye is seen as mystical and frightening. 'I get the evil eye from those who are more powerful than me', Stamos stated. The power attached to the evil eye and the vulnerability of its victims bring up a fundamental question concerning the sustainability of the pain of personal deficit. Within the Greek Orthodox community of Corfu, it appears that informants believe it is more bearable to acknowledge the lack of personhood in themselves, and act upon it by finding external experiences to fill that gap, than to accept the unbearable feeling of the deficits of others. In their attempt to sustain the pain of lack of personhood, the eyes of others thus become powerful and able to cause harm. In turn, the evil eye becomes something supernatural, with the ability to complete what is missing.

There is a significant difference between the data obtained from the fieldwork regarding the evil eye in relation to personhood and the common psychological views on human development and psychology of the self, which suggest that personhood is predicated on the sustainability of a clear distinction between self and others. Common to all the psychological theories about personhood is the process through which an individual develops personhood through individuation and separation. It is also maintained that failure to succeed in this process results in confusion about the self and psychopathology. Therefore, relational personhood is viewed with certain scepticism in the field of self-psychology. What I propose is a unique conceptualisation of personhood through vital relatedness of one with another through the initial process of being seen. 'There is something in the gaze of others that makes me feel that I exist. I am not sure who I would be without others', stated one informant, while another said that 'I would not be able to be me without others' eyes'. Similarities to this latter statement can be found in Asian traditions, which highlight the importance of relatedness in the development of personhood and in the reduction of psychopathology (Markus and Kitayama 1991). 'I think that we are scared to accept the fact that we are beings that are born from relationship to be in relationship', a priest pointed out, continuing:

> We would not exist without others. I think the evil eye exists because we refuse to accept the fact that we are interpersonal beings and we fight against our relational aspect. When others remind us through their gaze that we are needed for others to exist as well, we do not like it and we try to avoid it. It is then that we experience the negative aspects of the evil eye.

The significance of relationality in moulding personhood has been well recognised since antiquity. However, it has lately been forgotten, leading to psychopathological symptoms as people go against their nature. This notion was suggested by George, who is in his fifties. The fieldwork therefore indicated that personhood takes form only in socio-relational contexts where the interpersonality of human development is respected.

The evil eye highlights another element of personhood. Not only does it illustrate the importance of interpersonal relationships in the formation of personhood, it also explores what personhood means in a contemporary setting for each individual. The evil eye, therefore, underlines the importance and meaning of coexisting with each other in the development and definition of personhood. Father Nikodemos maintained that without others, the very notion of personhood loses its purpose and meaning. The evil eye in the Greek Orthodox tradition of Corfu thus has relationship at its core and is opposed to the Western concept of individualism. It could be argued that Greek Orthodox tradition advocates the absolute dissolution of individual personhood. Such an argument would not be accurate, however, because the Orthodox tradition in Corfu also values individual personhood, which is born through relationship. A strong sense of self is required in order to be able to reciprocate the relationship but also to be congruent to one's self and others. In Corfiot tradition, then, personhood supports both notions of self: self and self in others. An Orthodox mental health nurse stated that there is no such thing as one reality, and because of that, we can talk about distinctions between one and another; we can talk about relational personhood because each of us upholds a different reality. Nevertheless, in a country like Greece, and more specifically in Corfu, fluid self-boundaries are supported by ensconced Christian beliefs. The idea of the evil eye can be seen in the school of Pythagoras as an exchange of energies; and this can also be seen in Orphic mysteries in classical Greece. However, it has never been remotely accepted in the West. The fluidity of the boundaries of personhood implies that all human beings are considered as mutable and separate. The evil eye, then, is a form of mutation with regard to personhood. Through the evil eye, individuals become in touch with their core selves and start to develop a better sense of personhood. 'No matter how painful it might be to have the evil eye, there is always a sense of discovery, a sense of self-empowerment after I get rid of it', one mental health professional confessed. A question arises here that requires an answer: to what extent is belief in the evil eye regarding personhood elaborated, and even rationalised, in terms of magical thinking? The answer is not just a matter of a simple attempt to engage with magical thinking; rather, as Sampson (1988) suggests, it is a question with cultural dimensions.

In Greek Orthodox tradition there is opposition to the Western understanding of self. Greek Orthodox belief and tradition negate the Western centrality of personhood. It is believed that the self is not the centre of all things, and in fact cannot control everything. The sense of independence and sovereignty gives way to humility and the need for community. Thus, relational personhood is fully actualised in the societal networks with which people engage. In other words, as Katia said, personhood takes form:

> within the social arena where many actors interact and see each other. It is through the multiplicity of the gaze that one can develop a sense of self, a real sense of self that stems not only from our one view, but rather from the views of others as well, no matter how scary that might be.

Personhood is a dynamic network of forces that are encountered through the evil eye, and the stature of the individual being can be seen as insignificant; personhood, therefore, is actualised through finding equilibrium between one's gaze and that of others. The Greek Orthodox perspective of personhood through the gaze is characterised by relationality and reciprocity. Reciprocity is primary and suggests that personhood cannot be developed in isolation; in order to be able to consider one's self, others need to be considered as well. In other words, it is important to be able to be seen through self and others, and to accept things as they are, presented through the mirrors of others. There is an illusory sense that Western tradition upholds individuation and personhood, creating only egoistic beings, while overshadowing the true nature of personhood, which is relationality (Paranjpe 1988).

To recapitulate, the current picture of personhood necessitates a revisiting of history, but also a better understanding of the different cultural implications in the construction of self. It was interesting to observe that in the Greek Orthodox tradition of Corfu, the phenomenon of the evil eye regarding personhood has been kept subdued, not only by authoritarian institutions but also through psychological tendencies. There was also a tendency from a Westernised influence for any political opposition to the phenomenon to be disregarded, and at times 'crushed'. At times, the Christian religion has degenerated into superstition and materialism, departing further and further from its philosophical and existential roots. To expand the understanding of personhood we would need to consider the relational self that Christian Orthodoxy advocates, but this suggestion seems to be at an embryonic stage. Relational personhood 'has the ability to expand our understanding of self, cosmos and nature', as Stamos, an informant in his mid-twenties, put it.

Conclusion

Since the beginning of so-called civilisation, a great deal of evidence for belief in the evil eye has appeared and been witnessed among various cultures. Traces of this belief are found not only in ancient Greek and Roman culture, but also in the Bible. Important aspects to mention, as the literature to date has revealed, are that the evil eye is mostly associated with envy or admiration, and can cause misfortune; that it can negatively affect the sufferer's mental state; and that it is closely related to superstition. However, insufficient research has been done on the Orthodox Christian understanding of the evil eye in Greece, and specifically in Corfu, which was never ruled by the Ottoman Empire. The current study has therefore focused on the phenomenon of the evil eye in Corfu, a place which experientially appears to have different rituals and understandings of the phenomenon. In addition, the study has examined how individuals from Corfu interact with, understand and experience the phenomenon of the evil eye, based on extensive fieldwork.

It was surprising to observe that evil eye amulets were present in many of the households, offices and consulting rooms that I visited during the fieldwork. It was even easy to purchase these amulets from local churches or shops. However, Corfiots have a unique attitude towards the phenomenon that affects their understanding of their personhood and mental health. Thus, the phenomenon of the evil eye has become important for the structure and function of their society. It is my contention that this phenomenon has survived in the specific area of Corfu, and has been transformed into an existential phenomenon, because it is entrenched in social and family values. It also reflects the secrecy in Corfiot culture. Moreover, I observed that gender does not affect the symptoms or the healing of the phenomenon. The fact that the evil eye is informed by individuals' existential needs regardless of their gender is one of the significant contributions of the present study. In fact, those Corfiots who believe in the evil eye not only preserve but also revise their culture and transculture internally and externally.

Conclusion

The phenomenon of the evil eye as explored in this study has affected individuals ranging from peasants to professors; however, as with every other phenomenon, it has been subjected to generational changes. Recently, the evil eye has begun to emerge in mainstream culture as promoted in social media; however, what my research reveals is that the phenomenon has not lost its ancient origins. The results of this fieldwork thus illustrate how the evil eye has developed so far, and how it affects individuals' understanding of personhood and mental health, so that we can begin to comprehend the metamorphosis and value of the phenomenon in society. In my quest to bring to the fore all the existing literature about the evil eye, I realised that this phenomenon had only been partially explored, and only with regard to its element of misfortune. However, further examination of the evil eye has much more to offer to society and to our understanding of the development of an individual.

During the fieldwork, I observed the significant steps that informants took in order to understand and experience the phenomenon, and the ways in which they related to it inter- and intro-subjectively. However, despite the significant attitudes that individuals developed regarding the evil eye, this study discovered fundamental differences in attitude between laypeople, clergymen and mental health professionals. The results endorse and support the views of other scholars who have argued that the evil eye is fuelled by envy and admiration, and that its effects on the sufferer can be either physical or psychological, and in some cases can even cause death. However, based on the analysis of the results, I investigated the phenomenon further, and concluded that the evil eye has a more fundamental effect on mental health and the existential understanding of individuals.

The evil eye is a well-known phenomenon in Corfu, and arises from an understanding that individuals possess the ability to transmit energy (positive or negative) through the action of looking at someone. Such an action, especially when transmitting negative energy, results in psychical and physical distress, which is embodied through pain and low energy or motivation. To protect themselves from such attacks, Corfiots wear a panoply of various amulets, such as red-and-white threads on their wrists, blue birds and similar items, which are believed to carry prophylactic powers. Based on extensive fieldwork, this study examined how the phenomenon is approached and interpreted in Corfu; it also examined the relationship between self, religion and spirituality. The results support the view that the experience of possession is objectively real, as it stems specifically from clergymen, individuals and laypeople. The rituals related to the evil eye are based on the Greek Orthodox tradition and involve the intercession of religious figures such as Jesus, various saints (specifically St Spyridon, the patron saint of Corfu) and the Virgin Mary.

Despite the fact that many individuals, especially mental health professionals, find it difficult to associate misfortune and negativity with the evil eye, they continue to engage in rituals to protect themselves from it. One of these rituals is to wear blue evil eye beads in different shapes, mostly symbolising the eye. Another is to wear amulets in the shape of a phallus, as it is believed that this can ward off evil eye symptoms and protect the wearer.

This study supports the theoretical perspective of scholars who argue that envy is believed to generate and fuel the evil eye, causing harm not only to individuals but also to animals and objects. In addition, the study found similarities with those scholars who have pointed out that the evil eye can manifest in headaches, depression, male erectile dysfunction, female menstrual problems, anxiety and even death. This research also found that neonates are thought to be subject to the evil eye, as they have not yet developed spiritual defences to protect themselves. There was a clear description of the differences in spiritual robustness between adults and younger participants, with younger people being less able to resist evil eye attacks. Therefore, carers always hide amulets under children's clothes, and the study found that the majority of nurses and mothers hide amulets to protect the children in their care from the evil eye.

There are two significant outcomes from this study that may be derived from the empirical data. Firstly, the evil eye and the use of protective amulets is a reflection of the Corfiots' transhistorical and trans-generational heritage. The phenomenon is an attempt to understand and explain envy and jealousy, while the protective rituals are an attempt to shield those whom we love and value. Secondly, and most importantly, according to the findings of the fieldwork, the phenomenon of the evil eye certainly exists in the modern era and has fundamental effects on people's lives. The empirical data suggests that the evil eye is not just related to human expressions of envy and jealousy, but is rather a fundamental phenomenon that can enable scholars in this specific field to better understand the elements of a person's existence, based on the need of individuals to establish relationships. For many people – though not for the majority of the informants – the evil eye might appear to be a superstitious belief; however, such superstitious beliefs emerged during an early stage of human evolution, and human beings have now moved away from an understanding of the evil eye as a mere superstitious belief. This work proposes that it is rather a phenomenon which has effects on an individual's existence and formation of personhood. However, the evil eye brings with it its own complexities.

This study opposes the existing literature by revealing that the evil eye is not in fact fuelled by social inequality, but rather arises from the individual's internal need to be seen, as an internal way of understanding the self. This research did not find the phenomenon to be any more prevalent among those from low socio-economic or educational backgrounds; in fact, the study observed that belief in the evil eye occurs irrespective of social status. Surprisingly, it was actually more frequent among those with a good educational background.

The study therefore supports the position that the evil eye has not been fully examined or described in the existing literature on the subject, and that ethnographic studies to date have simply attempted to explain bad luck retrospectively through the evil eye. Spooner's (1976) theory finds support in this chapter; it led to a debate as to whether the evil eye is purely a social construct or whether there are other elements that need to be reobserved and re-examined. Therefore, based on the premise that ethnographic elements regarding a phenomenon are valid, in the case of the current study the statements by the informants guided me to depart from the explanation of misfortune and jealousy, as well as from the view that the evil eye is generated by social injustice. A closer look at the manifestations of the evil eye led to the understanding that the phenomenon needed to be viewed differently.

On one level, the fieldwork revealed that cultural and historical background and other influences that we all carry through our collective memory affect our interactions at an interpersonal level. Therefore, anyone can transmit the evil eye. On another level, the study supports the view that the more intimate a relationship we have with someone, the more perceptive their gaze becomes. Thus, the evil eye gains its power from the intensity of the relationships that we build with others, fuelled by envy or admiration. The evil eye is not related to the different social classes; in fact, it affects any individual regardless of their social status, as mentioned above. This anthropologically informed ethnographic study suggests, in contradiction to the literature, that the experience of the evil eye is related to the uniqueness of the individual, regardless of their social characteristics. It would also appear to be the uniqueness of the other person that defines the manner in which the evil eye manifests. Anything differing from the social norm, including individuals who stand out from the crowd, can attract the evil eye either through admiration or envy.

According to this study, belief in the evil eye expresses an awareness of a spiritual 'web' in which everyone is interconnected and therefore affected. In other words, our energies are connected in a web and are spiritually driven, whether by God through the saints, by the Virgin Mary or through the Devil via the evil eye. The informants placed the evil eye in the spiritual realm, because spiritual forces – which are beyond the natural and part of the cosmos – are seen as the power that activates the phenomenon. The results of the fieldwork therefore support the view that supernatural and natural events are interconnected. Young Corfiot informants, mostly those with higher education, engaged with the phenomenon of the evil eye differently from those who were middle-aged. The young informants seemed to actively engage with transmission of the evil eye in order to prove that the spiritual web exists, and that it can affect an individual's natural reality. The latter group engaged with the phenomenon in a more intellectual sense rather than experientially; individuals from this second group aimed to understand the evil eye scientifically.

Despite scientific attempts to understand the spiritual phenomenon of the evil eye, the analysis of the collected data shows that its anatomy is difficult to comprehend. It has a power that cannot be understood through natural laws, but only through mystical experience. It was clear that the majority of the informants associated the evil eye with *'the other side'* – the spiritual realm where the spirits of the dead exist. Therefore, the understanding of the supernatural for Corfiots assumes a different significance when it comes to thinking of those who have passed away; it is a natural process for them. Despite the informants' intention to understand the evil eye through a spiritual experience or scientific exegesis, it was commonly accepted that the evil eye is a natural phenomenon, as it can be observed with spiritual powers. Therefore, the evil eye can be understood not only through the individual's embodiment of the phenomenon, but also through its removal when it is cast out. Informants from the group of mental health professionals tried to understand the phenomenon scientifically; however, it was commonly accepted among them that despite their initial dismissive attitudes towards the evil eye, and although its powers can escape the physical world, it in fact belongs to it. The evil eye belongs to the physical world because it can be perceived through the body and experienced through the senses. Therefore, the concept of the evil eye can help to develop our understanding of the world and how we place ourselves in it. Despite initial support from the mental health workers for the argument that for a scientist, anything that does not belong to the rationale of sensory perception does not exist, medical practitioners could not and did not eliminate the possibility of spiritual communication through the evil eye. The study therefore concludes that whatever a person's occupation, educational background or other particular societal characteristics, it is still believed that the evil eye is a dynamic phenomenon that includes multiple perceptual elements; it is therefore observed not only in spiritual environments but also in the mundane.

The ethnographic research presented in this book, however, observed the phenomenon of the evil eye as it went beyond its previously established manifestations in the physical and spiritual world. The literature reveals that the evil eye is a deeply relational phenomenon which reflects the initial gaze of the mother's eyes; the study refers at this point to the first carer's eyes. The research suggests that the gaze is the most powerful bonding interaction that a human being can have. Following the ethnographic insights garnered during the fieldwork, the study points out that the evil eye is a representation of the initial bonding through the gaze of the mother. This moment provides a potent spiritual presence, beyond the normative time in which an individual starts to experience themselves and also begins to relate to others. The evil eye thus becomes a powerful psychical centre through which an individual starts to become in touch with the idea of selfhood. Further exploration revealed that it is through the evil eye's reflection of self that an individual is in touch with a sense of self. It is through the gaze that individuals start to look at themselves and feel their existence. However, this does not come without its price.

Despite the fact that the results refer to the specific geographical area of Corfu, the insights about the evil eye appear to be more universal. The universality of the phenomenon can be observed in the philosophical and ethnographic understanding of personhood. Indeed, the present study revealed that the field gives a different understanding of evil eye, that is, the relationship of the phenomenon with shame instead of envy and jealousy. This can be attributed to the specific nature of the field. However, due to the pivotal geographical area of the field as discussed in previous chapters, but also because of the triangulation method of collecting data, the results can be generalised to a more universal level. The study thus contributes significantly to the attempts to understand personhood through the relationship with others, as seen via the phenomenon of the evil eye.

The study began by outlining the idea that the evil eye is fundamentally a relational phenomenon and is manifested through the presence of the other's eyes. Undoubtedly, the evil eye affects the sense of self, but, as explored in this work, it reflects the initial gaze that a baby receives in the journey towards understanding and developing its selfhood. The question that the study engages with is: what is the effect in adulthood of the false mirror, if it occurred at such an early stage? The fieldwork's findings suggest that the evil eye reflects the early relationship, and it can only be experienced when the mother's eyes have had a petrifying effect in the early stages of a child's life. The fieldwork indicated common experiences of the evil eye among those who had experienced their mother's eyes as petrifying. It was these individuals who had been subjected to the evil eye, and who therefore started to experience the world as though they did not fit into it. The evil eye had therefore become a phenomenon that existed in the symbiotic state of the individual with the other and the world, and it forced the individual to separate and individuate in a healthier community that was not full of conditions and expectations.

During this symbiotic state, an individual develops anxieties about separation which are confronted via the evil eye through the idea of separation and therefore 'death'; this is the death of the symbiotic selfhood that does not exist apart from living through the other. The current study also suggests that the evil eye's symptomatology varies based on an individual's experience of the mother's mirror eyes. It is therefore a subjective experience. However, the findings show that the eyes become mirrors allowing an individual to see into another's psyche, which also affect the way a person sees and perceives themselves. A single look can have immense power, and can sometimes be so intense that it can shrivel an individual's self. The eye therefore has far more power than simple sight. To this extent, it may suffice to say that the evil eye is a phenomenon with existential significance and with both negative and positive effects on individuals.

This study therefore does not support the view that the evil eye is purely a negative phenomenon. However, it is a phenomenon that projects fear and malignity onto animate and inanimate objects, threatening them with suffering and damage. I agree however with current findings that the evil eye is embedded in individuals' collective unconscious, which reflects the existential fear of being deemed unworthy – a fear formed by the early gazes we encounter. The threat of being seen has equipped the evil eye with immense power, which can cause intense emotional turmoil to the one towards whom the reflection is directed through the eye. The intensity of the turmoil derives from the archetypal fear of being watched – especially without being aware of it – which reflects an existential anxiety of being exposed, visible and therefore vulnerable to attack. The evil eye is therefore correlated not only with envy, but also with shame. The fundamental functioning of the evil eye – the seeing – represents a threat to individuals who have been seen; their imperfections are revealed. The study therefore suggests that the fundamental element of the evil eye is shame, before all its associations with envy and its effects on a person's physical and psychical levels. Thus, shame is the major emotion that creates further embodied manifestations due to the individual's fear of being abandoned for not being good enough. To this extent, the evil eye becomes an entrapment of an individual's psychical and visual realm, which exposes the victim's flaws. Exposure to one's flaws creates a mental space in which the victim is confronted with their reflection in the process of better understanding themselves. This study therefore supports the idea that the phenomenon of the evil eye is associated with the journey of developing selfhood, but that this journey is not simply accompanied by envy.

In addition, the research showed that when the evil eye is observed in the context of Greek Orthodoxy, and particularly in Corfu, it is associated with shame as a deeper emotion than envy. During the fieldwork it was observed that the evil eye's manifestations are subjective and vary according to each individual's narrative; however, the emission of energy from the evil eye is connected to an internal sense of petrification, rather than 'paranoia' (the sense of being constantly watched and envied). The study highlights the fact that the fear of being watched is not an isolated emotion linked to psychopathology, but rather a fear that everyone can experience. The study also suggests that petrification is a result of the ultimate existential terror, which is associated with an individual's sense of selfhood. The element of petrification with regard to the evil eye was derived from the observations and the analysis of the collected data, and was understood as the transformation of organic matter into the stony replica of the individual's internal world. Instead of interacting with a dynamic internal world, the individual is now confronted with a stagnant image of self, with the effect of petrification.

After further analysis, this study therefore proposes that the paralysing element of the evil eye is not in fact related to envy, but rather to shame – and to be more precise, to deeply shaming moments derived from being watched. There is a psychical disturbance that stems from the contact with the evil eye. During that moment, the victim of the evil eye becomes an object rather than a subject, slowly losing their sense of existential presence. The individual then becomes a stony replica of the reflection that comes from the evil eye. It is important to mention that among the Corfiots in the study, it was commonly observed that those who suffered from the evil eye were experiencing deep shame, and at the same time that their mothers' eyes were constantly in their minds. There was a certain uncanny experience through the evil eye possession that created a shaming experience, which accordingly led to the individual becoming 'paralysed', or petrified, as when Medusa laid eyes upon her victims.

Examination of the existing literature confirms that the evil eye is commonly accepted as a global phenomenon that can be observed across history. There is a terror attached to the evil eye, and the findings of this fieldwork reveal that in the Orthodox Christian region of the Ionian Islands, and more specifically in Corfu, those who suffer from the evil eye exhibit intense emotional difficulties. The study concludes that wherever there is shame and guilt, the evil eye is not far away. To be more precise, in cases where informants were experiencing feelings of shame and guilt, the evil eye was playing a significant role in their internal process by expressing the fear of being watched, and of not being good enough or being bad. When individuals experienced these types of feelings, they actually started to believe that they needed to be punished in order to repent of their badness, and the only process for that was through the evil eye. The study frames the broader picture of the operation of the evil eye and its connection with selfhood, and it illustrates how the understanding of selfhood is related to the sense of selfhood as derived from the collected data.

The fieldwork revealed that the evil eye is not just about envy, and also that it is about the moment when a person is witnessed in a manner that provides a way for them to understand that they exist. Therefore, this study reveals that the evil eye reflects the process of being seen through the eyes of others, and the shame that is generated in the person at whom the gaze is directed. In addition, the study suggests that the evil eye is not only about the physical gaze, but also the metaphorical gaze. In other words, the evil eye is not only caused by the actual gaze towards someone, but also by the spiritual gaze that takes place even at a distance. Considering all the manifestations and functionality of the evil eye, the study concludes that it is undoubtedly a complex phenomenon, and is purely relational and strongly associated with the individual's subjective reality. The evil eye thus becomes a process through which an individual understands their own self through relationships with other(s) and the reflections that they project towards the subject.

The study therefore supports the view that the evil eye is the pathway through which an individual is confronted with the existential anxiety of their own self, in the process of understanding their own selfhood. The community has immense significance for this process, as do the relationships that the individual (sufferer) develops with members of their community. Were it not for the community and the relationships that individuals develop within it, the phenomenon of the evil eye would not exist; and, in turn, there would not be a journey to investigate the true self. The study also suggests that the evil eye provides an opportunity for an individual or sufferer to face their own existential anxieties regarding being watched. It is the gaze that allows an individual to be in touch with the shadow of the self in the process of discovering or redefining their true selfhood. One of the most important findings of the study was the discovery that the 'eye' in the evil eye is the fundamental element which creates personhood; the 'I', highlighting at the same time the importance for the individual to face their existential image as transmitted by the others' eye. This understanding led to further investigation and analysis of the phenomenon, and to the conclusion that the experience of the evil eye is an integrative process that allows the individual to accept all the elements of selfhood, both good and bad, and then suppresses or represses to the deepest level of consciousness elements that had never been witnessed and had therefore became monstrous. Finally, the study makes a pioneering breakthrough regarding the anatomy of the evil eye, which facilitates a holistic understanding of selfhood. This work reveals that the evil eye affects the three elements of human existence (body, soul, and agency or mind); each is affected based on where attention needs to be focused at different stages in the individual's lifespan. However, there are certain aspects that require further examination, as discussed below.

The significant increase in the variety of religious denominations in Corfu is an important trend that affects the societal and theological map of this particular area, and therefore increases the necessity for further studies that examine the relationship of the evil eye with the other religious denominations in the same sociocultural milieu, as well as how non-Orthodox people interact with and understand the phenomenon. In addition, attention should be given to the understandings of the evil eye of those who do not practise a religion or who do not have a belief in the supernatural and adopt a purely epistemological way of thinking. Their thinking appears to be present in everyday life, and has an effect on understandings of the phenomenon; but the effect on individuals' mental health also calls for further investigation. It is immensely important for further studies to focus on the development of the existential ethics which stem from the understanding of otherness and its contribution to the understanding of selfhood, as promoted through the reflection of the eye ('I') through the eyes of others.

Despite the limitations of this study and the further recommendations given above, it is important to conclude with what the book contributes to the field of the evil eye and the understanding of personhood. The evil eye is not a phenomenon that is solely related to envy or jealousy, but rather a more existential phenomenon that brings the individual to face existential shame. Within the intersubjective space of the others and 'I', the evil eye becomes the vehicle through which a meaningful reflection is carried to the (evil) eye's receptor. The moment of being seen through the 'I' of another activates an interaction of being in touch with the core relational aspects of human existence, which is the space where two individuals meet. The evil eye also carries the fundamental fear of being exposed and therefore rejected because of our nakedness. The 'I' therefore becomes the evil eye because it constantly reminds us of the need for the other, but also of the existential fear of being rejected if seen, which is attached to shame. I strongly support the notion that the evil eye might be associated with jealousy or envy, but dig deeper into the field to reveal that it is not only about envy, but rather shame of being seen. As in the story of Lady Godiva, the notion of being seen is associated with petrification. In that moment, the evil eye is transformed into an experience of suffering because of the reflection that it upholds, and it reminds us of the existential emptiness which is accompanied by shame. Finally, when that reflection is perceived it creates a strong reaction in the body, as the body holds the memory of the initial shame of being less than the initial eye. This study proposes that the evil eye is not a phenomenon that is associated with negative feelings, but rather a positive phenomenon that invites individuals to be in touch with their personhood, and to develop a better understanding through the witnessing of the other of what it is to be human in the brokenness of their existence.

References

Abu-Lughod, L. 1988. *Veiled Sentiments: Honor and Poetry in a Bedouin Society*. University of California Press.
Abu-Rabia, A. 2005. *Folk Medicine among the Bedouin Tribes in the Negev*. Ben-Gurion University of the Negev.
Abu-Ras, W., and S. H. Abu-Bader. 2008. 'The Impact of the September 11, 2001, Attacks on the Well-Being of Arab Americans in New York City', *Journal of Muslim Mental Health* 3: 217–39.
Abu-Saad, I. 2002. 'Licit and Illicit Drug Use and Social Change among Bedouin Arabs in Southern Israel', *Journal of Substance Use* 7: 141–46.
Acipayamli, O. 1962. 'Anadolu'da Nazarla İlgili Bazı Âdet ve İnanmalar' [Some Customs and Beliefs about Evil Eye in Anatolia], *Ankara Üniversitesi Dil ve Tarih Coğrafya Fakültesi Dergisi* 1: 1–5.
Adam, P. 2008. *Winnicott*: Harvard University Press.
Aeschylus. 1994. *Agamemnon*. The Ministry of Education and Religious Affairs.
Ajzen, I. 1991. 'The Theory of Planned Behavior', *Organizational Behavior and Human Decision Processes* 50: 179–211.
Ajzen, I., and M. Fishbein. 2005. 'The Influence of Attitudes on Behavior', in D. Albarracín, B. T. Johnson and M. P. Zanna (eds), *The Handbook of Attitudes*. Erlbaum, pp. 173–221.
Al-Ashqar, U. S. 2003. *The World of the Jinn and Devils in the Light of the Qur'an and Sunnah*. International Islamic Publishing House.
Al-Krenawi, A., and J. R. Graham. 1999. 'Social Work and Koranic Mental Health Healers', *International Social Work* 42: 53–65.
Al-Krenawi, A., J. Graham and B. Maoz. 2000. 'Gendered Utilization Differences of Mental Health Services in Jordan', *Community Mental Health Journal* 36: 501–11.
Alivizatos, N. 1999. 'A New Role for the Greek Church?', *Journal of Modern Greek Studies* 17: 23–40.
Allen, J., and D. Lester. 1994. 'Belief in Paranormal Phenomena and an External Locus of Control', *Perceptual and Motor Skills* 79: 226–29.
Aloud, N. 2004. *Factors Affecting Attitudes toward Seeking and Using Normal Mental Health and Psychological Services among Arab-Muslims Population*. Ohio State University.

Amanolahi, S. 2007. 'Supernaturalism among the Pastoral Societies of Iran', *Iran & the Caucasus* 11: 45–55.

American Psychiatric Association (APA). 2013. *Diagnostic and Statistical Manual of Mental Disorders*, 5th ed. Arlington, VA.

Anderson, R. 2003. 'Defining the Supernatural in Iceland', *Anthropological Forum* 13: 125–30.

Ankarloo, B., and S. Clark. 1999. *Witchcraft and Magic in Europe: Ancient Greece and Rome*: University of Pennsylvania Press.

Appel, W. 1976. 'The Myth of the Jettatura', in C. Maloney (ed.), *The Evil Eye*. Columbia University Press, pp. 16–27.

Aquaro, G. R. A. 2001. *Death by Envy: The Evil Eye and Envy in the Christian Tradition*. iUniverse.

Ardener, E. W. 1970. 'Witchcraft, Economics, and the Continuity of Belief', in M. Douglas (ed.), *Witchcraft Confessions and Accusations*. ASA Monographs, pp. 141–60.

Arensberg, C. 1965. *Culture and Community*. Harcourt, Brace & World.

Argyle, M., and M. Cook. 1976. *Gaze and Mutual Gaze*. Cambridge University Pres.

Atwood, G. E. 2011. *The Abyss of Madness*. Routledge.

Avgoustidis, A. G. 2001. 'Cooperation of Psychiatry and the Church as a Deinstitutionalization Project', *International Journal of Mental Health* 30: 42–48.

Ayers, M. Y. 2003. *Mother-Infant Attachment and Psychoanalysis: The Eyes of Shame*. Routledge.

Baghdiantz-McCabe, I., G. Harlaftis and M. I. Pepelase. 2005. *Diaspora Entrepreneurial Networks: Four Centuries of History*. Berg.

Bandura, A. 1963. *Social Learning and Personality Development:* Holt, Rinehart and Winston.

——. 1977. *Social Learning Theory*. Prentice Hall.

——. 2001. 'Social Cognitive Theory: An Agentic Perspective', *Annual Review of Psychology* 52: 1–26.

Banfield, G. 2004. 'What's Really Wrong with Ethnography?', *International Education Journal* 4: 53–63.

Barth, F. 2001. *Ethnic Groups and Boundaries: The Social Organization of Culture Difference*. Waveland Press.

Bartky, S. 1990. *Femininity and Domination: Studies in the Phenomenology of Oppression*. Routledge.

Bauman, Z. 2008. *Does Ethics Have a Chance in a World of Consumers?* Harvard University Press.

Bayer, R. S., and M. Shunaigat. 2002. 'Socio-Demographic and Clinical Characteristics of Possessive Disorder in Jordan', *Neurosciences* 7: 46–49.

Beidelman, T. O. 1970. 'Towards More Open Theoretical Interpretations', in M. Douglas (ed.), *Witchcraft Confessions and Accusations*. ASA Monographs, pp. 351–56.

Belensky, M. F., L. A. Bond and J. S. Weinstock. 1997. *A Tradition That Has No Name: Nurturing the Development of People, Families, and Communities*. Basic Books.

Bellali, T., and M. Kalafati. 2006. 'Greek Psychiatric Care Reform: New Perspectives and Challenges for Community Mental Health Nursing', *Journal of Psychiatric and Mental Health Nursing* 13: 33–39.
Berger, A. S. 1977. 'Notes on the Symbolism of the Eye', *Opthalmology Digest* 10: 32–43.
———. 2011. 'The Evil Eye: A Cautious Look', *Journal of Religion and Health* 5: 7–16.
Bermúdez, J. L. 1998. *The Paradox of Self-Consciousness*. MIT Press.
Beytut, D. K., et al. (2009) 'Pediatri Hemşirelerinin Ağrıya İlişkin Geleneksel İnanç ve Uygulamaları' [Traditional Beliefs and Practices of Paediatric Nurses About Pain], *Maltepe Üniversitesi Hemşirelik Bilim ve Sanatı Dergisi* 3: 12–18.
Black, R. 2007. *To the Hebrides: Samuel Johnson's Journey to the Western Islands and James Boswell's Journal of a Tour*. Birlinn.
Bloch, M. 2011. *Anthropology and the Cognitive Challenge*. Cambridge University Press.
Blum, R. H., and E. Blum. 1970. *The Dangerous Hour: The Lore of Crisis and Mystery in Rural Greece*. Scribner.
Bohigian, G. M. 1997a. 'The Staff and Serpent of Asclepius', *Missouri Medical Association Journal* 94: 210–21.
———. 1997b. 'The History of the Evil Eye and its Influences on Ophthalmology, Medicine and Social Customs', *Documenta Ophtalmologica* 94: 91–100.
Bollas, C. 1987. *The Shadow of the Object: Psychoanalysis of the Unknown Known*. Free Association Books.
Born, G. 1998. 'Anthropology, Kleinian Psychoanalysis, and the Subject in Culture', *American Anthropologist* 100: 372–86.
Bornstein, B. H., and M. K. Miller. 2009. *God in the Courtroom: Religion's Role at Trial*. Oxford University Press.
Bosco, J. 2003. 'The Supernatural in Hong Kong Young People's Ghost Stories', *Anthropological Forum* 13: 141–49.
Bouhoutsos, J. C., and K. V. Roe. 1984. 'Mental Health Services and the Emerging Role of Psychology in Greece', *American Psychologist* 39: 57–61.
Bowman, P. 1994. 'Xenophobia, Fantasy and the Nation: The Logic of Ethnic Violence in Former Yugoslavia', in V. Goddard, J. Llobera and C. Shore (eds), *The Anthropology of Europe: Identity and Boundaries in Conflict*. Berg, pp. 143–71.
Briggs, R. 2002. *Witches and Neighbours*. Blackwell.
Broucek, F. J. 1991. *Shame and the Self*. Guilford Press.
Brown, J. W. 1976. 'Consciousness and Pathology of Language', in R. W. Rieber (ed.), *Neuropsychology of Language: Essays in Honor of Eric Lenneberg*. Plenum Press, pp. 72–93.
Brower-Toland, S. 2012. 'Medieval Approaches to Consciousness: Ockham and Chatton', *Philosophers' Imprint* 12: 1–29.
Bruner, J. 1986. *Actual Minds, Possible Worlds*. Harvard University Press.
———. 2002. *Making Stories: Law, Literature, Life*. Harvard University Press.
Brunvand, J. H. 1996. *American Folklore: An Encyclopedia*. Gerland Publications.
Buber, M. 2002. *The Way of Man*. Routledge.
———. 2004. *Between Man and Man*. Routledge Classics.

Buhrmann, H. G., and M. K. Zaugg. 1981. 'Superstitions among Basketball Players: An Investigation of Various Forms of Superstitious Beliefs and Behavior among Competitive Basketballers at the Junior High School to University Level', *Journal of Sport Behavior* 4: 163–74.
Burke, J. 1988. *The Tyranny of Malice: Exploring the Dark Side of Character*. Summit Books.
Burns, R. B. 1994. *Introduction to Research Methods*. Longman Cheshire.
Butler, J. 1997. *The Psychic Life of Power*. Stanford University Press.
Calimach, A. 2001. *Lovers' Legends: The Gay Greek Myths*. Haiduk Press.
Campbell, J. K. 1964. *Honour, Family, and Patronage: A Study of Institutions and Moral Values in a Greek Mountain Community*. Clarendon Press.
Campion, J., and D. Bhugra. 1997. 'Experiences of Religious Healing in Psychiatric Patients in South India', *Social Psychiatry and Psychiatric Epidemiology* 32: 215–21.
Cartledge, P. 2003. *Nomos: Essays in Athenian Law, Politics and Society*. Cambridge University Press.
——. 2011. *The Great Philosophers*. Weidenfeld and Nicolson.
Carver, C. S., and M. F. Scheier. 2001. *On the Self-Regulation of Behaviour*. Cambridge University Press.
Case, T., et al. 2004. 'Coping With Uncertainty: Superstitious Strategies and Secondary Control', *Journal of Applied Social Psychology* 4: 848–71.
Cervone, D., et al. 2006. 'Self-Regulation: Reminders and Suggestions from Personality Science', *Applied Psychology: An International Review* 55: 333–85.
Charles, S. 1991. *Demons and the Devil: Moral Imagination in Modern Greek Culture*. Princeton University Press.
Church of Greece. 1999. *Εγκύκλιος αρ. 2565: Περί Νεοσατανισμού*. Encyclical.
Chusid, M. T. 2009. *Hearing Shofar: The Still Small Voice of the Ram's Horn*. Self-published.
Cinnirella, M., and K. M. Loewenthal. 1999. 'Religious and Ethnic Group Influences on Beliefs about Mental Illness: A Qualitative Interview Study', *British Journal of Medical Psychology* 72: 505–24.
Cochrane, R. 1983. *The Social Creation of Mental Illness*. Longman.
Cohler, B. J. 1992. 'Intent and Meaning in Psychoanalysis and Cultural Study', in T. Schwatz, G. M. White and C. A. Lutz (eds), *New Directions in Psychological Anthropology*. Cambridge University Press, pp. 269–93.
Codrington, R. H. 2006. *The Melanesians: Studies in Their Anthropology and Folklore*. Clarendon Press.
Conrad, J. 2012. *The Nigger Of The 'Narcissus': A Tale Of The Forecastle*. Hard Press.
Cory, T. S. 2013. *Aquinas on Human Self-Knowledge*. Cambridge University Press.
Creswell, J. W. 1998. *Qualitative Inquiry and Research Design: Choosing among Five Traditions*. SAGE.
Crick, M. 1976. *Explorations in Language and Meaning: Towards a Semantic Anthropology*. Halstead Press.
Crook, J., and T. Rabgyas. 1988. 'The Essential Insight: A Central Theme in the Philosophical Training of Mahayanist Monks', in A. C. Paranjpe, D. Y. F. Ho and R. W. Rieber (eds), *Asian Contributions to Psychology*. Praeger, pp. 149–83.

Cunningham, M. 2002. *Faith in the Byzantine World*. InterVarsity Press.
Currie, M. 1998. *Postmodern Narrative Theory*. St. Martin's Press.
Damasio, A. 2010. *Self Comes to Mind: Constructing the Conscious Mind*. Vintage.
Darmanin, M. 1999. 'The "Smallness" of Minimalist Tolerance', *Education Inquiry* 4: 31–62.
Davies, B., et al. 2004. 'The Ambivalent Practices of Reflexivity', *Qualitative Inquiry* 10: 360–89.
De Martino, E. 2000. *Sud e Magia*. Feltrinelli Editore.
De Quincey, C. 2005. *Radical Knowing: Understanding Consciousness through Relationship*. Park Street Press.
Deacon, T. W. 2011. *The Symbol Concept*. Oxford University Press.
Dein, S. 1997. 'ABC of Mental Health: Mental Health in a Multiethnic Society', *British Medical Journal* 315: 473–76.
Dein, S., M. Alexander and A. D. Napier. 2008. 'Jinn, Psychiatry and Contested Notions of Misfortune Among East London Bangladeshi', *Transcultural Psychiatry* 35: 31–55.
Denham, A. 2015. 'A Psychodynamic Phenomenology of Nankani Interpretive Divination and the Formation of Meaning', *Ethos* 43: 109–34.
Dennett, D. 2016. 'Conditions of Personhood', in A. Rorty (ed.), *The Identities of Persons*. University of California Press, pp. 170–96.
Denscombe, M. 2007. *The Good Research Guide: For Small-Scale Social Research*. Open University Press.
Derrida, J. 2008. *The Animal That Therefore I Am*. Fordham University Press.
Desrosiers, A., and S. St Fleurose. 2002. 'Treating Haitian Patients: Key Cultural Aspects', *American Journal of Psychotherapy* 56: 508–21.
Di Stasi, L. 1981. *Malocchio: The Underside of Vision*. North Point Press.
Diamond, J. 2001. *Snake Oil and Other Preoccupations*. Vintage.
Dickie, M. W. 1991. 'Heliodorus and Plutarch on the Evil Eye', *Classical Philology* 86: 17–29.
Dionisopoulos-Mass, R. 1976. 'The Evil Eye and Bewitchment in a Peasant Village', in C. Maloney (ed), *The Evil Eye*. Columbia University Press, pp. 42–62.
Domash, L. 1983. 'Self and Object Representations and the Evil-Eye', *Bulletin of the Menniger Clinic* 47: 217–24.
Douzenis, A. 2007. 'The Mentally Ill in Greece: Starvation During the Winter of the Nazi Occupation', *International Journal of Mental Health* 35: 42–46.
Du Boulay, J. 1974. *Portrait of a Greek Mountain Village*. Clarendon Press.
Dudley, T. R. 1999. 'The Effect of Superstitious Belief on Performance Following an Unsolvable Problem', *Personality and Individual Differences* 26: 1057–65.
Dundes, A. (ed.). 1981. *The Evil Eye: A Casebook*. University of Wisconsin Press.
———. 1992a. *The Evil Eye: A Folklore Casebook*. University of Wisconsin Press.
———. 1992b. 'Wet and Dry, the Evil Eye: An Essay in Indo-European and Semitic Worldview', in *The Evil Eye*. University of Wisconsin Press, pp. 257–12.
Eckman, P. 2003. *Emotions Revealed*. Times Books.
Edwards, D. 1971. *The Evil Eye and Middle East Culture*. Austin Press.

Eickelman, C. 1993. 'Fertility and Social Change in Oman: Women's Perspectives', *Middle East Journal* 47: 657–66.
Eisinga, R., M. T. Grotenhuis and B. Pelser. 2013. 'The Reliability of a Two-Item Scale: Pearson, Cronbach, or Spearman-Brown?', *International Journal of Public Health* 58: 637–42.
El-Islam, M. F. 1995. 'Cultural Aspects of Illness Behaviour', *The Arab Journal of Psychiatry* 6: 13–18.
Elliot, J. H. 1991. *Beware the Evil Eye: The Evil Eye in the Bible and the Ancient World*, vol. 1. Cascade Books.
Elliot, J. H. 1992. *Evil Eye: Mesopotamia*. Cascade Books.
Epictetus. 2012. *Discourses and Selected Writings*. Penguin Classics.
Erikson, E. H. 1987. *Dimensions of a New Identity: Jefferson Lectures in the Humanities*. W. W. Norton & Company.
Etchegoyen, H. 2005. *The Fundamentals of Psychoanalytic Technique*. Karnac.
Evans-Pritchard, E. E. 1937. *Witchcraft, Oracles and Magic Among the Azande*. Clarendon Press.
Fabrega, H. 2000. 'Culture, Spirituality and Psychiatry', *Current Opinion in Psychiatry* 13: 525–30.
Fenichel, O. 1953. *The Collected Papers of Otto Fenichel*. W. W. Norton & Company.
Ferenczi, S. 1963. 'Spiritism', *Psychoanalytic Review* 50: 139–44.
Ferenczi, S., and O. Rank. 1986. *The Development of Psychoanalysis*. International University Press.
Fern, E. F. 2001. *Advanced Focus Group Research*. SAGE.
Fine, G. A. 1993. 'Ten Lies of Ethnography: Moral Dilemmas of Field Research', *Journal of Contemporary Ethnography* 22: 267–94.
Finneran, N. 2003. 'Ethiopian Evil Eye Belief and the Magical Symbolism of Iron Working', *Folklore* 114: 427–33.
Fiske, S. T. 2004. *Social Beings: Core Motives in Social Psychology*. Wiley.
Flowers, P., et al. 1997. 'Health and Romance: Understanding Unprotected Sex in Relationships between Gay Men', *British Journal of Health Psychology* 2: 73–86.
Folklore Society. 2008. *County Folk-Lore*: BiblioBazaar.
Foster, G. M. 1965. 'Peasant Society and the Image of Limited Good', *American Anthropologist* 67: 293–15.
———. 1972. 'The Anatomy of Envy: A Study in Symbolic Behaviour', *Current Anthropology* 13: 165–202.
Foulks, E., et al. 1977. 'The Italian Evil Eye: Real Occhio', *Journal of Operational Psychiatry* 2: 28–34.
Frankfurt, H. 1971. 'Freedom of the Will and the Concept of a Person', *The Journal of Philosophy* 68: 5–20.
Freud, S. 1978. 'From the History of an Infantile Neurosis', in *Collected Papers*, vol. 3. Hogarth Press.
Gall, M. D., J. P. Gall and W. R. Borg. 2005. *Educational Research: An Introduction*. Pearson.

Gallagher, S. 2000. 'Philosophical Conception of the Self: Implications for Cognitive Science', *Trends in Cognitive Sciences* 4: 14–21.
——. 2006. 'How the Body Shapes the Mind: An Interview with Shaun Gallagher by Thomas Z. Ramsoy', *Science and Consciousness* 1: 22–35.
Gallese, V., and S. Sinigaglia. 2010. 'The Bodily Self as Power for Action', *Neuropsychologia* 48: 746–55.
Gallup, G. H., and F. Newport. 1991. 'Belief in Paranormal Phenomena among Adult Americans', *Skeptical Inquirer* 15: 137–46.
Galt, A. H. 1982. 'The Evil Eye as Synthetic Image and its Meanings on the Island of Pantelleria, Italy', *American Ethnologist* 9: 664–81.
Gammeltoft, T. H. 2017. *Refugee Policy as 'Negative Nation Branding': The Case of Denmark and the Nordics*. Danish Foreign Policy Yearbook.
Garrison, V., and A. Conrad. 1976. 'The Evil Eye: Envy or Risk of Seizure?', in C. Maloney (ed.), *The Evil Eye*. Columbia University Press, pp. 286–328.
Gaynesford, M. 2006. *I: The Meaning of the First-Person Term*. Clarendon Press.
Gedo, J. 1979. *Beyond Interpretation: Toward a Revised Theory for Psychoanalysis*. International University Press.
Gibson, A. 2004. *Towards a Postmodern Theory of Narrative*. Edinburgh University Press.
Gifford, E. S. 1960. 'The Evil Eye in Pennsylvania Medical History', *Keystone Folklore Quarterly* 5: 237–45.
Gill, M. 1982. *The Analysis of Transference*. International University Press.
Gillman, B. 2000. *The Research Interview*. Continuum.
Goffman, E. 2010. *Relations in Public: Microstudies of the Public Order*. Transaction Publishers.
Gomm, R. 2004. *Social Research Methodology: A Critical Introduction*. Palgrave Macmillian.
Gopaul-McNicol, S., D. Benjamin-Dartigue and M. Francois. 1998. 'Working with Haitian Canadian Families', *International Journal for the Advancement of Counselling* 20: 231–42.
Graham, A. C. 1989. *Disputes of the Tao: Philosophical Arguments in Ancient China*. Open Court.
Gravel, P. B. 1995. *The Malevolent Eye: An Essay on the Evil Eye, Fertility and the Concept of Mana*. Peter Lang.
Green, A. 1983. *On Private Madness*. Hogarth Press.
Greenfield, R. P. H. 1988. *Traditions of Beliefs in Late Byzantine Demonology*. Adolf M. Hakkert.
Grolnick, S. 1987. 'Reflection on Psychoanalytic Subjectivity and Objectivity as Applied to Anthropology', *Journal of the Society for Psychological Anthropology* 15: 136–43.
Gubrium, J. F., and J. A. Holstein. 1997. *The New Language of Qualitative Method*. Oxford University Press.
——. 2009. *Analyzing Narrative Reality*. SAGE.
Habimana, E., and L. Masse. 2000. 'Envy Manifestations and Personality Disorders', *European Psychiatry* 15: 15–21.

Hadot, P. 1995. *Philosophy as a Way of Life: Spiritual Exercises from Socrates to Foucault*. Oxford University Press.
Halliday, M. A. K. 1978. *Language as Social Semiotic: The Social Interpretation of Language and Meaning*. Edward Arnold.
Hallowell, I. 1955. *Culture and Experience*. University of Pennsylvania Press.
Hamilton, V. P. 2010. *The Book of Genesis*. Eerdmans Publishing.
Hardie, M. M. 1981. 'The Evil Eye in Some Greek Villages of the Upper Haliakmon Valley in West Macedonia', in A. Dundes (ed.), *The Evil Eye: A Folklore Casebook*. University of Wisconsin Press, pp. 107–23.
Harris, H. S. 1983. *Hegel's Development*, vols. 1 and 2. Clarendon Press.
Harris, J. 2007. *Constantinople: Capital of Byzantium*. Hambledon & London.
Hartocollis, P. 1966. 'Psychiatry in Contemporary Greece', *American Journal of Psychiatry* 123: 457–62.
Hasse, C. 2012. 'Psychological Anthropology, Mind, Culture, and Activity', *Psychological Anthropology* 19: 385–87.
Hay, I. 2005. *Qualitative Research Methods in Human Geography*. Oxford University Press.
Heald, S., and A. Deluz. 1994. *Anthropology and Psychoanalysis: An Encounter Through Culture*. Routledge.
Heelas, P., and L. Woodhead. 2005. *The Spiritual Revolution: Why Religion is Giving Way to Spirituality*. Blackwell.
Heliodorus. 1997. *Ethiopian Story*. Phoenix.
Hellenic Statistical Authority. 2011. *Population Census*. General Directorate of Administration & Organisation Division of Statistical Information & Publications Division Statistical Data Dissemination Section.
Henelly, J. M. 1998. 'The "Surveillance of Desiree": Freud, Foucault, and Villette', *Victorian Literature and Culture* 26: 421–40.
Herbermann, C. G. 1912. *Selected Illustrations*. The Catholic Encyclopedia.
Herman, L., and B. Vervaeck. 2005. *Handbook of Narrative Analysis*. University of Nebraska Press.
Heron, J. 1996. *Co-operative Inquiry: Research Into the Human Condition*. SAGE.
Herzfeld, M. 1981. 'Meaning and Morality: A Semiotic Approach to Evil Eye Accusations in a Greek Village', *American Ethnologist* 8: 560–74.
——. 1986. 'Closure as Cure: Tropes in the Exploration of Bodily and Social Disorder', *Current Anthropology* 27: 107–20.
Hinshelwood, R. D. 1989. *A Dictionary of Kleinian Thought*. Free Association Books.
Hira, K., et al. 1998. 'Influence of Superstition on the Date of Hospital Discharge and Medical Cost in Japan: Retrospective and Descriptive Study', *British Medical Journal* 317: 1680–83.
Ho, D. Y. F. 1994. 'Filial Piety, Authoritarian Moralism, and Cognitive Conservatism', *Genetic, Social, and General Psychology Monographs* 120: 347–65.
Hollan, D. 2016. 'Psychoanalysis and Ethnography', *Ethos* 44: 507–21.
Holy Bible: King James Version. 2011. Collins.
Homer. 2003. *Iliad*. Wildside Press.

Hood, R. W., P. C. Hill and B. Spilka. 2009. *The Psychology of Religion: An Empirical Approach*. Guilford Press.
Hsu, F. L. K. 1989. *Psychoanalytic Aspects of Fieldwork*. SAGE.
Hunt, Shelby D. 1989. 'Naturalistic, Humanistic, and Interpretive Inquiry: Challenges and Ultimate Potential'. In Elizabeth Hirschman (ed.), *Interpretive Consumer Research*. Association for Consumer Research, pp 185–198.
Hussain, R. 2002. 'Lay Perceptions of Genetic Risks Attributable to Inbreeding in Pakistan', *Pakistan: American Journal of Human Biology* 14: 264–74.
Hussein, F. M. 1991. 'A Study of the Role of Unorthodox Treatments of Psychiatric Illnesses', *Arabian Journal of Psychiatry* 12: 170–84.
Jahoda, G. 1969. *The Psychology of Superstition*. Allen Lane.
James, W. 1983. *Principles of Psychology*. Harvard University Press.
Johnson, F. 1985. *Culture and Self: Asian and Western Perspectives*. Tavistock.
Johnson, M. 1987. *The Body in the Mind: The Bodily Basis of Meaning, Imagination and Reason*. University of Chicago Press.
Jones, L. C. 1951. *The Evil Eye among European-Americans*. UW Press.
Joseph, J., et al. 1969. *Folklore*. Folklore Society.
Jung, C. C. 2006. *The Psychology of the Transference*. Princeton University Press.
———. 2015. *Archetypes and the Collective Unconscious*. Routledge.
Kakar, S., and K. Kakar. 2007. *The Indians: Portrait of a People*. Penguin-Viking.
Kakar, S. 2012. *The Inner World: A Psychoanalytic Study of Childhood and Society in India*. Oxford India Perennials.
Karastergiou, A., et al. 2005. 'The Reform of the Greek Mental Health Services', *Journal of Mental Health* 14: 197–203.
Kaufman, R. 1985. 'Is the Concept of Pain Incoherent?', *The Southern Journal of Philosophy* 23: 279–83.
Kearney, R. 2001. *The God Who May Be*. Indiana University Press.
Khalifa, N., and T. Hardie. 2005. 'Possession and Jinn', *Journal of Royal Society of Medicine* 98: 351–53.
Khalifa, N., et al. 2011. 'Beliefs About Jinn, Black Magic and Evil Eye among Muslims: Age, Gender and First Language Influence', *International Journal of Culture and Mental Health* 4: 68–77.
Khan, M. S. 1986. *Islamic Medicine*. Routledge and Kegan Paul.
Killeen, P. R. 1978. 'Superstition a Matter of Bias, not Detectability', *Science* 199: 88–90.
Kingdon, B. L., et al. 2002. *The Illusory Beliefs Inventory: A New Measure of Magical Thinking and Its Relationship with Obsessive Compulsive Disorder*. Cambridge University Press.
King Solomon. 2008. *The Key of Solomon the King: Translated from Ancient Manuscripts in the British Museum*. Forgotten Books.
Klein, M. 1984. *Envy and Gratitude and Other Works 1946–1963*. Hogarth Press.
Klonick, K. 2016. 'Re-Shaming the Debate: Social Norms, Shame, and Regulation in an Internet Age', *Maryland Law Review* 75: 1029–65.
Kluckhohn, C. 1970. *Navaho Witchcraft*. Beacon Press.

Knoblauch, H. 2008. 'Spirituality and Popular Religion in Europe', *Social Compass* 55: 140–53.
Koenig, H., D. King and V. Carson. 2012. *Handbook of Religion and Health*. Oxford University Press.
Kohut, H. 1971. *The Analysis of the Self.* International Universities Press.
Koltko-Rivera, M. E. 2004. 'The Psychology of Worldviews', *Review of General Psychology* 8: 3–58.
Kosmatou, E. 2000. *La Population des îles Ioniennes XVIIIème à XIXème Siècle*. Paris I.
Kracke, W., and G. Herdt. 1987. 'Introduction: Interpretation in Psychoanalytic Anthropology', *Ethos* 15: 3–7.
Kristeva, J. 1991. *Strangers to Ourselves*. Columbia University Press.
Krueger, R. A., and M. A. Casey. 2000. *Focus Groups: A Practical Guide for Applied Research*. SAGE.
Kuper, A. 1999. *Culture: The Anthropologists' Account*. Harvard University Press.
Kurtz, E. 1981. *Shame and Guilt: Characteristics of the Dependency Cycle*. Hazelden.
Kvale, S. 1996. *Interviews: An Introduction to Qualitative Research Interviewing*. SAGE.
Lacan, J. 1949. *Ecrits*. W. W. Norton & Company
Lacan, J., and B. Fink. 2007. *Ecrits: The First Complete Edition in English*. W. W. Norton & Company.
Lange, R., H. J. Irwin and J. Houran. 2000. 'Top-Down Purification of Tobacyk's Revised Paranormal Belief Scale', *Personality and Individual Differences* 29: 131–56.
Laplanche, J. 1999. *Essays on Otherness*. Psychology Press.
Larkin, M., S. Watts and E. Clifton. 2006. 'Giving Voice and Making Sense in Interpretative Phenomenological Analysis', *Qualitative Research in Psychology* 3: 102–120.
Lawn, J. E., et al. 2004. 'Why are 4 Million Newborn Babies Dying Each Year?', *Lancet* 364: 399–401.
Lazarus, R. S. 2006. 'Emotions and Interpersonal Relationships: Toward a Person-Centered Conceptualization of Emotions and Coping', *Journal of Personality* 74: 9–46.
Leary, M. R., and J. P. Tangney. 2014. *Handbook of Self and Identity*. Guilford Press.
Lefcourt, H. M. 1982. *Locus of Control: Current Trends in Theory and Research*. Psychology Press.
Levi, S. 1987. *The Bedouin in Sinai Desert*. Schocken Books.
Levinas, E. 1998. 'Uniqueness', in *Entre Nous: On Thinking-of-the-Other*. Columbia University Press.
Levine, J. A., and A. B. Levine. 2011. 'The Psychodynamics of Shame and Guilt in Great Expectations', *International Journal of Applied Psychoanalytic Studies* 9: 62–66.
LeVine, R. A. 1982. *Culture, Behavior and Personality*. Aldine.
Levine, R. A., and D. T. Campbell. 1995. *Ethnocentrism: Theories of Conflict, Ethnic Attitudes, and Group Behaviour*. John Wilson & Sons.
Levy, R., and D. Hollan. 1998. 'Person-Centred Interviewing and Observation in Anthropology'. In H. R. Bernard (ed.), *Handbook of Methods in Cultural Anthropology*. AltaMira Press, pp. 333–364.

Levy, I. J., and R. Z. Levy. 2002. *Ritual Medical Lore of Sephardic Women*. University of Illinois Press.
Lewis, M. D. 1995. 'Cognition-Emotion Feedback and the Self-Organization of Developmental Paths', *Human Development* 38: 71–102.
Loewenthal, K. M. 1995. *Mental Health and Religion*. Chapman & Hall.
Loewenthal, K. M., et al. 2001. 'Faith Conquers All? Beliefs about the Role of Religious Factors in Coping with Depression among Different Cultural-Religious Groups in the U.K', *British Journal of Medical Psychology* 74: 293–303.
Lofland, J., and L. Lofland. 1995. *Analyzing Social Settings*. Wadsworth.
Lohmann, R. I. 2003. 'The Supernatural is Everywhere: Defining Qualities of Religion in Melanesia and Beyond', *Anthropological Forum* 13: 175–85.
Louis, C. J. 1951. 'The Evil Eye among European-Americans', *Western Folklore* 10: 11–25.
Luttwak, E. 2009. *The Grand Strategy of the Byzantine Empire*. Harvard University Press.
Machovec, F. J. 1976. 'The Evil Eye: Superstition or Hypnotic Phenomenon?', *The American Journal of Clinical Hypnosis* 19: 74–79.
Madianos, M. G. 1999. 'The Diachronic Beliefs in the Evil Eye in Athens: Some Quantitative Evidence', *European Journal of Psychiatry* 13: 176–82.
Madianos, M. G., et al. 2000. 'Geographical Variation in Mental Hospital Discharges in Greece and Socioeconomic Correlates: A Nationwide Study (1978–1993)', *Social Psychiatry and Psychiatric Epidemiology* 34: 477–83.
Maduro, P. 2013. 'Five Points of Interplay between Intersubjective-Systems Theory and Heidegger's Existential Philosophy, and the Clinical Attitudes They Foster', *A Quarterly Psychoanalytic Forum* 7: 37–41.
Makris, G., and D. Bekridakis. 2013. 'The Greek Orthodox Church and the Economic Crisis since 2009', *International Journal for the Study of the Christian Church* 13: 111–32.
Migliore, S. 1997. *Mal'uocchiu: Ambiguity, Evil Eye, and the Language of Distress*. University of Toronto Press.
Malinowski, B. 1954. *Magic, Science and Religion and Other Essays*. Doubleday.
Maloney, C. (ed.). 1976. *The Evil Eye*. Columbia University Press.
Marcais, P. 1960. *Ayn and Evil Eye*. Brill.
Marchese, R. T. 2001. *The Fabric of Life: Cultural Transformation in Turkish Society*. Global Academic Publishing.
Marci, I. 2001. 'Medical Psychology in Greece', *Journal of Clinical Psychology in Medical Settings* 8: 27–30.
Marcus, G., and M. Cushman. 1986. *Ethnographies as Texts*. University of Chicago Press.
Markham, J. G. 1985. *Forerunners to Udug-hul: Sumerian Exorcistic Incantations*. Wiesbaden and Stuttgart.
Markus, H. R., and S. Kitayama. 1991. 'Culture and the Self: Implications for Cognition, Emotion and Motivation', *Psychological Review* 98: 224–53.
Merleau-Ponty, M. 1962. *Phenomenology of Perception*. Routledge.
———. 1973. *Consciousness and the Acquisition of Language*. Northwestern University Press.

Marsh D. R., et al. 2002. 'Advancing Newborn Health and Survival in Developing Countries: A Conceptual Framework', *Journal of Perinatology* 22: 572–76.
Marshall, C., and G. B. Rossman. 2010. *Designing Qualitative Research*. SAGE.
Massey, G. 2012. *Ancient Egypt: The Light of the World*. Create Space Independent Publishing Platform.
Matute, H. 1995. 'Human Reactions to Uncontrollable Outcomes: Further Evidences for Superstitions Rather Than Helplessness', *The Quarterly Journal of Experimental Psychology* 48: 142–57.
Mauss, M. 1983. 'A Category of the Human Mind: The Notion of the Person; the Notion of Self', in M. Carrithers, S. Collins and S. Lukes (eds), *The Category of the Person*. Cambridge University Press, pp. 45–125.
McCrae, R. R., and A. Terracciano. 2005. 'Personality Profiles of Cultures: Aggregate Personality Traits', *Journal of Personality and Social Psychology* 89: 407–25.
McGee, R. J., and R. L. Warms. 2004. *Anthropological Theory: An Introductory History*. McGraw Hill.
McGuire, M. 1990. 'Religion and the Body: Rematerializing the Human Body in the Social Sciences of Religion', *Journal for the Scientific Study of Religion* 29: 283–97.
McKinley, N. M. 2011. 'Feminist Perspectives on Body Image', in T. F. Cash and L. Smolak (eds), *Body Image: A Handbook of Science, Practice, and Prevention*, 2nd ed. Guilford Press, pp. 48–55.
Metzinger, T. 2003. *Being No One*. Mass Press.
Mikkelsen, H. H. 2016. 'Unthinkable Solitude: Successful Aging in Denmark through the Lacanian Real', *American Anthropological Association* 44: 448–63.
Miller, A. 1988. *The Drama of Being a Child*. Virago.
Mitchell, J. 2000. *The Selected Melanie Klein*. Penguin-Viking.
Mohammad, S. I., et al. 2014. 'Beliefs about Jinn, Black Magic and Evil Eye in Bangladesh: The Effects of Gender and Level of Education', *Mental Health, Religion & Culture* 16: 719–28.
Moore, C. 1996. 'Theories of Mind in Infancy', *British Journal of Developmental Psychology* 14: 19–40.
Moore, D., and W. Notz. 2006. *Statistics: Concepts and Controversies*. H. Freeman.
Morgan, D., S. Morgan and D. L. Morgan. 1993. *Successful Focus Groups: Advancing the State of the Art*. SAGE.
Morris, B. 1994. *Anthropology of the Self: The Individual in Cultural Perspective*. Pluto Press.
Moss, L. W., and S. C. Cappannari. 1976. 'Mal'occhio, Ayin ha ra, Oculus Fascinus, Judenblick: The Evil Eye Hovers Above', in C. Maloney (ed.), *The Evil Eye*. Columbia University Press, pp. 1–15.
Muensterberger, W. 1996. 'Review of the Work of Culture by Gananath Obeyesekere', *The Psychoanalytic Quarterly* 62: 299–304.
Murdock, G. P. 1962. *The Ethnographic Atlas*. Pittsburgh Press.
Murgoci, A. 1923. 'The Evil Eye in Roumania, and Its Antidotes', *Folklore* 34: 357–62.
Murguia, A., R. A. Peterson and M. C. Zea. 2003. 'Use and Implications of Ethnomedical Health Care Approaches among Central American Immigrants', *Health and Social Work* 28: 43–51.

Murphy, J. 2009. *Inner Excellence*. McGraw-Hill.
Myers, T. 2003. *Slavoj Žižek*. Routledge.
Nachmais, C. F., and D. Nachmais. 2008. *Research Methods in the Social Sciences*, 7th ed. Worth Publishers.
Nayha, S. 2002. 'Traffic Deaths and Superstition on Friday the 13th', *American Journal of Psychiatry* 159: 2110–13.
Neil, G. 1980. 'The Place of Superstition in Sport: The Self-Fulfilling Prophecy', *Coaching Review* 3: 40–42.
Newport, F., and M. Strausberg. 2001. *Americans' Belief in Psychic and Paranormal Phenomena is up over Last Decade*. Gallup News Service, Poll Analyses.
Nichol, D. M. 1992. *Byzantium and Venice: A Study in Diplomatic and Cultural Relations*. Cambridge University Press.
Nicholson, M. 1999. 'Male Envy: The Logic of Malice in Literature and Culture', in C. Maloney (ed.), *The Evil Eye*. Columbia University Press, pp. 1–15.
Nietzsche, F. 2003. *The Will to Power*. Independently published.
Nurani, L. M. 2008. 'Critical Review of Ethnographic Approach', *Journal Sosioteknologi* 17: 441–47.
Nussbaum, M. C. 1994. *The Therapy of Desire: Theory and Practice in Hellenistic Ethics*. Princeton University Press.
———. 1995. 'Objectification', *Philosophy and Public Affairs* 24: 249–91.
Obeyesekere, G. 1981. *Medusa's Hair*. University of Chicago Press.
Ögenler, O., and G. Yapici. 2012. 'Bir Grup Üniversite Öğrencisinin Batıl İnanışlar ve Hastalıklara Karşı Tutum ve Davranışlarının Değerlendirilmesi' [Evaluation of Attitudes and Behaviour Against Superstitious Beliefs and Diseases in the Group of University Students], *Cumhuriyet Tıp Dergisi* 34: 1–8.
Olusesi, O. A. 2008. 'The Relationship between Causal Beliefs about Mental Illness and Marital Instability, and Help Seeking Preferences of Nigerian Immigrants'. PhD dissertation. School of Social Work, New York University.
Onians, R. B. 1954. *The Origins of European Thought about the Body, the Mind, the Soul, the World, Time, and Fate*. Cambridge University Press.
———. 1988. *The Origins of European Thought about the Body, the Mind, the Soul, the World, the Time and the Fate*, 2nd ed. Cambridge University Press.
Orange, D. M. 2011. *The Suffering Stranger: Hermeneutics for Everyday Clinical Practice*. Routledge.
Oulis, D., G. Makris and S. Roussos. 2010. 'The Orthodox Church of Greece: Policies and Challenges under Archbishop Christodoulos of Athens (1998–2008)', *The International Journal for the Study of the Christian Church* 10: 192–210.
Özden, T. 1987. 'Beliefs and Traditions about Pregnancy, Delivery and Lactation'. PhD dissertation. Nursing Department, Hacettepe University Health Science Institute, Ankara.
Özkan, S., and L. Khorshıd. 1995. 'Beliefs and Traditional Practices among Mothers with 0-1-Year-Old Babies' Lactation'. PhD dissertation. Nursing Department, Aegean University School of Nursing, İzmir.
Özyazıcıoğlu, N., and S. Polat. 2004. 'Traditional Health Care Practices among Mothers with 12-Month Babies', *Atatürk University School of Nursing Journal* 72: 63–71.

Page, S. H. T. 1995. *Powers of Evil: A Biblical Study of Satan and Demons*. Baker Books.
Palmer, G. B. 2007. 'Cognitive Linguistics and Anthropological Linguistics', in D. Geeraerts and H. Cuyckens (eds), *The Oxford Handbook of Cognitive Linguistics*. Oxford University Press, pp. 1045–73.
Papademetriou, G. C. 1974. 'Exorcism and the Greek Orthodox Church', in A. Nauman (ed.), *Exorcism through the Ages*. Christopher Newport College, pp. 66–72.
Papanikolas, H. 2002. *An Amulet of Greek Earth: Generations of Immigrant Folk Culture*. Ohio University Press.
Paranjpe, A. C. 1988. 'A Personality Theory According to Vedanta', in A. C. Paranjpe, D. Y. F. Ho and R. W. Rieber (eds), *Asian Contributions to Psychology*. Praeger, pp. 185–213.
Parish, H., and W. G. Naphy. 2003. *Religion and Superstition in Reformation Europe*. Manchester University Press.
Parrott, W. G., and R. H. Smith. 1993. 'Distinguishing the Experiences of Envy and Jealousy', *Journal of Personality and Social Psychology* 64: 906–20.
Patai, A. 1976. *The Arab Mind*. Charles Scribner's Sons.
Peabody, P. J. 2001. *Old Greek Folk Stories Told Anew*. US Trade Paper.
———. 2006. *Old Folk Greek Stories*. Houghton Mifflin.
Pereira, S., K. Bhui and S. Dein. 1995. 'Making Sense of Possession States: Psychopathology and Differential Diagnosis', *British Journal of Hospital Medicine* 53: 582–86.
Peterson-Bidoshi, K. 2006. 'The "Dordolec": Albanian House Dolls and the Evil Eye', *The Journal of American Folklore* 119: 337–55.
Petrus, T. 2006. 'Engaging the World of the Supernatural: Anthropology, Phenomenology and the Limitations of Scientific Rationalism in the Study of the Supernatural', *Indo-Pacific Journal of Phenomenology* 61: 1–12.
Pfeifer, S. 1994. 'Belief in Demons and Exorcism in Psychiatric Patients in Switzerland', *British Journal of Medical Psychology* 67: 247–58.
Phillips, J. 2008. *Winnicott*. Harvard University Press.
Pieroni, A., and C. Quave. 2005. 'Traditional Pharmacopoeias and Medicines among Albanians and Italians in Southern Italy', *Journal of Ethnopharmacology* 101: 258–70.
Pilch, J. J. 2000. *Healing in the New Testament: Insights from Medical and Mediterranean Anthropology*. Fortress.
Pirandello, L. 1964. 'The Licence', in *Pirandello's One-Act Plays*. Doubleday.
Plass, R., and J. Cofield. 2014. *The Relational Soul: Moving from False Self to Deep Connection*. IVP Books.
Plato. 2003. *Apologia Socrates and Kriton*. Zitros.
Plutarch. 2012. *Plutarch's Morals*. Dodo Press.
———. 2013. *Complete Works of Plutarch*. Delphi Classics.
Prince, G. A. 1995. *Power from on High: The Development of Mormon Priesthood*. Signature Books.
Prišlin, R. 1991. Kada se i Kako Ponašanje Slaže s Našim Stavovima. U: *Uvod u psihologiju* [When and How Behaviour Agrees with Our Attitudes: Introduction to Psychology]. Grafički zavod Hrvatske.

Pronin, E., et al. 2006. 'Everyday Magical Powers: The Role of Apparent Mental Causation in the Overestimation of Personal Influence', *Journal of Personality and Social Psychology* 91: 218–31.
Quave, C. L., and A. Pieroni. 2005. 'Ritual Healing in Arbëreshë Albanian and Italian Communities of Lucania, Southern Italy', *Journal of Folklore Research* 42: 57–97.
Rachman, A. 1997. *Sandor Ferenczi: The Psychoanalyst of Tenderness & Passion.* Aronson.
Racker, H. 2001. *Transference and Countertransference.* International Universities Press.
Rao, K. R. 1988. 'Psychology of Transcendence: A Study of Early Buddhistic Psychology', in A. C. Paranjpe, D. Y. F. Ho and R. W. Rieber (eds), *Asian Contributions to Psychology.* Praeger, pp. 123–48.
Rasmussen, S. 2008. 'Personhood, Self, Differences, and Dialogue (Commentary on Chaudhary)', *International Journal for Dialogical Science* 3: 31–54.
Raz, J. 2011. *Value, Respect and Attachment.* Cambridge University Press.
Reid, K., P. Flowers and M. Larkin. 2005. 'Exploring Lived Experience: An Introduction to Interpretative Phenomenological Analysis', *The Psychologist* 18: 20–23.
Reis, B. 2005. 'The Self is Alive and Well and Living in Relational Psychoanalysis', *Psychoanalytic Psychology* 22: 86–95.
——. 2009. 'Commentary on Papers by Trevarthen, Ammaniti and Trentini and Gallese', *Psychoanalytic Dialogue* 19: 565–79.
Reiter, R. 1981. 'Zur Augensymbolic', *International Zeitschrift fur Artzliche Psychoanalyse* 1: 159–63.
Ricoeur, P. 1981. *Freud and Philosophy: An Essay on Interpretation.* Yale University Press.
——. 1992. *Oneself as Another.* University of Chicago Press.
——. 2005. *The Course of Recognition.* Harvard University Press.
Ritchie, J., and J. Lewis. 2003. *Qualitative Research Practice: A Guide for Social Science Students and Researchers.* SAGE.
Roberts, J. M. 1976. 'Belief in Evil Eye in World Perspective', in C. Maloney (ed.), *The Evil Eye.* Columbia University Press, pp. 223–78.
Roderick, H., and E. Davidson. 1977. *Symbols of Power.* Folklore Society.
Rogoff, B. 2011. *Developing Destinies: A Mayan Midwife and Town.* Oxford University Press.
Rohrbaugh, R. L. 2006. 'Hermeneutics as Cross-Cultural Encounters: Obstacles to Understanding', *HTS Theological Studies* 62: 559–76.
Rolleston, J. D., C. F. Gordon and B. Lee. 1961. 'The Evil Eye', *Hebrew Medical Journal* 34: 292–304.
Rosenwein, B. H. 2006. *Emotional Communities in the Early Middle Ages.* Cornell University Press.
Ross, C. A., and S. Joshi. 1992. 'Paranormal Experiences in the General Population', *Journal of Nervous and Mental Disease* 180: 357–61.
Rossman, G., and S. F. Rallis. 2003. *Learning in the Field: An Introduction to Qualitative Research.* SAGE.
Roussou, E. 2005. 'To Kako Mati: Ekfrazontas ton Popiko Politismo' [The Evil Eye: Expressing the Local Culture], *Ditikomakedoniko Grammata* 17: 373–83.

———. 2011a. 'Orthodoxy at the Crossroads: Popular Religion and Greek Identity in the Practice of the Evil Eye', *Journal of Mediterranean Studies* 20: 85–106.
———. 2011b. 'When Soma Encounters the Spiritual: Bodily Praxes of Performed Religiosity in Contemporary Greece', in R. Blanes and A. Fedele (eds), *Beyond Body and Soul: Anthropological Approaches to Corporeality in Contemporary Religion*. Berghahn Books, pp. 133–50.
Rouvelas, M. 1993. *A Guide to Greek Traditions and Customs in America*. Attica Press.
Russell, J. B. 1981. *Satan: The Early Christian Tradition*. Cornell University Press.
———. 1986. *Mephistopheles: The Devil in the Modern World*. Cornell University Press.
———. 1998. *A History of Heaven: The Singing Silence*. Princeton University Press.
Rustin, M. 1991. *The Good Society and the Inner World: Psychoanalysis, Politics and Culture*. Verso.
Ryan, J. 2005. *How Does Psychotherapy Work?* Karnac.
Ryder, A. G., and Y. E. Chentsova-Dutton. 2012. 'Depression Sociocultural Context: "Chinese Somatization," Revisited', *Psychiatric Clinics of North America* 35: 15–36.
Saenko, I. V. 2005. 'The Superstitions of Today's College Students', *Russian Education & Society* 47: 76–89.
Said, E. 1978. *Orientalism*. Penguin.
Sampson, E. E. 1988. 'The Debate on Individualism', *American Psychologist* 43: 15–22.
———. 1989. 'The Deconstruction of the Self', in J. Shotter and K. J. Gergen (eds), *Texts of Identity*. SAGE, pp. 1–19.
Sartre, J. P. 1992. *Being and Nothingness*. Washington Square Press.
Schaefer, R. 1976. *A New Language for Psychoanalysis*. Yale University Press.
Schmemann, A. 1974. *Of Water and the Spirit: A Liturgical Study of Baptism*. St Vladimir's Seminary Press.
———. 1997. *The Eucharist*. St Vladimir's Seminary Press.
Schore, A. N. 2009. 'Relational Trauma and the Developing Right Brain: An Interface of Psychoanalytic Self Psychology and Neuroscience', *Annals of the New York Academy of Science* 1115: 189–203.
Schroeder, P. W. 1996. *The Transformation of European Politics 1763–1848*. Oxford University Press.
Scotland, N. A. D. 1989. *Eucharistic Consecration in the First Four Centuries and Its Implications for Liturgical Reform*. Latimer House.
Sedgwick, P. 1982. *Psychopolitics*. Pluto Press.
Sedikides, C., and S. J. Spencer. 2007. *The Self*. Psychology Press.
Segal, H. 1979. *Klein*. Fontana.
———. 1982. *Introduction to the Work of Melanie Klein*. Hogarth Press.
———. 1986. *The Work of Hanna Segal: A Kleinian Approach to Clinical Practice*. Free Association Books.
Seidler, G. H. 2000. *In Others' Eyes: An Analysis of Shame*. International Universities Press.
Seremetakis, N. C. 2009. 'Divination, Media and the Network Body of Modernity', *American Anthropological Association* 36: 337–50.

Shaffir, W. B., and R. A. Stebbins. 1991. *Experiencing Fieldwork: An Inside View of Qualitative Research*. SAGE.

Shaner, A. 1999. 'Delusions, Superstitious Conditioning and Chaotic Dopamine Neurodynamics', *Medical Hypothesis* 52: 119–23.

Sharma, U. 1998. *Complementary Medicine Today: Practitioners and Patients*. Routledge.

Shaun, G., and D. Zahavi. 2010. *Phenomenological Approaches to Self-Consciousness*. The Stanford Encyclopedia of Philosophy.

Sheldrake, R. 2003. *The Sense of Being Stared At, and Other Aspects of the Extended Mind*. Hutchinson.

Shermer, M. 1998. *Why People Believe Weird Things: Pseudoscience, Superstition, and Other Confusions of Our Time*. W. H. Freeman and Company, pp. 63-173.

Siebers, T. 1983. *The Mirror of Medusa*. University of California Press.

Silverman, D. 2004. *Qualitative Research: Theory, Method and Practice*. SAGE.

Simmons, L., and R. Schindler. 2003. 'Cultural Superstition and the Price Endings Used in Chinese Advertising', *Journal of International Marketing* 11: 101–11.

Skinner, B. F. 1938. *The Behavior of Organisms: An Experimental Analysis*. Appleton-Century.

——. 1948. '"Superstition" in the Pigeon', *Journal of Experimental Psychology* 38: 168–72.

——. 1953. *Science and Human Behavior*. Appleton-Centrury.

Smith, J. A., M. Jarman, and M. Osborn. 1999. 'Doing Interpretative Phenomenological Analysis'. In M. Murray and K. Chamberlain (eds), *Qualitative Health Psychology: Theories and Methods*. SAGE, pp. 218–240.

Smith, J. M. H. 2005. *Europe After Rome: A New Cultural History, 500–1000*. Oxford University Press.

Smith, J. 2007. 'Hermeneutics, Human Sciences and Health: Linking Theory and Practice', *International Journal of Qualitative Studies on Health and Well-Being* 2: 3–11.

Smith, J., P. Flowers and M. Larkin. 2009. *Interpretative Phenomenological Analysis: Theory Method and Research*. SAGE.

Sorabji, R. 2006. *Self: Ancient and Modern Insights about Individuality, Life, and Death*. Clarendon Press.

Souvlakis, N., and M. C. Cross. 2008. 'People's Attitude to Counselling', *Psicoterapia cognitiva e comportamentale* 14: 188–90.

Sperber, D. 1985. *On Anthropological Knowledge*. Cambridge University Press.

Spillius, E. B. 1988. *Melanie Klein Today: Developments in Theory and Practice*, vol. 1. Routledge.

Spinks, B. 2010. *The Blackwell Companion to Eastern Christianity*. Wiley-Blackwell.

Spiro, M. E. 1965. *Context and Meaning in Cultural Anthropology*. Free Press.

——. 1993. 'Is the Western Conception of the Self "Peculiar" Within the Context of the World Cultures?', *Ethos* 21: 107–53.

Spooner, B. 1976. 'Concluding Essay 1: Anthropology and the Evil Eye', in C. Maloney (ed.), *The Evil Eye*. Columbia University Press, pp. 279–85.

Stan, L. 2017. *Selfhood and Otherness in Kierkegaard's Authorship: A Heterological Investigation*. Rowman & Littlefield.

Steffen, V. 2016. 'Public Anxieties and Projective Identification: Therapeutic Encounters between Danish Clairvoyants and Their Clients', *Ethos* 44: 485–506.

Stegemann, E. W., and W. Stegemann. 1995. *Urchristliche Sozialgeschichte: Die Anfänge im Judentum und die Christusgemeinden in der mediterranen Welt*. Kohlhammer.

Stein, H. E. 1981. 'Envy and the Evil Eye: An Essay in the Psychological Ontogeny of Belief and Ritual', in C. Maloney (ed.), *The Evil Eye*. Columbia University Press, pp. 193–222.

Stein, H. F. 1981. 'Psychoanalytic Anthropology and Psychohistory: A Personal Synthesis', *Journal of Psychoanalytic Anthropology* 4: 239–251.

Steiner, F. 2006. 'Taboo', in J. Adler and R. Fardon (eds), *Taboo, Truth and Religion*. Berghahn Books, pp. 3–15.

Stephenson, P. H. 1979. 'Hutterite Belief in Evil Eye: Beyond Paranoia and towards a General Theory of Invidia', *Culture, Medicine, and Psychiatry* 3: 247–65.

Stewart, A. 1998. *The Ethnographer's Method*. SAGE.

Stigler, S. M. 1992. 'A Historical View of Statistical Concepts in Psychology and Educational Research', *American Journal of Education* 101: 60–70.

Stipik, D. J. 1983. 'A Developmental Analysis of Pride and Shame', *Human Development* 26: 42–54.

Stolorow, R. D., G. E. Atwood and D. M. Orange. 2002. *Worlds of Experience: Interweaving Philosophical and Clinical Dimensions in Psychoanalysis*. Basic Books.

Strawson, G. 1999. 'The Self and the SESMET', *Journal of Consciousness Studies* 6: 99–135.

Subramuniyaswami, S. S. 2002. *Merging with Silva: Hinduism's Contemporary Metaphysics*. Himalayan Academy.

Summer, W. G. 1906. *Folkways*. Ginn.

Sutcliffe, S. 2003. *Children of the New Age: A History of Spiritual Practices*. Routledge.

Sutton, P. 2003. *Native Title in Australia: An Ethnographic Perspective*. Cambridge University Press.

Thiel, U. 2011. *The Early Modern Subject: Self-Consciousness and Personal Identity from Descartes to Hume*. Oxford University Press.

Thomas, K. 1971. *Religion and the Decline of Magic*. Weidenfeld and Nicolson.

Thomsen, M. L. 1992. 'The Evil Eye in Mesopotamia', *Journal of Near Eastern Studies* 51: 19–32.

Tobacyk, J., and G. Milford. 1983. 'Belief in Paranormal Phenomena: Assessment Instrument Development and Implications for Personality Functioning', *Journal of Personality and Social Psychology* 44: 648–55.

Tobacyk, J., E. Nagot and M. Miller. 1987. 'Paranormal Beliefs and Locus of Control: A Multidimensional Examination', *Journal of Personality Assessment* 52: 241–46.

Tourney, G., and D. Plazak. 1954. 'Evil Eye in Myth and Schizophrenia', *The Psychiatric Quarterly* 28: 478–95.

Triandis, H. C. 1995. *Individualism and Collectivism*. Westview.

Tripp-Reimer, T. 1982. 'Cultural Influence on the Potential for Natural Selection', *Central Issues in Anthropology* 4: 49–57.

Troianos, Spyros. 2013. *I Elliniki Idiaiterotita: apo ti Byzantini Synallilia stin 'Epikratousa Thriskia'* [The Hellenic Specificity: From the Byzantine Synallilia to Prevailing Religion], http://www.acadimia.gr/content/view/143/76/lang,el/ (accessed 4 March 2013).

Tsai, J. L., B. Knutson and H. H. Fung. 2006. 'Cultural Variation in Affect Valuation', *Journal of Personality and Social Psychology* 90: 288–307.

Turkle, S. 1992. *Psychoanalytic Politics: Jacques Lacan and Freud's French Revolution*. Guildford Press.

Ullmann, M. 1978. *Islamic Medicine*. Edinburgh University Press.

Van Maanen, J. 1988. *Tales of the Field: On Writing Ethnography*. University of Chicago Press.

Van Raalte, J., et al. 1991. 'Chance Orientation and Superstitious Behavior on the Putting Green', *Journal of Sport Behavior* 14: 41–50.

Vecchiato, N. 1994. 'Evil Eye, Health Beliefs and Social Tensions among the Sidama', in H. Marcus (ed.), *New Trends in Ethiopian Studies: Proceedings of the 12th International Conference of Ethiopian Studies*. Red Sea Press, pp. 1033–43.

Veikou, H. 1998. *To Kako Mati: I Koinoniki Kataskevi tis Optikis Epikoinonias* [Evil Eye: The Social Construction of Visual Communication]. Ellinika Grammata.

Vyse, S. A. 2000. *Believing in Magic: The Psychology of Superstition*. Oxford University Press.

Walcot, P. 1978. *Envy and the Greeks: A Study of Human Behavior*. Aris and Phillips.

Waldram, J. B. 1993. 'Aboriginal Spirituality: Symbolic Healing in Canadian Prisons', *Culture, Medicine and Psychiatry* 17: 354–62.

Ware, K. 1993. *The Orthodox Church*. Penguin.

———. 1996. *The Orthodox Way*. St Vladimir's Seminary Press.

Waud, K. H., and G. H. Herdt. 1987. 'Introduction: Interpretation in Psychoanalytic Anthropology', *Ethos* 15: 3–7.

Wazana, N. 2007. 'A Case of the Evil Eye: Qohelet 4:4–8', *Journal of Biblical Literature* 126: 685–702.

Weatherhead, S., and A. Daiches. 2010. 'Muslim Views on Mental Health and Psychotherapy', *Psychology and Psychotherapy: Theory, Research and Practice* 83: 75–89.

Wegner, D. M., and T. Wheatley. 1999. 'Apparent Mental Causation: Sources of the Experience of Will', *American Psychologist* 54: 480–92.

———. 2002. *The Illusion of Conscious Will*. MIT Press.

Weinstein, D. 1991. *Heavy Metal: A Cultural Sociology*. Lexington Books.

West, S. A., A. S. Griffin and A. Gardner. 2007. 'Social Semantics: Altruism, Cooperation, Mutualism, Strong Reciprocity and Group Selection', *Journal of Evolutionary Biology* 20: 415–32.

Westermarck, E. 1926. *Ritual and Belief in Morocco*. Macmillan.

Wheen, F. 2005. *How Mumbo-Jumbo Conquered the World*. Harper Perennial.

Whitehouse, H. 2004. *Modes of Religiosity: A Cognitive Theory of Religious Transmission*. AltaMira Press.

Whitson, J. A., and A. D. Galinsky. 2008. 'Lacking Control Increases Illusory Pattern Perception', *Science* 322: 115–17.
Wilk, S. R. 2000. *Medusa: Solving the Mystery of the Gorgon*. Oxford University Press.
Winch, P. J., et al. 2005. 'Bangladesh Projahnmo Study Group: Local Understandings of Vulnerability and Protection during the Neonatal Period in Sylhet District, Bangladesh: A Qualitative Study', *Lancet* 366: 478–85.
Wing, D. 1998. 'A Comparison of Traditional Folk Healing Concepts with Contemporary Healing Concepts', *Journal of Community Health Nursing* 15: 143–54.
Winnicott, D. W. 1960. 'The Theory of the Parent-Infant Relationship', *International Journal of Psycho-Analysis* 41: 585–95.
———. 1965. *Maturational Processes and the Facilitating Environment: Studies in the Theory of Emotional Development*. Hogarth Press.
———. 1971. *Therapeutic Consultation in Child Psychiatry*. Hogarth Press.
Wirt, E. 1982. 'The Seal of Solomon: Some Metaphysical and Theological Implications', *Religion and Psychical Research Journal* 5: 233–38.
Wolfradt, U. 1997. 'Dissociative Experiences, Trait Anxiety and Paranormal Beliefs', *Personality and Individual Differences* 23: 15–19.
Wood, M. 2007. *Possession, Power and the New Age: Ambiguities of Authority in Neoliberal Societies*. Ashgate.
World Health Organization. 1992. *The ICD-10 Classification of Mental and Behavioral Disorder*.
Wright, K. 1991. *Vision and Separation between Mother and Baby*. Jason Aronson.
Yalin, S. 1998. 'Traditional Patient Care Practices'. PhD dissertation. Nursing Department, Hacettepe University Health Sciences Institute, Ankara.
Yannaras, C. 2004. *Relational Ontology*. Ikaros.
———. 2006. *Against Religion*. Ikaros.
———. 2012a. *The Enigma of Evil*. Holy Orthodox Press.
———. 2012b. *The Meaning of Reality: Essays on Existence and Communion, Eros and History*. Sebastian Press.
Younis, Y. O. 2000. 'Possession and Exorcism: An Illustrative Case', *Arabic Journal of Psychiatry* 11: 56–59.
Zahavi, D. 2008. *Subjectivity and Selfhood. Investigating the First-Person Perspective*. MIT Press.
Zauberdiagnose, C., and M. Schwarze. 1992. *Magie in Mesopotamien*. Carsten Niebuhr Institute Publications.
Žeželj, I., et al. 2009. 'Construction and Behavioral Validation of Superstition Scale', *Psihologija*, 42: 141–58.
Žeželj, I., et al. 2017. 'The Role of Inter-Ethnic Online Friendships in Prejudice Reduction in Post-Conflict Societies: Evidence from Serbia, Croatia and Cyprus', *Computers in Human Behavior* 76: 386–95.
Zimmerman, M. 1981. *The Eclipse of the Self: The Development of Heidegger's Concept of Authenticity*. Pluto Press.

Zissi, A., and M. M. Barry. 1997. 'From Leros Asylum to Community-Based Facilities: Levels of Functioning and Quality of Life Among Hostel Residents in Greece', *The International Journal of Social Psychiatry* 43: 104–15.
Žižek, S., and G. Daly. 2004. *Conversations with Žižek*. Polity Press.
Žižek, S. 2006. *Interrogating the Real*. Continuum.
——. 2007. *The Universal Exception*. Continuum.
Zoysa, I., et al. 1998. 'Careseeking for Illness in Young Infants in an Urban Slum in India', *Social Science & Medicine* 47: 2101–11.
Zusne, L., and W. Jones. 1989. *Anomalistic Psychology: A Study of Magical Thinking*. Lawrence Erlbaum Association.

Index

A

abbot, 110, 111, 201
Aeschylus, 22, 225
Agamemnon, 22, 23, 225
agnostic, 67
Albania, 20, 46
alchemical, 25, 35, 111, 167
aloneness, 205–7
altruism, 206, 243
ambiguous, 108, 133
amulets, 30, 37–40, 45, 59, 86, 97, 106, 121, 122, 124, 126, 129, 157, 214–16
Anatolian, 37
ancient, 20, 22–24, 40, 49, 105, 214, 215, 226, 230, 231, 233, 236, 241
anger, 22, 23, 35, 45, 53, 67, 68, 99, 100, 142, 148, 166, 167
anthropological, 1, 8, 10, 61–63, 69, 71, 73, 85, 226, 227, 235, 236, 238, 240, 241
anthropology, 63–69, 179, 180, 227, 228, 230–32, 234, 236, 238, 241–43
Aristotle, 23
Asclepius, 227
ashamed, 42, 90, 140, 145, 148, 164
Asia, 46, 179
austerity, 53, 55
authoritarian, 76, 213, 232
autonomy, 49, 147, 167, 206, 209
awareness, 14, 43, 81, 94, 111, 115, 132, 146, 150, 193, 217

B

baby, 36, 37, 41, 87, 88, 190, 219, 244
Balkans, 19, 38, 46
Bangladesh, 36, 236, 244
bankrupt, 53
baptism, 29, 41, 240
Bedouin, 18, 19, 46, 225, 234
Beelzeboul, 32
beings, 8, 11, 15, 18, 20–22, 25, 26, 30, 32, 33, 44, 47, 92, 102, 103, 105, 108, 109, 121, 132, 134, 135, 141, 145, 150, 159, 162, 164, 178, 179, 182, 183, 185, 191, 200, 206, 209, 211, 212, 216, 230
belief, 8–17, 19, 24–38, 40, 41, 44, 45, 51, 52, 65, 67, 69, 73, 74, 84, 86, 93, 95, 102, 106, 109, 112, 113, 117, 122, 125–31, 136, 137, 141, 143–45, 159, 176, 200, 212, 214, 216, 217, 223, 225, 226, 229–31, 234, 237–39, 242, 243
believers, 12, 13, 28, 31, 45, 54, 90, 124, 132, 181
biological, 96, 132, 176
biomedical, 27, 29
blasphemy, 84
blessing, 40, 41, 119
blob, 176
blood, 40, 41, 117, 144
blue, 30, 38–40, 52, 121, 122, 215, 216
body, 19, 25, 33, 36, 38, 40, 46, 51, 74, 88–98, 100, 102, 104, 111–14, 116,

119, 120, 125, 133, 137, 138, 143–45, 148, 151, 152, 154, 156–63, 165, 177, 178, 181, 191, 194, 198, 199, 201, 218, 223, 224, 231, 233, 236, 237, 240, 241
boundaries, 47, 68, 79, 89, 94, 96, 102, 108, 112, 148, 156, 159, 182, 192, 209, 212, 226, 227
British, 43, 49, 117, 228–30, 232, 233, 235, 236, 238
buda, 18
Byzantine, 30, 50, 51, 229, 231, 235, 243

C

calamities, 1, 2, 5, 25, 27, 31, 102
caster, 29, 96–98, 105, 106, 134, 152–54, 163–66, 169, 173, 175, 194, 205
Catholic, 29, 49, 232
charlatans, 101, 122, 134
charms, 28, 37, 45, 121
childhood, 15, 67, 147, 152, 167, 198, 203, 233
children, 36, 40, 41, 52, 75, 91, 99, 101, 129, 154, 161, 216, 242
China, 36, 62, 231
Christian, 1, 11, 13, 28–30, 32, 38, 40–42, 49–51, 55, 87, 90, 91, 93, 95, 96, 99, 101, 102, 106, 108, 112–15, 118, 122, 129, 134, 136, 138, 139, 141, 147, 149, 150, 153, 162, 165, 167, 171, 177, 183, 184, 186, 188–90, 196, 201, 202, 208, 209, 212–14, 221, 226, 235, 237, 240
clairvoyant, 94, 95
clergymen, 4, 48, 52, 55, 58, 76, 86, 90, 101, 108, 109, 113, 133, 134, 215
clinicians, 115, 125–27
coexistence, 26, 149, 152, 205
cognitive, 11, 12, 22, 86, 97, 127, 128, 136, 157, 158, 162, 168, 172, 177, 191, 226, 227, 231, 232, 238, 244
complex, 14, 16, 62, 63, 128, 153, 162, 187, 192, 194, 222
Confucianism, 188

consciousness, 8, 10, 16, 27, 37, 50, 51, 60, 93, 102, 106, 110, 111, 144, 156, 160, 179–83, 188, 194, 196, 202, 222, 227, 229, 231, 235, 242
Constantinople, 50, 54, 232
construct, 14, 16, 35, 61, 79, 130, 134, 148, 154, 168, 170, 184, 188, 191, 200, 201, 207, 217
contemporary, 4, 5, 7, 10, 13, 20, 42, 43, 52, 62, 87, 159, 173, 180, 207, 208, 211, 230, 232, 240, 242, 244
Corfu, 2, 5, 9, 16, 39, 46–50, 52, 55, 58–60, 64, 66, 71, 74–76, 79, 86–89, 94, 109, 110, 112, 114–17, 119, 122, 123, 125, 133, 134, 136–41, 147, 149, 153, 171, 173, 176, 177, 182, 187, 190, 193, 195, 196, 202, 208–15, 219, 221, 223
craziness, 138, 142
crisis, 50–55, 57, 74, 118, 141, 142, 153, 182, 227, 235
cultural, 8, 10, 16, 27, 28, 45, 48, 60–63, 65–68, 70, 73, 78, 79, 84, 115, 124, 135–37, 151, 161, 168, 169, 172, 176–81, 199, 200, 208, 212, 213, 217, 228–30, 234–37, 241, 243
cure, 31, 101, 143, 171, 232

D

damage, 18, 34, 35, 46, 90, 91, 99–101, 105, 126, 128, 129, 131, 134, 183, 205, 220
death, 19, 22, 25–27, 30–32, 35, 38, 40, 41, 46, 47, 51, 102, 103, 112, 118, 127, 145, 159, 166, 183, 215, 216, 220, 226, 241
deisidaimonia (δεισιδαιμονία), 106
defences, 18, 65, 68, 69, 144, 145, 154, 216
demons, 10, 32, 33, 41, 42, 44, 84, 89, 91, 92, 104, 105, 109, 132–34, 140, 142, 143, 228, 238
depression, 35, 46, 136, 138, 140, 141, 216, 235, 240

destroy, 20, 21, 68, 99, 100, 103, 107, 142, 155, 160, 164–68, 181, 209
diagnosis, 29, 44, 140, 144, 171, 198, 238
dissociative, 23, 45, 144, 244
distress, 15, 44, 62, 89, 100, 101, 136–38, 142, 144, 168, 171, 215, 235
divination, 12, 13, 28, 229, 241
doctor, 41, 88, 109, 139
DSM-V, 45
dualism, 25, 26, 33, 35, 188
dysfunction, 16, 52, 105, 115, 183, 216

E

ecclesiastical, 40, 50, 51, 72, 121, 122
ecology, 19, 54, 116, 179, 180, 182, 186, 192, 200, 203
ego, 15, 101, 144, 162
Egypt, 20, 236
embodied, 69, 113, 121, 145, 148, 149, 153, 156–58, 172, 173, 179, 181, 215, 220
envy, 17–19, 21–26, 29–33, 35, 38, 45–47, 103, 105, 107, 108, 118, 134, 139, 141, 144, 155, 165–67, 169, 172, 174, 199, 200, 206, 214–17, 219–23, 226, 230, 231, 233, 237, 238, 242, 243
Epictetus, 21, 230
Ethiopians, 18
ethnographic, 1–3, 5, 8, 9, 16, 27, 59, 61–67, 69–71, 80–85, 87, 116, 175, 176, 178–80, 182–84, 207, 217–19, 236, 237, 242
Euchologion, 30
evil, 1–5, 7–13, 15–48, 50, 51, 53, 57–60, 62–67, 69–77, 79, 84, 86–227, 229–33, 235–40, 242–44
existence, 8, 10, 21, 26, 28, 30, 44, 45, 51, 61, 63, 67, 75, 95–97, 110, 111, 121, 130, 137, 144–48, 150, 151, 153, 158, 160, 177, 181–83, 185, 187, 189, 194–201, 203–5, 207, 216, 219, 223, 224, 244
exorcism, 28, 29, 31, 32, 39–42, 122, 238, 244

eye (Βασκανία), 1–5, 7–13, 15–48, 50, 51, 53, 57–60, 62–67, 69–77, 79, 84, 86–227, 229–33, 235–40, 242, 243

F

faith, 27, 29, 33, 40, 44, 45, 47, 67, 75, 90, 109, 115, 117, 134, 137, 139, 141, 144, 147, 229, 235
fascination, 22, 23, 36, 37, 44, 205
fear, 2, 9–17, 19, 22, 24–27, 32, 34, 35, 47, 53, 67, 68, 73, 74, 87, 90, 93, 106–9, 111, 115, 116, 120, 123, 124, 126, 127, 129–31, 133–36, 140, 145, 148–51, 153, 154, 158–61, 164, 166–70, 173, 174, 181, 183, 185, 186, 189, 190, 197–200, 202–6, 208–10, 220, 221, 223
fieldwork, 2, 4, 5, 19, 31, 35–37, 46, 48, 59–67, 69–76, 79–82, 87, 91, 94, 95, 100, 106, 108, 110, 112, 122, 124, 128, 129, 134–37, 139, 142, 145, 146, 151, 152, 154–56, 158, 161–69, 172–77, 181, 185, 189–91, 194, 198, 199, 204, 206, 208–11, 214–17, 219, 221, 222, 233, 241
folklore, 25, 37, 84, 227–33, 235, 237–39
Freud, 68, 162, 164, 230, 232, 239
frozen, 144, 198

G

Gaelic, 18, 37
gaze, 17, 19, 21, 23, 38, 100, 135, 136, 147–60, 163–65, 173, 180, 181, 185, 187, 188, 197–99, 202, 207–9, 211, 212, 217, 219, 222, 226
Godiva, 165, 223
God, 22, 92, 104, 107, 111, 114, 133, 134, 146, 148
gorgon, 23, 244
Greek, 3, 4, 7–10, 12, 16, 18, 21–36, 39–55, 58–60, 67, 72, 73, 84, 86, 87, 89–91, 97, 111, 114, 124, 132–34, 137, 141, 144, 169–71, 177, 179,

210–15, 221, 225, 227–29, 232, 233, 235, 238, 240
guilt, 89, 102, 128, 136, 146, 161, 164, 173, 209, 221, 234

H
hallucinations, 46, 138
harm, 1, 17, 20, 32, 34, 35, 38, 40, 44–46, 62, 92, 101, 105, 109, 183, 201, 205, 210, 216
hate, 35, 100, 105, 109, 134
headaches, 26, 35, 46, 97, 98, 101, 116–18, 154, 201, 202, 216
healers, 4, 27, 38, 39, 44–46, 55, 58, 59, 72, 73, 84–86, 101, 114–22, 132, 134, 138, 141, 143, 144, 155, 170, 225
healing, 2, 4, 27, 36–38, 41, 42, 50, 58, 59, 69, 70, 72, 73, 98, 113, 115, 116, 119–22, 147, 168, 170–72, 188, 201, 214, 228, 238, 239, 243, 244
health, 1–4, 8, 9, 17, 21–23, 27, 28, 32, 42–47, 50, 53, 55, 58, 59, 65, 69, 72, 73, 76, 78, 85, 86, 115, 116, 122–28, 130–32, 134, 135, 137–44, 151, 161, 165, 170–73, 175, 184, 190, 211, 212, 214–16, 218, 223, 225–27, 229, 230, 233–38, 241, 243, 244
holy, 29, 36–38, 40–42, 50–52, 54, 92, 110, 112, 117, 119, 120, 183, 232, 244
Homer, 49, 232
hope, 10, 12, 16, 90, 125, 140, 153, 171

I
illness, 17, 18, 22–25, 30, 35, 37, 42–45, 47, 100, 124, 128, 135–41, 144, 170, 172, 228, 230, 237, 245
illusory, 9, 12, 15, 130, 209, 212, 233, 244
India, 63, 228, 233, 245
individuation, 146, 167, 180, 182, 183, 186, 190, 210, 212
informants, 2, 3, 31, 48, 55, 57, 58, 60–62, 64–66, 69–72, 75–79, 81, 82, 85–87, 89–101, 114, 119, 133–38, 142, 144, 146, 148–64, 166, 167, 169, 170, 172, 174, 185, 186, 191, 194, 198–202, 204, 205, 207–10, 215–18, 221
insomnia, 35, 46, 136, 141
intersubjective, 63, 69, 120, 121, 163, 186, 197, 205, 206, 223
Ionian, 48–50, 138, 140, 169, 221
Islamic, 20, 45, 225, 233, 243
Italy, 37, 45, 46, 49, 231, 238, 239

J
jealousy, 17, 19, 24, 30, 31, 36, 105, 108, 141, 144, 216, 217, 219, 223, 238
Jesus, 8, 18, 30, 33, 36, 39–41, 114, 117, 215
jinns, 18, 20
Jung, 68, 200, 203, 233

K
Korkira, 49
koutsompolio, 31

L
Lacan, 64, 78, 150, 209, 234, 243

M
magic, 13, 17, 18, 30, 32, 40, 45, 84, 101, 120, 226, 230, 233, 235, 236, 242, 243
Malawi, 179
malevolent, 1, 24, 26, 31, 44, 45, 70, 86, 93, 231
masochistic, 161, 164, 167
mati, 35, 117, 118, 240, 243
matiasma, 18, 29, 35, 91, 93, 122, 177
matiasmenos (ματιασμένος), 117
Mediterranean, 26–28, 30, 49, 60, 169, 238, 240
mental, 1–4, 8, 9, 17, 18, 21–25, 27, 28, 32, 35, 37, 42–47, 50, 55, 58, 59, 65, 69, 72, 73, 76, 78, 85, 86, 89, 93, 100–102, 115, 120–44, 151, 156,

161, 165, 170–73, 175, 184, 190, 211, 212, 214–16, 218, 220, 223, 225–29, 233, 235–37, 239, 240, 243, 244
mirror, 2, 99, 118, 119, 145, 148, 150, 151, 156, 158, 160–62, 172, 183–85, 193, 195, 197, 198, 200, 219, 220, 241
misfortune, 5, 10, 11, 16, 19, 22, 23, 29, 31, 40, 86, 99, 100, 102, 109, 112, 113, 124, 126, 134, 137, 153, 157, 170, 172, 214–17, 229

N

narcissistic, 15, 22, 99, 103, 144, 155, 173, 209

O

omnipotence, 15, 68, 99
orthodox, 1, 3–5, 7–12, 16, 18, 26–35, 39, 41–47, 49–51, 54, 55, 58, 59, 72–74, 86, 87, 89–91, 96, 99, 101, 102, 105–8, 112, 114, 115, 119, 132, 133, 136–38, 141, 143, 144, 151, 153, 161, 162, 166–71, 177, 179, 190, 196, 201, 202, 208–15, 221, 235, 237, 238, 243, 244
otherness, 173, 179, 181, 183, 184, 194, 195, 206, 223, 234, 242

P

pain, 12, 22, 33, 35, 46, 68, 86, 89, 90, 93, 97, 98, 100, 102, 111, 115, 116, 118, 121, 122, 135, 142, 144, 148, 150, 151, 153, 154, 156, 158, 159, 162, 164–68, 170, 172, 173, 184, 194, 195, 200, 204, 210, 215, 227, 233
paranoia, 45, 106, 221, 242
persecutory, 35, 68, 106, 168
personality, 22, 45, 60, 189, 226, 228, 229, 231, 234, 236, 238, 239, 242–44
personhood, 1–3, 5, 16, 62, 63, 67–69, 99, 147, 150, 151, 153, 156, 158–61, 173–216, 219, 222–24, 229, 239

petrification, 22, 46, 184, 199, 221, 223
Phthonos, 108, 109
Plutarch, 21, 23, 25, 105, 229, 239
possessed, 18, 24, 32–34, 36, 39, 41, 44, 46, 58, 73, 90, 91, 95, 96, 98, 106, 136, 137, 139, 165, 181, 184, 189, 194, 205
power, 13, 14, 18–24, 29–32, 36, 37, 39, 40, 42, 49, 51, 53, 58, 59, 69, 70, 90–92, 94–97, 99, 100, 102–5, 107, 113, 114, 119, 121, 129–31, 133, 135, 137, 150, 151, 159, 162, 163, 168, 171, 210, 217, 218, 220, 228, 231, 237, 239, 244
prayers, 29–31, 38, 39, 41, 42, 87, 90, 113–15, 117, 119, 121, 125, 137, 147
priests, 28, 29, 39, 41, 44, 45, 58, 72–74, 76, 84, 85, 87, 90, 92, 99, 101, 102, 104–7, 109, 112, 113, 117, 122–24, 133, 134, 137, 144, 195
psychiatric, 44, 45, 115, 123–25, 127–32, 134, 226–28, 233, 235, 238, 240, 243
psychiatrist, 123, 125, 127–30, 138
psychoanalytic, 60–65, 67–69, 77, 146, 147, 230, 231, 233–36, 239, 240, 242, 243
psychology, 1, 3, 11, 60, 61, 67, 210, 226–28, 230, 232–36, 238–43, 245
psychopathology, 126, 210, 211, 221, 238
psychosomatic, 35, 115, 120, 121, 144
Pythagoras, 212

R

religion, 4, 7, 9, 12–14, 21, 36, 47, 50, 58, 67, 71, 73, 74, 87, 91, 94, 96, 102, 123, 126, 129, 130, 141, 169, 213, 215, 223, 227, 232–36, 238, 240, 242–44
rituals, 4, 9–15, 20, 23, 27–31, 34, 36, 37, 39, 40, 42, 52, 53, 58, 59, 64, 66, 70, 72, 76, 98, 110, 112, 114–22, 126, 130, 134, 137, 147, 167, 169, 173, 184, 201, 203, 210, 214–16

S

Satan, 7–9, 30, 32, 33, 42, 91, 94, 95, 183, 238, 240
self, 5, 11, 15, 22, 46, 63, 64, 68, 111, 113, 117, 118, 135, 136, 146, 148–54, 156–63, 166, 167, 173, 175, 176, 178–93, 195–98, 200–213, 215, 217, 219–22, 227, 229, 231, 233–36, 238–42, 244
selfhood, 116, 219–23, 242, 244
shame, 43, 128, 135, 136, 140, 142, 144–52, 155, 156, 158–61, 164, 173, 199, 208, 219–24, 226, 227, 233, 234, 241, 242
sin, 8, 30, 102, 103, 133, 135, 145, 165
Socrates, 20, 232, 238
somatic, 35, 89, 111, 115, 136, 141, 156, 162, 163, 168, 172
soul, 26, 33, 88, 89, 97, 98, 104, 124, 127, 128, 138, 140, 145, 146, 156, 158, 159, 178, 183, 199, 223, 237, 238, 240
spiritual, 4, 20, 34–39, 41, 42, 44, 46, 47, 50, 52, 54, 58, 70, 73, 89, 90, 92–98, 111, 113–16, 118, 121, 123, 125–27, 130–39, 141–43, 161, 168, 170–72, 188, 197, 216–19, 222, 232, 240, 242
sufferer, 23, 27, 28, 36, 38, 39, 42, 95, 96, 98, 105, 106, 110, 111, 114, 115, 117, 119–21, 138, 140, 143, 152–56, 163–66, 170, 172, 173, 175, 183, 184, 215, 222
supernatural, 1, 2, 9, 13, 14, 67, 93–96, 108, 109, 133, 137–39, 210, 217, 218, 223, 226, 227, 235, 238
superstition, 9–13, 19, 213, 214, 232, 233, 235, 237, 238, 241, 243, 244
symptomatology, 2, 3, 34, 42, 45, 46, 59, 70, 106, 114, 115, 119, 120, 126, 128, 130, 135, 140–43, 155, 170, 172, 173, 198, 201, 220

T

terror, 34, 68, 106, 161, 221
tradition, 7, 8, 10, 12, 16–20, 25, 28–36, 38–42, 45, 46, 57, 59, 60, 67, 74, 91, 96, 99, 103, 114–16, 121, 122, 134, 138, 146, 168, 177, 186, 211–13, 215, 226, 240
trauma, 12, 15, 74, 140–42, 167, 170, 240
treatment, 9, 27, 29, 43, 44, 115, 121–23, 125, 126, 131, 132, 134, 137, 138, 143, 170–72
Trinitarian, 183, 188

V

vaskania, 7, 18, 31, 32, 35, 41, 91, 108
Vietnamese, 62
void, 68, 141, 152, 155, 183, 184

W

witchcraft, 10, 13, 16, 17, 31, 37, 40, 101, 133, 226, 230, 233
witnessing, 98, 118, 133, 161, 166, 178, 184, 194, 224

X

xematiasma (ξεμάτιασμα), 118

Y

Yugoslavia, 38, 227

CPSIA information can be obtained
at www.ICGtesting.com
Printed in the USA
BVHW091838070621
608955BV00002B/65